**MCSA/MCSE
Windows 2000 Professional
(70-210) Exam Preparation**

Editor in Chief: Stephen Helba
Assistant Vice President and Publisher: Charles E. Stewart, Jr.
Production Editor: Alexandrina Benedicto Wolf
Design Coordinator: Diane Ernsberger
Production Manager: Matthew Ottenweller
Cover Designer: Karrie Converse-Jones
Cover Photo: Esther F. Brooks
Illustrations: Cathy J. Boulay and Stuart C. Palmer

This book was set in Futura MD BT, Times New Roman, and Arial by Cathy J. Boulay, EITPrep. It
was printed and bound by R.R. Donnelley & Sons Company. The cover was printed by Phoenix
Color Corp.

Pearson Education Ltd., *London*
Pearson Education Australia Pty. Limited, *Sydney*
Pearson Education Singapore, Pte. Ltd.
Pearson Education North Asia Ltd., *Hong Kong*
Pearson Education Canada, Ltd., *Toronto*
Pearson Educacion de Mexico, S.A. de C.V.
Pearson Education–Japan, *Tokyo*
Pearson Education Malaysia, Pte. Ltd.
Pearson Education, *Upper Saddle River, New Jersey*

eITPrep Managing Director: Charles J. Brooks

Written by Jerald A. Dively

On the cover:
Out of the Fog – A powerful steam locomotive rushes out of the fog at a crossing near Milton, West
Virginia. This 70-210 PassIT exam prep book can give you the power to roar through the first
crossing of the Microsoft MCSA and MCSE tracks.

10 9 8 7 6 5 4 3 2 1

ISBN 0-13-097305-X

Preface

This book condenses the material associated with the Microsoft 70-210 Installing, Configuring, and Administering Windows 2000 Professional exam into a neat little handbook to make your life easier as you prepare for the 70-210 MCSA/MCSE Professional examination. It presents only the material that is relevant for the exam, and eliminates any underlying "theory" material that is not.

When using this test preparation tool, you must remember that we have provided only the information necessary to pass the examination. What does this mean? Well, it means that you should pass the test, but may not have a detailed understanding of the subject. Ideally, the people who should use this book are those who are already working with Windows 2000 Professional, but haven't passed the test yet. This book will provide you with the exam-specific knowledge to successfully take the test.

On the other hand, getting an MCSA/MCSE certification will open many doors to you that were previously closed. If you don't have any experience, but you want to get into the IT field, you may want to use this book to challenge the exam, and then try to get the job that you want. Afterward, you should be able to get the experience needed to keep the job through on-the-job training.

Don't worry if you feel like a "paper MCSA/MCSE." Put first things first—pass the test, then go out and get that 30-pound technical book to help you prepare for the real world. After all, how does anybody get experience with operating systems and networks if they are not given the opportunity to try?

ACKNOWLEDGMENTS

I give my acknowledgements to my loving wife, Denise, and my two wonderful children, Ashley and Nicole; and to my toy poodle, Cookie. Without the assistance of my two daughters this book would not have been possible. I would also like to thank Charles Brooks whose staff has done an excellent job making sure that the book was properly put together. I also want to thank the Mindloft Corporation for allowing me to apply hands-on experience while writing this book.

HOW TO USE THIS BOOK

You might ask yourself, "How do I use this Pass IT book?" Well, the explanation is simple. We have designed this book for anyone to study and take the 70-210 examination. We provide you with exam-specific pointers throughout the text.

First, review the chapter objectives, and then read the chapter. Go back to the chapter objectives to see if you can remember the material covered. Then, read the chapter again. The more times you expose yourself to information, the better chance that it will remain in your long-term memory.

Each chapter begins with an introduction that basically takes the objectives and defines them in easy-to-understand terms. As we discuss material, you may see some of the information highlighted *in bold italic letters* with an "*" preceding the information. Pay very close attention to this information: The likelihood of seeing it on the test is very high. Not only do we highlight the really important information, but we also place this information in what we call "Exam Tips". Exam Tips are just that—tips to pass the exam. Sometimes we also include Notes to help you further understand the information.

Most chapters contain special Challenges that simulate the types of situations that Microsoft likes to use in its exam questions. Solutions for these Challenges are provided at the end of the chapter.

Finally, we have created questions at the end of each chapter to jog your memory. These are important questions because they concentrate on the subject areas that are tested on the 70-210 MCSA/MCSE Professional Examination. The questions are only samples that closely resemble actual test content. This book is accompanied by a comprehensive 70-210 Professional test bank that is sealed on the back cover of the book. The CD testing material was developed to simulate the MCSA/MCSE Certification Exam testing process and contains materials that will enable you to complete practice tests, determine your weak points, and study more strategically. You will not be disappointed when it comes time to take the test.

Now, take the test and good luck!

After you take the test, we would appreciate an e-mail at *admin@eitprep.com*. Your input will be used to make this book better.

Table of Contents

Chapter 1   Installing/Upgrading Windows 2000 Professional

Chapter 2   Automated Windows 2000 Professional Installation

Chapter 3   Managing Windows 2000 Professional

Chapter 4   Users and Groups

Chapter 5   User and Hardware Profiles

Chapter 6   Disk Management

Chapter 7   Local Computer Security

Chapter 8   Accessing Files and Folders

Chapter 9   Networking

Chapter 10   Printing

Chapter 11   Dial-up Networking

Chapter 12   Optimizing Windows 2000 Professional

Chapter 13   System Recovery

Chapter 1

Installing/Upgrading
Windows 2000 Professional

These are the areas that are generally testable on the MCSE Server 2000 examination:

1. Perform an attended installation of Windows 2000 Professional.

2. Upgrade a computer from previous versions of Windows.

3. Apply update packs to installed software applications.

4. Prepare a computer to meet upgrade requirements.

5. Troubleshoot failed installations.

Installing/Upgrading
Windows 2000 Professional

Introduction

This chapter will provide you with the information you need to perform an attended installation of Windows 2000 Professional. What does "attended" mean? It means that you are going to physically sit in front of the computer and manually install the operating system. We will discuss minimum requirements of the processor, disk space, and memory for the installation process to be successful. Then we will discuss what the HCL is and what it means if your hardware is not listed there. You will be shown that the /checkupgradeonly switch can be used with the WINNT32.EXE command to check your current hardware configuration.

Then you will learn that when you upgrade your operating system you retain users and groups, desktop settings, applications, preferences, program groups, and items. Windows 95/98, Windows NT 3.51, and NT 4.0 are the only operating systems that have a direct path to be upgraded to Windows 2000 Professional. You will also learn which operating systems cannot be directly upgraded.

Next, you will be shown how to properly dual boot Windows 2000 Professional with another operating system. If you dual boot Windows 98 with Windows 2000 Professional, then the file system used to install Windows 2000 Professional must be FAT32. This will enable the operating systems to recognize each other. We will then inform you how to properly configure a dual boot with Windows NT 4.0 Workstation.

You will learn when to use the WINNT32.EXE command to perform a Windows 2000 Professional installation. If you are upgrading a 16-bit operating system you should use WINNT.EXE. You must use the proper setup command, which depends on the current operating system, or the installation will not proceed properly.

There are different ways to install Windows 2000 Professional. You will discover that you can install the OS from the current operating system, from the CD-ROM (if your computer supports it), or from the Windows Professional 2000 setup boot disks. You can create the setup boot disks by using the MAKEBT32 or MAKEBOOT command. You will find out which operating systems use these commands. Setup boot disks are not computer-specific and can be used to help you start another machine that is having problems with the installation process.

You will learn how to install tha operating systemover the network, provided that you have a distribution server with the OS files located in a shared folder. Another important thing to be aware of is that two executable files—WINNT and WINNT32—are used to install Windows 2000 Professional. They are located in the WINNT shared folder. You will also discover that, if the CD-ROM is unavailable or you cannot boot to the CD, installing over the network is the next best option.

Before you upgrade your operating system you must know that Windows 2000 Professional supports DOS, Windows 16-bit, and Windows 32-bit applications. It does not support third-party applications without thorough testing and possible reprogramming of the application.

Finally, you will be introduced to common error messages that you may receive during a typical installation, along with steps that can be used to correct these problems. To assist you in pinpointing problems, two logs are created: the Setuperr.log and the Setupact.log, which are located in the WINNT folder.

FEATURES OF WINDOWS 2000 PROFESSIONAL

Windows 2000 Professional was not created as an upgrade to Windows 98 or Windows NT 4.0, but it integrates the best features of both operating systems into one improved operating system. Some of the features that were taken from Windows 98 and Windows NT 4.0 Workstation are listed in Table 1-1. Please note that we have only listed the most popular features taken from both operating systems. Windows 2000 Professional also increased the types and number of hardware that could be supported. In fact, many additions were made to the Hardware Compatibility List (HCL) so that Windows 2000 Professional would be compatible with a wider range of hardware.

This is a big departure from Windows NT 4.0 Workstation, since it only supported a limited range of hardware. This caused additional expense to companies because they had to change many pieces of hardware before the operating system could be installed properly.

In fact, many additions were made to the Hardware Compatibility List (HCL) so that Windows 2000 Professional would be compatible with a wider range of hardware.

Table 1-1: Features from Windows 98 and Windows NT 4.0

Feature	Description
Plug-and-Play	Supports a wide range of hardware through the use of Plug-and-Play capability. This feature enables the system to automatically detect and configure hardware without user interaction.
Advanced Configuration and Power Interface (ACPI)	ACPI works hand-in-hand with Plug-and-Play by providing automatic/dynamic detection of hardware. This includes the allocation of system resources, such as IRQ and I/O addresses. It also provides the means for a device driver to be installed if it is readily available.
Universal Serial Bus (USB)	USB is an external high-speed serial bus system that enables the computer to support 127 devices through a single USB port. The USB standard permits devices to be attached or detached to the computer without powering down the system first.
Greater reliability	Windows 2000 Professional was designed to be more robust than Windows 98. This decreases the chances of system crashes.
Local security	Windows 2000 has a security enhancement feature from Windows NT 4.0 that provides local security by requiring the user to log on locally with a valid user name and password. It also uses the NTFS file system that allows you to provide local file security.

After examining Table 1-1, you can see that Windows 2000 Professional incorporates features from both operating systems to make your life easier when using this new operating system. Windows 2000 also incorporates some new features that were previously only available through additional third-party software. We have listed the most important new features in Table 1-2.

Table 1-2: New Features

Feature	Description
Disk quotas	Disk quotas enable administrators to limit the amount of disk space a user is able to use on the local system.
Internet Printing Support	This feature enables users to print over the Internet with the use of a new protocol called the Internet Printing Protocol.
Encrypting File System (EFS)	The Encrypting File System enables users to encrypt their personal data through the use of private keys.
Additional Virtual Private Networking (VPN) support	With Windows 2000, VPN operation is enhanced by including support for IPSec and L2TP protocols.

NOTE: You will learn more about these features later in this book.

INSTALLING WINDOWS 2000 PROFESSIONAL

Installing Windows 2000 Professional requires some preplanning. First, you should be aware of the minimum hardware requirements, and know how to determine which hardware is supported by Windows 2000 Professional. You must know the difference between an upgrade installation and a clean installation. Finally, you must finally decide which file system you wish to install.

Hardware Requirements

Before you can install Windows 2000 Professional, you must make sure that the minimum hardware requirements are met. Refer to Table 1-3, which lists the minimum and recommended hardware requirements. Be aware that the minimum requirements are defined by Microsoft, but in many cases are not sufficient for your computer system to perform effectively. However, for the exam you must know the minimum requirements.

Table 1-3: Minimum/Recommended Hardware Requirements

Item	Minimum Requirement	Recommended
Processor	Pentium 133MHz or higher	Pentium 166 MHz or higher
Disk Space	650 MB of free disk space and a total hard drive space of 1 GB	Variable, depending on the applications and data to be installed
Memory	64 MB	128 MB
Network Card	N/A	A NIC is needed if the user wants to connect to a network
Display	Standard VGA	Standard VGA or higher

NOTE: The minimum requirements listed in Table 1-3 are Microsoft's posted minimum. They should enable you to successfully install Windows 2000 Professional. However, the operating system may operate slowly.

EXAM TIP: It is important that you know the minimum requirements set for the processor, disk space, and memory. It is possible that you will receive at least three questions in this area.

Using the Hardware Compatibility List (HCL)

After you have met the minimum hardware requirements, you must review the HCL to make sure that your computer's hardware is compatible with Windows 2000 Professional. The HCL, a listing provided by Microsoft, guarantees that the hardware on the HCL is certified to operate properly with Windows 2000 Professional. For the most current HCL go to *http:www.microsoft.com/hcl*. *You should note that software applications are not listed on the HCL.* Another point to consider is that if you install a piece of hardware that is not listed on the HCL and you have problems afterward, Microsoft will not provide you with any technical support. An example of an HCL is shown in Figure 1-1.

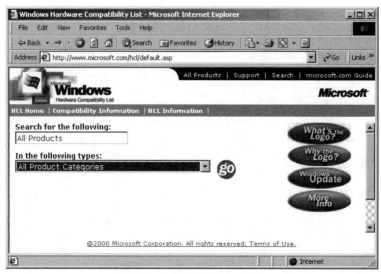

Figure 1-1: HCL Example

To upgrade systems, you can manually review the HCL, or you can use the Windows 2000 Professional CD-ROM. Go to the computer that you want to upgrade and put in the CD. Then use the ***WINNT32.EXE command with the /checkupgradeonly switch*** to evaluate the system. Note that the WINNT32.EXE command is used with 32-bit operating systems such as Windows 98 and Windows NT 4.0 Workstation. It will check your current hardware configuration and inform you on whether the upgrade will be successful. Be aware that you have to use the WINNT.EXE command for upgrading older 16-bit operating systems.

Finally, you can also go the Microsoft website and use the ***CHKUPGRD.EXE*** command to check the hardware configuration of the computer you are considering for an upgrade to Window 2000 Professional.

Let's apply the HCL to the real world. If you have to upgrade 1,000 systems for a large company with offices worldwide, what would you do?

Refer to the Challenge Solutions at the end of the chapter for the answer to this problem.

Challenge #1

Chapter 1

To Upgrade or a Clean Installation

After checking your hardware, the next step is to determine whether you want to perform an upgrade or a clean installation. *You should upgrade if you currently have Windows NT 4.0 Workstation, Windows 95/98, or Windows NT 3.51 installed.* When you upgrade you retain certain options such as *users and groups, desktop settings, applications, preferences, program groups, and items.* When you install an upgrade you actually install Windows 2000 Professional on top of (in the same folder as) the current operating system. Remember, that you cannot upgrade to Windows 2000 Professional from an operating system other than those mentioned earlier. For other operating systems, you must perform a clean installation. Any other operating system that you are not able to upgrade to Windows 2000 Professional can also be installed in a separate folder and used in a dual-boot situation.

A clean installation should be used if there is no operating system installed, or when you have an operating system that cannot be upgraded to Windows 2000 Professional. *Examples of operating systems that cannot be upgraded are DOS, Windows 3.x, Windows NT 3.5, and any other operating system; (i.e., NetWare.)* When you perform a clean installation, the systems files are copied to the WINNT folder.

Installation Options

Before you install the operating system, you must make some choices. Will your hard disk be partitioned? What file system will you use on the partitions? What licensing method will you use? Will the computer be part of a workgroup or a domain? And finally, what language will the computer use?

Your first consideration is how you will partition your hard disk. When you install Windows 2000 Professional you need 650 MB of free disk space and a total disk space of 1 GB. This means that the minimum partition size for installing the OS should be at least 1 GB.

Picking a File System

Windows 2000 Professional supports the following file systems: FAT16, FAT32, and NTFS. FAT16 (or just FAT) is the file system used by DOS and Windows 3.x. FAT16 only supports partitions up to 2 GB. It does not provide for local file security, but NTFS does. FAT16 also supports Windows 3.1 and Windows 9x.

FAT32 is a 32-bit version of FAT that first shipped with Windows 95 OEM (OSR2). It can support partitions up to 2 TB. FAT32 also improved disk storage efficiency by reducing cluster sizes. This file system does not provide local file security, compression, disk quotas, or file encryption, as does NTFS. *Note that Windows NT 4.0 Workstation does not support FAT32.*

NTFS can recognize FAT32 partitions, but Windows 98 cannot recognize NTFS partitions.

Challenge #2

Let's say that you want to dual boot your Windows 2000 Professional computer with Windows 98. "Dual boot" means that you wish to retain Windows 98 and do a clean installation of Windows 2000 Professional in a different location. What file system should you choose?

If you elect to use FAT as your file system, the partition will automatically be formatted with FAT16 if its size is less than 2 GB. If the partition is over 2 GB, it will be formatted as FAT32. FAT16 and FAT32 do not support local security and provide only network security through shares. As a side note, FAT16 does not recognize FAT32.

If you dual boot FAT16 with NTFS, the NTFS file system can recognize the FAT16 partition, but the FAT16 partition cannot recognize the NTFS file system.

Now comes the file system that made Windows 2000 popular—the New Technology File System (NTFS). NTFS-5 that ships with Windows 2000 permits you to provide local security for files and folders. *NTFS also provides support for data compression, disk quotas, and file encryption. NTFS can recognize FAT16, FAT32, and NTFS. *You must also use NTFS if you wish to use Active Directory.* You will learn more about Active Directory later. Take note that Windows NT 4.0 Workstation shipped with NTFS-4 and if you are planning to have a dual-boot configuration between this OS and Windows 2000 Professional, the NT 4.0 computer must be upgraded with Service Pack 4 installed. This configures the NTFS-4 file system to NTFS-5.

EXAM TIP: Know that Windows NT 4.0 does not support FAT32. What this means is that if you have a computer that has both Windows NT 4.0 and Windows 98, then the file system must be NTFS on both operating systems. If you dual boot Windows 98 with Windows 2000 Professional, the file system used to install Windows 2000 Professional must be FAT32. This will permit the operating systems to recognize each other. If you are going to use Active Directory you must use NTFS. Finally, know that NTFS supports local security for files and folders, data compression, disk quotas, and file encryption.

Installation into a Domain or Workgroup

You sould consider installing Windows 2000 Professional into a Workgroup if you have a small, decentralized network, or if the Windows 2000 Professional operating system is installed on a non-networked computer. Normally, you would choose to install the operating system into a Workgroup if a server is not configured on the network. You would use the domain installation method if you have a network server and want to implement tighter security on the network.

Installation Methods

There are two installation methods to choose from. You can install from the Windows 2000 Professional Setup CD or from a network share.

Using the Windows 2000 Professional Setup CD, there are three ways to perform the install. They are:

1. Boot to the operating system currently installed on the computer and use the *WINNT.EXE or WINNT32.EXE* commands. An example of the WINNT32.EXE command is shown in Figure 1-2. You must use the WINNT.EXE command if you are booting from a 16-bit operating system such as DOS or Windows 3.1. You would use WINNT32.EXE if you are booting from a 32-bit operating system such as Windows 9x or Windows NT 4.0.

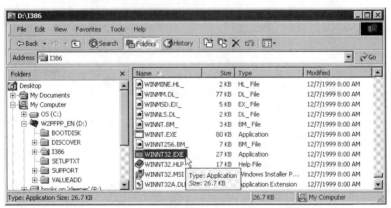

Figure 1-2: Using the WINNT32.EXE Command

> **EXAM TIP:** Know that if you have Windows 98 on your computer, for example, and you wish to install Windows 2000 Professional, you would use the WINNT32.EXE command. If you have a 16-bit operating system you would, of course, use WINNT.EXE. This small section can result in at least two questions.

2. If your computer can boot from the CD, all you have to do is insert the CD into the drive and reboot the machine. The installation process will start automatically.

3. If there is no operating system installed you must use the Windows 2000 Professional Setup boot disks. These disks will boot your computer to a command prompt and load the CD-ROM drivers.

To create Windows 2000 Professional Setup boot disks you need four disks. These disks can be created from a 32-bit operating system such as Windows 2000, Windows NT, or Windows 9x. The command used with these operating systems is *\MAKEBT32.EXE*. This utility can be found on the Windows 2000 Professional CD in the *BOOTDISK folder*.

You can also create Setup boot disks from 16-bit operating systems, such as DOS and Windows 3.1, with the *MAKEBOOT.EXE command*. This command is entered through the Start\Run dialog box and produces the inquiry screen shown in Figure 1-3.

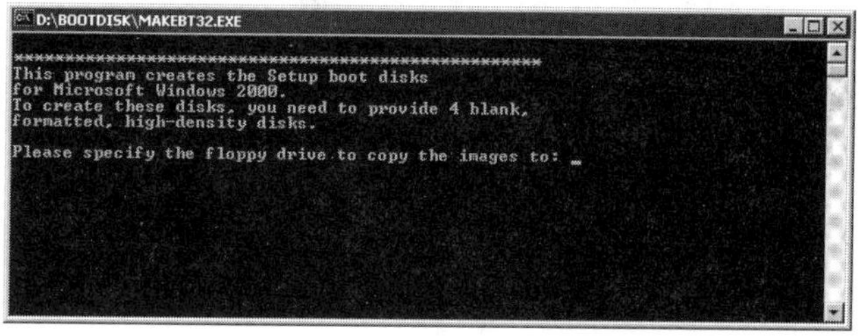

Figure 1-3: MAKEBT32.EXE

NOTE: The Setup boot disks can be used to install the OS, or to boot your computer to the Recovery Console, when the computer will not boot up on its own. We will examine the Recovery Console later in this book.

EXAM TIP: You must be aware that you can install Windows 2000 Professional from the current operating system, the CD-ROM (if your computer supports it), and from the Setup boot disks. Know that to create the Setup boot disks you use the MAKEBT32 or MAKEBOOT command. You must know which operating system uses which command. Finally, be aware that these utilities can be found in the BOOTDISK folder of the Windows 2000 Professional CD.

The Setup boot disks are not specific to a particular computer. This means that you can use the disks on different computers.

You are upgrading two Windows NT 4.0 Workstation computers to Windows 2000 Professional and one of the computers installs successfully, but the other experiences a power loss and cannot boot into NT 4.0. What action can you undertake to get the second machine to operate?

EXAM TIP: Know that the Setup boot disks are not computer-specific and can be used to start another machine that is having problems with the installation process.

Installation Over the Network

You have seen that you can install the Windows 2000 operating system from the CD. Now we will show you how to install the operating system over the network.

The first thing you need to establish is a distribution server. A distribution server is a computer that has the Windows Professional distribution files stored in a shared folder. Here are the steps used to install Windows 2000 from a network share:

- First, start the computer that will receive the operating system.

- Connect to the distribution server and find the *WINNT shared folder*.

- Use the WINNT.EXE or WINNT32.EXE command.

NOTE: *If the CD-ROM is unavailable*, or you cannot boot to the CD, then installing the operating system over the network is the best option. For this process you must create a bootable floppy disk and boot the system from that disk. Then, connect to the distribution server, locate the \I386 folder, and then click the Winnt.exe file. The installation process will start. Follow the instructions to install Windows 2000 Professional.

EXAM TIP: Know that in order to install Windows 2000 over the network you must first have a distribution server with the operating system files located in a shared folder. Also, know that the executable files WINNT and WINNT32 are located in the WINNT shared folder. Finally, know that if the CD-ROM is unavailable or you cannot boot to the CD, installing over the network is the next best option.

The Setup Program

After you decide how you will install the operating system, you must understand the setup process. You need to understand the setup process, not only to know how to make the installation successful, but also to be able to troubleshoot a failed installation. The setup process goes as follows:

Start the setup process with the WINNT.EXE or WINNT32.EXE command, depending on the operating system you are installing or upgrading from. The Windows 2000 Setup dialog box will appear and ask you where you would like the operating system installed. It is normal to accept the default of WINNT by pressing ENTER.

At this point, the setup files are copied to your hard drive. Figure 1-4 provides an example of this process. After they have been copied, you will be prompted to remove any floppy disks and restart the computer.

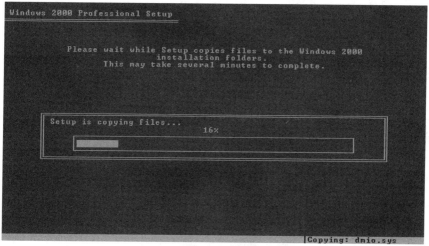

Figure 1-4: Setup Files Being Copied to the Hard Drive

After the computer restarts, you will be presented with the Windows 2000 Professional Setup dialog box, shown in Figure 1-5. You can continue the setup process by clicking on the Next button or pressing ENTER.

Figure 1-5:
Windows 2000
Setup Dialog Box

The next screen will ask you which partition you want to use to set up Windows 2000. The default folder name is \WINNT. The installation files will be copied to the installation folder and the computer will automatically reboot.

After the computer reboots, the Windows 2000 Setup Wizard will start automatically. When the Setup Wizard starts it will detect and install device drivers. It will also gather information about your locale, name, product key, licensing mode, computer name, and password. When this information gathering is complete, you must remove the CD and click the Finish button to restart the computer.

After the computer restarts, the Network Identification Wizard starts, as shown in Figure 1-6. The wizard will prompt you to input a user name and password to be used to log on to the computer.

NOTE: During the installation you must make sure that the computer name is unique to the network. Then, after installation you have to ensure that the proper protocol and network adapter are configured in Network Settings. If either of these settings is not configured properly you will receive an error message at startup stating that a dependency service failed to start.

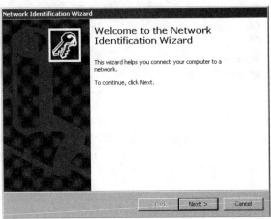

Figure 1-6: Network Identification Wizard

We have not listed the entire setup process here. Instead, we have only highlighted the important processes. One other important item to consider is that during the installation of Windows 2000 Professional, if you choose *"Typical Settings" in the Network Settings screen*, the operating system will install the following default items:

- TCP/IP using automatic configuration using a DHCP server
- Client for Microsoft Networks
- Microsoft File and Print Sharing

Other Installation Considerations

Application Compatibility - Before you upgrade to Windows 2000 Professional you must make sure that the applications currently on the computer will be compatible with the new operating system. Windows 32-bit applications are compatible and usually do not require testing prior to the installation. Windows 16-bit and DOS applications, are supported with Windows 2000 Professional. However, we recommend that you test these applications prior to installation. In addition, if you have any third-party applications, they should be thoroughly tested before you install the operating system. As a general rule, third-party applications are not usually supported under Windows 2000 Professional.

In the real world, the applications that you have on the computer prior to the upgrade may not operate properly after the upgrade has been accomplished. Upgrading to Windows NT usually required the applications to be reinstalled after the upgrade process. The main reason that applications may not work properly after upgrading to Windows 2000 Professional is that configuration information is stored in different locations in Windows 2000, Windows 95/98, and Windows NT. Before performing the upgrade, you should apply an *Upgrade Pack (called "Update Pack" on the exam)* to the computer. The Update Pack provides a migration DLL that will enable the application to operate properly in Windows 2000 Professional. You can tell the computer to use Upgrade Packs during the Windows 2000 Professional upgrade process.

Dual-Boot Support

As stated before, Windows 2000 Professional supports dual booting. This means that if you currently have an operating system on the computer, you can perform a clean installation of Windows 2000 Professional into a different folder. Why would you want to dual boot? This arrangement is normally used when you do not have enough test computers in your lab and you want to test the current systems with Windows 2000 Professional. Another reason for dual booting is for backward compatibility with legacy applications that will not operate properly under Windows 2000 Professional. If you currently have an operating system on your computer and install Windows 2000 Professional, it will automatically be configured for dual booting.

One thing to consider before dual booting is putting each operating system into a different partition. You also need to *install the simplest operating system first*. This means that you should install Windows 2000 Professional after the other operating system has been installed. Another thing to consider is that when you dual boot with Windows 2000 Professional you *cannot convert your disks to Dynamic Disks* because the other operating system will not be able to recognize them. (Dynamic Disks will be covered later in this book). You must also consider using a file system that both operating systems will be able to access. Finally, if you are going to be dual booting with Windows NT 4.0 Workstation, you should upgrade it to *Service Pack 4*, which provides NTFS version 5 support. Remember that NTFS-5 is the file system that ships with Windows 2000 Professional.

UPGRADING TO WINDOWS PROFESSIONAL

As stated previously, you should upgrade to Windows 2000 Professional if you currently have Windows NT 4.0 Workstation, Windows 95/98, or Windows NT 3.51 installed. These operating systems have a direct upgrade path. Any other Windows operating system must first be upgraded to one of these versions, and then to Windows 2000 Professional. You must also be aware that whether you upgrade or do a clean installation, the hardware requirements are the same.

Upgrading from Windows NT 4.0 Workstation

Troubleshooting the Upgrade Process

When Windows 2000 Professional is installed some log files are created by the Setup program. These log files can be reviewed to identify any problems detected during the installation process. There are two particular log files that should be used to troubleshoot installation problems.

The Action Log includes all the actions that were performed during the installation process and provides a description of each action. It also provides a list of actions in chronological order. This log is located at: *\Windir\setupact.log. Note that the Windir directory is usually the WINNT folder.

The next log file is the Error Log, which lists the errors, if any, that occur during the installation process. Each error also includes a description and an indication of its severity. This log is located at: *\Windir\setuperr.log.

Table 1-4 lists the most common installation errors:

Table 1-4: Common Installation Errors

Error	Description
Insufficient disk space	To install Windows 2000 Professional you need at least 650 MB of free disk space and a total disk space of 1GB. If Windows does not detect at least 650 MB of free space during installation, the installation will not continue.
Not enough memory	You must have 64 MB of RAM to ensure a proper installation. If you do not have enough memory, the installation may succeed, but your system will not operate properly.
Not enough processing power	You must have at least a Pentium 133 MHz processor to install the OS. If your processor is too slow, the installation may succeed, but your system will not operate properly.
Incorrect CD key	You must have a valid CD key or the installation cannot continue.
Failure to access TCP/IP network resources	If you use the default installation, the computer is set up to use DHCP. If a DHCP server is not set up on the network, you will not receive a TCP/IP address and, therefore, will not be able to access network resources.
Failure to connect to a domain controller when joining a domain	You must have a domain controller and a DNS server to join a domain. If neither is available, you will receive this message. You may also receive this message if the domain name is not entered properly.

EXAM TIP: You must know what the error messages in Table 1-4 mean and how to correct the problems. Also, be aware of the two logs created: the Setuperr.log and the Setupact.log. Finally, know the location of each log, which typically is the \WINNT folder.

Common Installation Problems

One common problem that occurs during Windows 2000 installations is that the installation process fails and freezes while copying installation files. This frequently occurs when the IDE controllers are not configured properly in the system's BIOS.

If you have an older computer with a Uninterruptable Power Supply (UPS) attached and you want to upgrade to Windows 2000 Server, you must disconnect the UPS serial cable before running the installation. Windows 2000 will view the UPS as another device and try to detect it in the PnP startup process. Under this scenario, the UPS will not operate properly.

EXAM TIP: Be aware that the problems in Challenges 4 and 5 can occur and know what actions will correct these problems.

You are installing Windows 2000 Pro on an older computer that has four 10 GB IDE drives installed. It also has an in-line UPS attached for data security purposes. In the middle of the installation routine, the system locks up and does not proceed. What is one likely cause of this problem and what action should be taken to recover from it?

Challenge #4

After you correct the problem causing the symptoms in Challenge #4, the system boots up fine. However, power in the building goes out and the system crashes. What has caused the system to crash, how do you correct the problem, and what is the condition of the data on the computer?

Challenge #5

1. You install Windows 2000 Professional on a new computer that has Windows 98 installed. It has a single 1 GB hard drive with a single partition. The partition, which is the same size as the hard drive, is formatted with FAT32. Which of the following answers gives the correct procedure to prepare the hard drive for this computer?

   a. Install Windows 2000 Professional on top of the Windows 98 operating system. Create a second partition with the Convert command and format it with NTFS. Apply the default NTFS permissions on the second partition with the secedit command.

   b. Install Windows 2000 Professional in the current system partition. Then use Disk Management to create a second partition formatted with NTFS.

   c. Install Windows 2000 Professional and choose the option to select the location of the system partition. Create a second partition with the Convert command and format it with NTFS. Apply the default NTFS permissions on the second partition with the secedit command.

   d. Repartition the hard drive, define the size of the partition for the installation of Windows 2000 Professional, and format it as NTFS, FAT32, or FAT16 during the installation. After installation use Disk Management to format the remaining hard disk space.

2. You need to upgrade five Windows NT 4.0 Workstations to Windows 2000 Professional, but you are not sure that you have enough memory in the NT 4.0 computers. What is the recommended minimum amount of memory for installing Windows 2000 Professional?

   a. 64 MB
   b. 128 MB
   c. 256 MB
   d. 1 GB

3. Which of the following items can be viewed on Microsoft's Hardware Compatibility List (HCL)? (Select all that apply.)

   a. Hard drives
   b. NIC cards
   c. Tape backup drives
   d. Software applications

4. You are new on the job and must install Windows 2000 Professional on all the computers on the network. You are not sure whether you should upgrade or perform a clean installation. Which of the following would prompt you to upgrade instead of performing a clean installation?

   a. When the computer is running NT 3.51 or NT 4.0 Workstation
   b. If you want to keep existing applications and preferences
   c. If you want to preserve existing users and groups
   d. If the computer will dual boot between Windows 2000 and a previously installed operating system

5. Someone has been breaking into your network and you want to use the improved security features of Windows 2000 Professional to stop them. Which of the following versions of Windows cannot be upgraded to Windows 2000 Professional?

   a. DOS
   b. Windows 95
   c. Windows NT 3.5 Workstation
   d. Windows 3.1
   e. NT Server 4.0

6. You have a DOS machine that you need to install Windows 2000 Professional on. Which of the following commands could you use with this machine?

   a. Setup
   b. Install
   c. WINNT
   d. WINNT32

7. You must upgrade 500 computers located all over the world. You discuss the upgrade with your assistants. One of your assistants reminds you to check the hardware compatibility list before upgrading the computers. You are also told that the best way to check whether the hardware is compatible with Windows 2000 is to use the Windows 2000 Professional CD-ROM with the WINNT32.EXE file. Which of the following switches can be used to check the hardware of the computers that you are planning to upgrade?

   a. /Checkupgradeonly
   b. /Checkupgrade
   c. /Hardwaretest
   d. /Onlycheckupgrade

8. You are the administrator of a Windows 2000 network. Tommy, your head administrator, needs to install Windows 2000 Professional on a DOS computer. After he completes the installation he wants to make boot disks in the event the computer cannot boot properly. Which of the following commands can Tommy use from the \i386 directory to make the Setup boot disks?

   a. MAKEBT32.EXE
   b. MAKEBOOT.EXE
   c. BOOTDISK.EXE
   d. MB.EXE

9. Julie has a laptop computer that she uses at work and at home. She wants to upgrade to Windows 2000 Professional, but she is concerned that her hardware may not be sufficient to perform the upgrade. Here is a list of hardware that is currently installed on her laptop computer:

   Pentium Pro 200 MHz
   32 MB of RAM
   650 MB of free space

   Which of the following answers correctly states whether her laptop computer has sufficient system resources to perform the upgrade?

   a. Her system meets the minimum system requirements for running Windows 2000 Professional.
   b. Her system must have the processor upgraded before installing Windows 2000 Professional.
   c. Her system must have the memory upgraded before installing Windows 2000 Professional.
   d. Her system must have the hard disk upgraded before installing Windows 2000 Professional.

10. You are planning to upgrade 50 network computers to Windows 2000 Professional. You are not sure of what type of hardware this operating system will support. Which of the following hardware types are supported by Windows 2000 Professional?

    a. Plug-and-Play
    b. Non-Plug-and-Play
    c. Items on the HCL
    d. All the above

11. Joe needs to upgrade the following network computer types to Windows 2000 Professional: Windows 3.1, Windows 95, Windows 98, Windows NT Workstation 3.51, and Windows NT 4.0 Workstation. Which of the following can Joe directly upgrade to Windows 2000 Professional? (Select all that apply.)
   a. Windows 3.1
   b. Windows 95
   c. Windows 98
   d. Windows NT 3.51 Workstation
   e. Windows NT 4.0 Workstation

12. Jerald currently has a Windows NT 4.0 Workstation located on a network segment. He would like to install Windows 2000 Professional on this computer in a dual-boot configuration. Both operating systems must be able to access each other's data files. Which of the following activities must Jerald perform prior to installing Windows 2000 Professional?
   a. Run Check Disk in Windows NT 4.0 Workstation.
   b. Disable disk compression in Windows NT 4.0 Workstation.
   c. Install Service Pack 4 or later for Windows NT 4.0 Workstation.
   d. Install the DFS client in Windows NT 4.0 Workstation.

13. Ken is testing operating systems to check their compatibility with each other. He chooses to use a new computer as the test machine. This computer has three hard drives: Disk 0, Disk 1, Disk 2. Each disk has a storage capacity of 5 GB and will be configured in a way that each partition encompasses an entire hard drive. His first test configuration will be a dual boot of Windows 98 and Windows 2000 Professional. Disk 0 will be used to install Windows 2000 Professional and must be able to provide for local security. Windows 98 will be installed on Disk 1. He also wants to allow both operating systems to save documents to Disk 2 and to retrieve them at will. Select the following disk configuration that will meet all of Ken's requirements?
   a. Disk 0 NTFS, Disk 1 FAT32, Disk 2 FAT32
   b. Disk 0 FAT32, Disk 1 FAT32, Disk 2 FAT32
   c. Disk 0 FAT16, Disk 1 FAT32, Disk 2 FAT32
   d. Disk 0 NTFS, Disk 1 FAT32, Disk 2 NTFS

14. Tony is the software manager of a small Windows 2000 network. He needs to install Windows 2000 Professional on a new computer on the network. After a typical installation, he needs to confirm the location of the system files, but he is not sure where to look. Which of the following describes the location that Tony should search for the system files?

a. The \Winnt directory
b. The \I386 folder
c. The \Windows\system folder
d. The \Windows directory

1. **d.** FDISK the hard drive, create a partition with a minimum size of 650 MB (1 GB total disk space), and format it as NTFS, FAT32 or FAT16 during installation. You cannot create a second partition because Windows 2000 Professional requires a total disk space of 1 GB which is the size of the only drive you have.

2. **a.** According to Microsoft, this is the minimum required amount of RAM, but in our opinion, more RAM is needed for the computer to perform properly. 128 MB is the minimum required amount of RAM need to install Windows 2000 Server.

3. **a, b, c.** The key to this question is to identify all the hardware items. That is what the Hardware Compatibility List (HCL) is used for.

4. **a, b, c.** These operating systems provide for a direct upgrade to Windows 2000 Professional. If you want to keep existing applications and preferences, you must upgrade to Windows 2000 Professional. If you perform a clean installation your applications and preferences will be lost. If you want to preserve existing users and groups, you must upgrade to Windows 2000 Professional. If you conduct a clean installation your existing users and groups will be lost. Upgrading to Windows 2000 Professional will not provide for a dual boot between Windows 2000 Professional and the previous operating system. In this case you would perform a clean installation.

5. **a, c, d, e.** You cannot directly upgrade DOS, Windows 3.1, or Windows NT 3.5 to Windows 2000 Professional. These operating systems do not have a direct upgrade path to Windows 2000 Professional. You must first upgrade these operating systems to Windows NT 4.0 Workstation and then to Windows 2000 Professional.

6. **c.** If you want to install Windows 2000 Professional from a 16-bit operating system such as DOS, use the WINNT command. WINNT32 is used when you are installing Windows 2000 Professional from a 32-bit operating system like Windows 9x or Windows NT 4.0. Windows 2000 Professional does not recognize the Install and Setup commands to install the operating system.

7. **a.** This switch, when used with the WINNT32.EXE command, will check the hardware on the machine you intend to upgrade to Windows 2000 Professional.

8. **b.** When you make Setup boot disks in a 32-bit operating system, the MAKEBT32.EXE is the command that you would use. MAKEBOOT.EXE is the command to use when you want to make setup disks on a 16-bit operating system such as DOS. BOOTDISK.EXE and MB.EXE are not commands in Windows 2000 Professional.

9. **c.** The memory must upgraded to at least 64 MB.

10. **d.** All the items are supported by Windows 2000 Professional. One item to note is that if you try to install a piece of hardware that is not listed on the HCL, Microsoft will not provide you any technical support.

11. **b, c, d, e.** These are the operating systems that have a direct upgrade path to Windows 2000 Professional. You cannot upgrade Windows 3.1, DOS, or Windows NT 3.5 directly. These operating systems must first be upgraded to Windows NT 4.0 Workstation and then to Windows 2000 Professional.

12. **c.** Installing Service Pack 4 or later on the Windows NT 4.0 Workstation will enable this operating system to access the Windows 2000 Professional data files. This Service Pack actually upgrades the NTFS-4 file system to NTFS-5, which is the file system used in Windows 2000 Professional.

13. **a.** Disk 0 is configured with NTFS to permit Windows 2000 Professional to provide for local file security. Disk 1 is formatted with FAT32 because that is the default file system for Windows 98. Disk 2 must be formatted to enable Windows 98 to use this disk. Disk 0, which is Windows 2000 Professional, can recognize Disk 2, which is a FAT32 disk.

14. **a.** In a typical installation the Windows Setup utility will install the Windows 2000 Professional files in the \Winnt directory.

Challenge Solutions

1. To upgrade systems, you can manually review the HCL or you can use the Windows 2000 Professional CD-ROM. Go to the computer that you want to upgrade and put in the CD. Then use the WINNT32.EXE command with the /checkupgradeonly switch. Note that the WINNT32.EXE is used from 32-bit operating systems like Windows 98 and Windows NT 4.0 Workstation. This will check your current hardware configuration and inform you on whether the upgrade will be successful. Be aware that you may have to use the WINNT.EXE command for older 16-bit applications.

   You can also go the Microsoft website and use the CHKUPGRD.EXE command to check the hardware configuration of the computer you are considering for upgrade to Window 2000 Professional.

2. The trick here is to pick a file system that both operating systems will recognize. NTFS can recognize FAT32, but Windows 98 cannot recognize NTFS.

3. To assist you with this problem you can use the computer that installed successfully to make Setup boot disks to start the other computer. Remember that the command to use is MAKEBT32.EXE because Windows NT 4.0 Workstation is a 32-bit operating system.

4. There is a chance that the system's IDE controllers have not been configured properly in the BIOS. You should restart the system, move into the CMOS Setup utility and correct the settings. Then, restart the system again and attempt to install Windows again.

5. With older computers, the Windows 2000 installation routine will try to detect the UPS as a device, rendering it useless. In Challenge 4 it was mentioned that the UPS was attached to the system. However, the problem did not show up until the power outage occurred. You must reinstall the UPS software to return it to its normal function. Any data that was not saved before the power went off is lost.

Chapter

2

Automated Windows 2000 Professional Installation

These are the areas that are generally testable on the MCSE Professional 2000 examination:

1. Perform an unattended installation of Windows 2000 Professional.

   • Install Windows 2000 Professional using Windows 2000 Server Remote Installation Services.

   • Install Windows 2000 Professional using the System Preparation tool

   • Create unattended answer files using Setup Manager to automate the installation of Windows 2000 Professional.

2. Install applications using Windows Installer packages.

Introduction

In this chapter you will learn how to automate your Windows 2000 Professional installations. This chapter may be short, but the information has been condensed and you can expect at least five possible exam questions from this material. You will learn that the Sysprep and Setupmgr utilities are located on the Windows 2000 Server CD under this path: Support\Tools\Deploy.cab. They are called deployment utilities. You will also learn that the Extract command is used while in Windows Explorer to enable you to use these utilities.

Yoy will also discover that the Sysprep utility is used to prepare a disk image used in the automated setup process. You will learn the switches that are used with the Sysprep utility. You will then learn how the source computer is configured with the Sysprep utility. One item of importance is that in order for the installation to be successful using the Sysprep utility, the source (master) and target computer must have the same hardware installed.

The Setup Manager utility is used to prepare answer Files. You will learn that Setup Manager enables you to prepare answer files for unattend installations, Sysprep installations (disk images), and Remote Installation Services. Then you will discover that Sysprep answer files can only be used to install Windows 2000 operating systems.

Then you will learn how to set up a RIS server to enable PXE-compatible clients to install Windows Professional on computers on your network.

Finally, we will show you how to distribute application packages to network clients.

AUTOMATED DEPLOYMENT OF WINDOWS 2000 PROFESSIONAL

Coming up with a plan to deploy Windows 2000 Professional throughout your network could save you a lot of time. As you discovered in Chapter 1, you can manually install Windows Professional on each computer, or you can choose to automate the process. You should choose to automate the installation process if you have many computers that you must install or upgrade to Windows 2000 Professional. The automated process can be used in the following ways:

• Remote installation process

- Disk imaging process (We call this the "snapshot process")

- Unattended installation process

The first process we will discuss is the Remote Installation Services (RIS) process. This process is new to Windows 2000 and enables you to remotely install Windows 2000 Professional on computers located on your network. For the process to operate properly you must first set up an RIS Server that will be configured to remotely install the operating system. Each computer that will receive the operating system must have a *Pre-boot Execution Environment (PXE) network card installed, or use an RIS boot disk with a PXE-compatible network card to ensure the RIS process is successful. A PXE network card has a small computer chip on it that allows the computer to connect to the network.*

EXAM TIP: Know that in order for the RIS process to operate properly either the client computer must have a PXE network card installed or you must use an RIS boot disk to reach the RIS server.

RIS Server Defined

The RIS server can be configured to install Windows 2000 Professional using a CD-based image, or with a Remote Installation Preparation (RIPrep) image. The CD-based image only contains the Windows 2000 Professional operating system installation files. This is important because if you also want to install certain applications as part of your deployment you will need to use the RIPrep image method. The RIPrep image method is actually called "disk imaging", which we prefer to call the "shapshot process." This process configures a source computer with Windows 2000 Professional, all the needed applications, and any system configurations that you would like to establish on the destination computer. The destination computer will be a mirror image of the source computer.

Disk Imaging Defined

Let's begin with some basic terminology. The computer that the image is created from may be referred to as: the source, master, or reference computer. The computer that receives this image is the target or destination computer. The disk imaging process is carried out as follows:

First, the source computer must have Windows 2000 Professional installed, along with any applications that you wish to install. Next, the source computer must have its hardware configured in the manner that you wish the target computer to be set up. After the source computer has been set up the way you want it, *the System Preparation (Sysprep) tool* utility must be used to prepare (ghost) the image on a hard disk. Next, the disk is removed from the source computer and placed into a disk duplicator, which is used to copy the image on the disk to other hard drives. The copied disks are then removed and placed into the target computers that will receive the image. When the target computer is first turned on, the disk image goes through a mini-setup process. We refer to the source computer a "snapshot" system because you take a snapshot of the disk drive as it is currently configured and transfer it to another computer. Disk images are generally used when you have many computers that need to be configured with the same settings and applications. For disk imaging to work properly the source and the target computers must meet these requirements:

- *The SCSI or IDE controllers must be the same type on the source and target computers*

- *The processor type must be the same type on the source and destination computers*

- *The target computer's hard drive must have at least the same amount of space as that of the source computer.*

EXAM TIP: You must realize that in order for the disk imaging process to work properly the source computer must be configured with the operating system, additional applications, and hardware configurations first, and then the Sysprep utility can be used. Also know that the target computers must meet the three requirements listed above.

NOTE: Plug-and-Play devices on the source and destination computers do not need to be identical. The drivers just need to be available.

Unattended Installation Defined

The unattended method of automated installation is used when the computers that will receive Windows 2000 Professional are not PXE-compliant. This method employs a master computer, normally referred to as a distribution server, which is used to install the operating system on the target or destination computers. The master computer usually has an answer file that assists in the automated installation process. The only requirement for this process to operate properly is that the target computer must be able to connect to the distribution server over the network. When the network connection has been established the installation process can proceed.

Answer files are scripts used to answer questions that would normally occur during an installation of Windows Professional. They can be used with unattended installations, RIS installations, or Sysprep installations (disk image). An answer file is generally used when the computers that will receive the Windows Professional operating system are not configured exactly the same. The answer file can be configured to permit no user intervention. *Answer files are created by using the Setup Manager utility.* The Setup Manager enables you to create answer files using a GUI interface that provides a user-friendly environment. This utility enables you to automate the installation of user-specific or computer-specific configuration information that will be used on the target computers. It also provides a vehicle for including application setup scripts. When you use this utility, it actually creates the distribution folder that will be employed for the Windows 2000 Professional installation process. *In order to gain access to the Setup Manager, you must first extract the utility from the Windows 2000 Deployment Tools located on the Windows 2000 Server CD.*

EXAM TIP: Definitely know that answer files are created with the Setup Manager utility. Also, know that before you can use the Setup Manager, it must first be extracted from the Windows 2000 Deployment Tools.

USING THE DEPLOYMENT TOOLS

What are deployment tools? Well, they consist of two utilities that are used for automated installations. One is the System Preparation (Sysprep) tool, which is used to prepare disk images. The other utility is the Setup Manager (Setupmgr), which is used to create answer files. These utilities are located on the Windows 2000 Professional CD under the path: *Support\Tools\Deploy.cab*. In order to use these utilities, they must first be converted with the *Extract command in Windows Explorer*. Figure 2-1 shows how to use the Extract command.

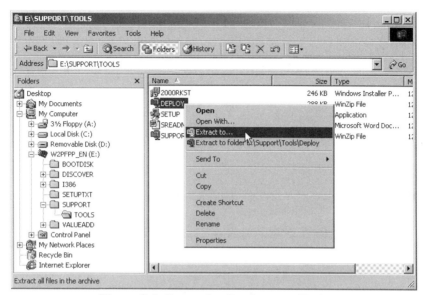

Figure 2-1: Extracting Deployment Tools

You must be logged on as the Administrator to use the "Extract" command. Before you use the Extract command, you should first create a location for the extracted files to reside. A folder named Deployment Tools should be created in the root folder of your C: drive as the destination of the extracted files.

EXAM TIP: You must be aware that the Sysprep and Setupmgr utilities are located on the Windows 2000 Professional CD under the path: Support\Tools\Deploy.cab. Then you must know that the Extract command should be used from Windows Explorer to enable you to use these utilities.

Setup Manager

As stated before, the Setup Manager is used not only to create a new answer file, but also to edit an answer file that was previously configured. *Setup Manager enables you to prepare answer files for Windows 2000 unattended installation, Sysprep installations, and Remote Installation Services. Sysprep answer files are created with an .inf extension. Another important consideration is that Sysprep answer files can only be used to automatically install Windows 2000. No other operating system can be installed using these files.* After you have properly extracted the Deployment Tools, you start the Setup Manager utility by double-clicking the "setupmgr" icon in the Deployment Tools folder. When the Setup Manager starts, you will be given a welcome screen, just press the Next button. The New or Existing Answer File screen, shown in Figure 2-2, provides you with three choices:

- Create a new answer file
- Create an answer file that duplicates this computer's configuration
- Modify an existing answer file

NOTE: When the answer file is created, the default name is "remboot.txt".

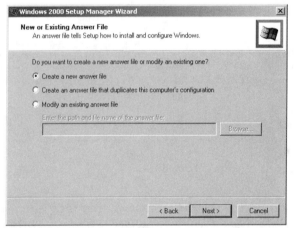

Figure 2-2: New or Existing Answer File Dialog Box

EXAM TIP: Know that the Setup Manager utility can be used to prepare answer files. Also, know that Setup Manager will permit you to prepare answer files for unattended installations, Sysprep installations, and Remote Installation Services. Also, be aware that Sysprep answer files are created with an .inf extension. Finally, know that Sysprep answer files can only be used to install Windows 2000.

The System Preparation Tool

The System Preparation (Sysprep) tool is used to take an image of the source computer and copy it to a target computer. When the image is placed on the target computer, a smaller version of the Windows 2000 Professional setup program runs. An answer file can be created to perform the installation without user input. Table 2-1 describes the sysprep command switches that can be used.

Table 2-1: The Sysprep Command Switches

Switch	Description
-quite	Performs the installation with no user interaction
-pnp	Informs the Setup program to detect Plug-and-Play hardware
-reboot	Restarts the target computer
-Nosidget	Does not create a SID on the target computer. A SID is a security ID that identifies the computer on the network.

NOTE: After the System Preparation tool is used on the source computer, the Setup Manager Wizard must be used to identify the unique computer information.

EXAM TIP: You must understand that the Sysprep utility is employed to prepares a disk image used in the setup process. You must also know the switches that are used with the Sysprep utility. Learn all of these, but pay particular attention to the –quite switch.

Now, to consider some real world information about the Sysprep utility. Let's say that you have just received 20 computer systems that currently have Windows 98 installed on them. Each system has dual processors. You want to upgrade these systems to Windows 2000 Professional. After running Setup on the deployment machine, only one of the processors was detected. What should you do now?

Challenge #1

An important item to consider when using the Sysprep utility is that the source (master computer) and the target computer must have the *same hardware installed* to ensure that the installation is successful. If the hardware is different, you will have to install the operating system locally using the Setup boot disks or a bootable CD.

EXAM TIP: Be aware that the configuration of the source computer at the time the Sysprep utility is run will establish the configuration that the target computers will receive. You must also know that in order for the installation to be successful using the Sysprep utility, the source (master) and target computer must have the same hardware installed.

Planning Unattended Installations

Unattended Windows 2000 Professional installations are performed using a distribution server. Remember, a distribution server has the operating system installation files located in a shared folder. The distribution server can also have answer files to assist with the automated installation process. Answer files are used to provide information that is normally entered by the user, such as computer name, acceptance of the license agreement, networking details, etc.

Challenge #2

Let's say Timmy has created an unattended answer file with the Setup Manager. He has configured this file for 20 computers. He just received two new computers and he wants to add them to the unattended answer file. How would he accomplish this task?

Unattended installations work best when the target computers have been tested to ensure that their hardware is compatible with Windows 2000 Professional.

You want to use the unattended installation method to automatically install Windows 2000 Professional on 50 computers. You have some hardware drivers that are not digitally signed, but you want to use them anyway. Describe the procedure that will enable you to use these unsigned drivers and not display a warning message on the destination computers?

Challenge #3

Planning to Use Remote Installation Services (RIS)

Remote Installation Services (RIS) can be used to remotely install Windows 2000 Professional to computers on your network. In order to use RIS you must first set up an RIS server to store the Windows 2000 Professional operating system files. These files are actually stored in a shared image folder that is used by the clients to install the operating system. Answer files are normally used with this process to permit the installation to proceed without user interaction.

Remote Installation Services must be installed on a Window 2000 Server configured as a domain controller or as a member server. The RIS server must meet the general hardware requirements of a typical Windows 2000 Server installation as follows: an 133 MHz processor or higher and 128 MB of RAM. *The only difference is that the hard drive on the RIS server must have at least two disk partitions. One partition will be used for the operating system and the other partition will be used for the RIS image. The partition that will hold the RIS image must be at least 2 GB in size and formatted with the NTFS file system. Of course, the RIS server must also have a network adapter installed.*

In order for the RIS process to be successful a *DHCP server must be available on the network* and it must be configured to assign IP addresses to the RIS clients. A DNS server configured as an Active Directory integrated server must also be available to locate the RIS server and RIS clients.

Automated Windows 2000 Professional Installation   **39**

To install the RIS server you must use the "Configure Your Server" utility located in the Administrative Tools folder. While you are in the utility, select the Advanced option and then select Optional Components. This will start a wizard that installs the RIS Server. After the RIS server has been installed, it must be configured to provide installation services.

To help you with the installation, the items required for the RIS process to operate properly are:

1. Windows 2000 Server with RIS installed

2. DNS server

3. DHCP server (Authorized in Active Directory)

4. Windows 2000 domain with Active Directory, which means a domain controller

5. Client computer that can connect to the network, with either a PXE NIC or PXE-compliant NIC and a RIS client boot disk

6. Ability of the client to reach the DHCP server

NOTE: *The most common cause of the RIS process failing is when the client is behind a router (or a server acting as a router) that does not forward BOOTP information. This information would include DHCP requests. To make sure that the client can receive DHCP information, you can either install a DHCP Relay Agent or add another DHCP server to the network segment in which the client resides.*

EXAM TIP: Know all the required items needed to ensure that the RIS process operates properly.

Detailed Instructions on Installing a RIS Server

To configure an RIS server to install the Windows 2000 Professional operating system you can use a CD-based image, or an RIPrep image, as explained earlier. To start the process you must select Start and, in the Run dialog box, type "RISETUP". This will start the RIS Setup Wizard. During this process, you will be prompted to provide the location of the Remote Installation Folder. *This folder cannot be placed on the system or boot partition. It must be located on a partition formatted with NTFS (version 5).* You can also define whether the server will respond to client computers that request the service, or not respond to unknown client computer requests.

After the RIS server has been installed, the DHCP server must be authorized to operate in the Active Directory environment by using the DHCP Manager. (Remember that the DHCP server automatically configures the RIS clients with dynamic IP address information.) This authorization is necessary for security reasons. The authorization process is initiated by first accessing the DHCP Manager and then, in the left pane, right-clicking the DHCP server and selecting the "Authorize" option. This process is shown in Figure 2-3.

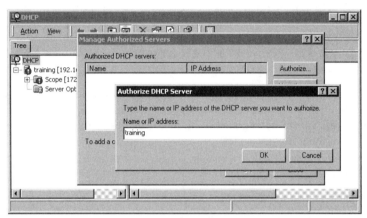

Figure 2-3: Authorizing a DHCP Server

Users must be granted the right to create a computer account. This is accomplished in the Active Directory Users and Computers utility. by right-clicking on the domain or organization unit for which you would like users to create computer accounts and then selecting the "Delegate Control" option from the pop-up menu. This will start the Delegation of Control Wizard that enables you to designate which users or groups will be authorized to create computer accounts and, thereby, install the Windows 2000 Professional operating system using RIS. The option to select is "Join a computer to the domain". The user must then be granted the user right "Log on as a Batch Job". This right is granted through the Group Policy snap-in.

Setting up the RIS Client

An RIS client is a computer that will have the Windows 2000 Professional operating system installed. Of course, the target computer must meet the hardware requirements for a typical installation of Windows 2000 Professional. The client must also have a network adapter card that has a PXE-based boot ROM installed. The ROM chip works with the computer's BIOS to connect to the RIS server. If the network card supports PXE, then the client can use an RIS boot disk to contact the RIS server. To create an RIS boot disk, enter the following command in the Run dialog box: *\\RIS_Server\\Reminst\Admin\I386\Rbfg.exe*. This will take you through the process of creating the RIS boot disk. You will normally choose to browse the network and find the RIS server. From here you can simply click the Reminst folder, the Admin folder, the I386 folder, and finally the *Rbfg.exe* file to start the process.

EXAM TIP: Know that the Rbfg.exe executable file will actually create an RIS client boot disk.

Windows Installer Packages

You can use Windows Installer Packages when you want to deploy a new application to your network clients. For this process to operate properly, your network must have a Windows 2000 Server acting as a domain controller. This process works with applications of the following types:

- Microsoft Installer (MSI) format files
- Repackaged applications (MSI files)
- Transform files (MST patch files)
- ZAP files

You should use MSI files when they are available and use ZAP files when MSI files are not available. ZAP files usually install applications in their native Setup program. You can also use MST transform files to create customized application installations that provide specific features for those applications. *You can only use MST files if the application includes a modification tool to create customized configurations.*

Windows Installer Packages can be used in the following two ways:

- *Published Applications.* This method is used when you want to give the user a choice to install the application with the Add/Remove Program utility in the Control Panel.

- *Assigned Applications.* This method automatically installs the application when a user attempts to open the application on the Programs menu.

To initiate the Windows Installer Packages process, you must perform the following steps:

1. Create a network share and copy the MSI application to it.

2. Create a Group Policy Object (GPO) for the application. This step is accomplished using the Active Directory Users and Computers utility. After you enter the utility, right-click your domain name, select Properties, then click the Group Policy tab, as illustrated in Figure 2-4. Notice the "New" button near the bottom of this figure. This button is used to create a new GPO.

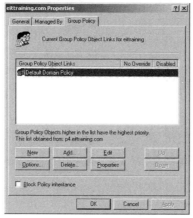

Figure 2-4: Domain Properties Dialog Box, Group Policy Tab

3. Authorize users or groups to access the application. After the GPO has been created, you must identify the users or groups that will be permitted to install the package. This is accomplished through the Group Policy tab of the domain Properties dialog box by highlighting the package you just created, then clicking the Properties button. This will bring up the new Domain Policy's Properties dialog box. You must select the Security tab as shown in Figure 2-5.

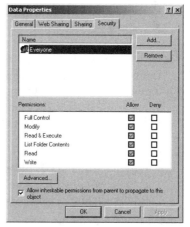

Figure 2-5: Default Domain Policy Properties Dialog Box, Security Tab

4. Add the package to the GPO. This is where the package is identified as published or assigned to a user or computer. The process goes like this: Use the Group Policy tab of the domain Properties dialog box, highlight the package, and click the Edit button. This will bring up the Group Policy window, expand the User Configuration, expand Software Settings, right-click Software Installation, and select New then Package. After the package is added to the GPO, users with permissions will be able to install the package with the Add/Remove Programs utility in the Control Panel.

EXAM TIP: Become familiar with all the processes required to properly configure Windows Installer Packages to deploy "assigned" or "published" applications to your network users. Don't forget to pay particular attention to the CHALLENGES. They should be treated just like EXAM TIPS. In other words, you may very likely see some of this information on the exam.

Review Questions

1. Tommy is the lead administrator and wants to create an answer file. He creates the answer file and now he cannot find it. Which of the following files should he be looking for?
   a. sysprep.txt
   b. sysprep.msi
   c. sysprep.ini
   d. sysprep.inf

2. Timmy has created an unattended answer file using the Setup Manager. He has configured this file for 20 computers. He just received two new computers and wants to add them to the unattended answer file. Which of the following will enable him to add the new computers for an unattended installation over the network?
   a. Edit the unattend.txt file with Notepad.
   b. Edit the unattend.udf file with Notepad.
   c. Edit the winnt.sif file with Notepad.
   d. Edit the unattend.bat file with Notepad.

3. Tony must automate the installation of 30 computers with Windows 2000 Professional. An answer file is needed to ensure that the process operates properly. Which of the following is the best tool to use to create an answer file?
   a. syprep.exe
   b. unattend.exe
   c. Setup Manager Wizard
   d. RIS

4. Jerry needs to perform an unattended installation of 200 Windows 2000 Professional computers located on the network. He is not sure of which answer file to use. Which of the following is the correct file to use? (Select two answers.)
   a. unattend.txt
   b. sysprep.inf
   c. RIS.txt
   d. attend.txt

5. You have 20 computer systems that currently have Windows 98 installed on them. Each system has dual processors. You want to upgrade these systems to Windows 2000 Professional. After running Setup on the deployment machine, only one of the processors was detected. Which of the following must you accomplish to complete the upgrade?
   a. Use sysprep.exe and update the other machines after deployment.
   b. Use sysprep.exe with the –pnp option.
   c. On the deployment machine use Device Manager to make the system recognize the second processor. Then run sysprep.exe.
   d. Windows 2000 Professional does not support dual processors.

6. You are the assistant to the network manager and want to learn more about the Sysprep answer file. You are told that this file can be used to remotely install which of the following operating systems?
   a. Windows 3.1
   b. Windows 98
   c. Windows NT 4.0 or 3.51
   d. Windows 2000

7. You currently have a Windows NT 4.0 Workstation and want to use the /syspart switch when installing Windows 2000 Professional. Which of the following commands can you use with the /syspart switch in this situation?
   a. WINNT
   b. WINNT32
   c. Setup
   d. Install

8. You are the administrator for a small Windows 2000 network and you wish to install Windows 2000 Professional on 20 computer systems that currently have Windows 98 installed. The source computer and the Windows 98 systems have different hardware configurations. Each system is currently connected to the network to allow it to connect to the source server. In this case, which of the following installation methods can be utilized? (Select two answers.)
   a. Sysprep method
   b. Syspart method
   c. Setup disks method
   d. Bootable CD method

9. Jimmy is the network administrator of a company in the midwest. He has been asked to automate the installation of Windows 2000 Professional on 10 DOS systems and 4 Windows 3.x systems. Each system has network connectivity and can connect to the distribution server. Which of the following processes will enable you to automate the installation? (Select two.)
   a. Create a /I386 folder on the distribution share on the network server. Copy the contents of the /I386 folder from the Windows 2000 Professional CD and answer file to the folder that you created.
   b. On the local hard disk, share the installation files by copying them from /I386 folder on the CD-ROM to the A: drive.
   c. Go to the distribution folder that contains the installation files on the computers running MS-DOS or Windows 3.x and run the command : WINNT/u:/s:/t:
   d. Go to the distribution folder that contains the installation files on the computers running MS-DOS or Windows 3.x and run the command: WINNT32/unattended: /d:

10. You are preparing your 20 new computers to utilize the sysprep.exe program to duplicate Windows 2000 Professional to each new system. You wish to perform the automated duplication and prepare the master computer image in an hour. Which of the following switches can be used along with sysprep.exe to accomplish this task?
    a. -reboot
    b. -auto
    c. -quiet
    d. -pnp

11. Timmy has 25 Windows 98 computers on his network that he would like to upgrade to Windows 2000 Professional. Each computer is PXE-compliant and all have the same hardware configuration. During the installation process five of the computers are upgraded properly and the setup process suddenly stops. Which of the following is the best solution for completing the upgrade process?
    a. Change the BIOS settings.
    b. Add more IP addresses in the DHCP server.
    c. Make startup disks using RBFG.EXE.
    d. Use the PXE-boot disks to connect to the RIS server.

12. You have 10 Windows 98 client computers that you would like to upgrade to Windows 2000 Professional. Before you start the process, you confirm that the network currently has a DNS server, a domain controller is configured to use Active Directory, the RIS server is correctly installed, and the client computer has network connectivity. The client is behind a router that is non-BOOTP compliant. Which of the following will ensure that the automated installation will be successful?
    a. Install a DHCP Relay Agent on the network segment on which the client resides.
    b. Install a WINS server on the network segment on which the client resides.
    c. Install a DNS server on the network segment on which the client resides.
    d. Nothing is wrong; the installation will proceed as normal.

13. Jerry is the network administrator for your network. He has 30 new computers that he must install Windows 2000 Professional on. Fifteen of the computers are PXE-compliant and the other 15 are not PXE-compliant. Before he proceeds, he verifies that all the computers contain hardware that is on the HCL. He creates the RIS image and configures the RIS Server to deploy the operating system. He starts all the computers to initiate the installation process. Later, he learns that the 15 PXE-compliant computers successfully installed the operating system, but the other non-PXE-compliant computers were not able to connect to the RIS server. Which of the following enables these computers to contact the RIS server?

    a. Run Rbfg.exe to create a non-PXE-compliant startup disk.
    b. Run Riprep.exe to create a non-PXE-complaint startup disk.
    c. Grant the everyone group NTFS Read permission for the RIS image.
    d. Grant Administrators group NTFS Read permission for the RIS image.

Answers and Explanations

1. **d.** He would look for the sysprep file with the .inf extension.

2. **a.** The unattend.txt file must be edited to include the additional computers required for installation.

3. **c.** The Setup Manager is used to create answer files.

4. **a, b.** Unattend.txt and sysprep.inf are types of answer files that can be used. Look at the extensions carefully.

5. **c.** The deployment machine must be configured to recognize the second processor. Then run the SysPrep utility.

6. **d.** The SysPrep answer file can only be used to install Windows 2000 Server or Professional.

7. **b.** This command is used to install Windows 2000 Professional from a 32-bit operating system like Windows NT 4.0 Workstation. Winnt is used to install Windows 2000 Professional from a 16-bit operating system like DOS. Windows 2000 Professional does not use the Setup and Install commands to install the operating system.

8. **c, d.** Because the computers that are to receive the operating system do not have the same hardware they must be installed locally from setup disks or the bootable CD.

9. **a, c.** These are the correct answers. But before you copy the contents of the /I386 folder, the share on the network server must shared. The WINNT /u:/s:/t command enables the client computers to copy the operating system from the network share. Remember that the WINNT command is used to install Windows 2000 Professional on a 16-bit operating system.

10. **c.** This is the correct switch to do the automated duplication and prepare the master computer image. This switch can be used in conjunction with sysprep.exe to accomplish this.

11. **b.** Because all the computers are PXE-compliant and have the same hardware configuration the installation processes should have been successful. The only other reason that the process failed is because the DHCP server did not have enough dynamic IP addresses to issue to the clients.

12. **a.** Because the automated installation process must use DHCP services, the client must be able to contact the DHCP server. The best choice is a DHCP Replay Agent located on the network segment on which the client resides.

13. **a.** The non-PXE-compliant computers need to connect to the RIS server and the Rbfg.exe program can be used to create an RIS client boot disk. Granting the Everyone group NTFS Read permissions has nothing to do with installation of the operating system. The Administrators group already has full permission for the RIS image.

Challenge Solutions

1. Simply, use Device Manager on the deployment machine to make the system recognize the second processor. At this point you can use the Sysprep utility, take a snapshot of the computer, and deploy the image to the other Windows 98 systems. You configure the source computer the way you want the target system to be configured when that image of the operating system is installed.

2. Locate the unattend.txt file, open it with Notepad, and edit the file to include the additional computers that will receive the operating system.

3. Simply go the source computer on the System Properties Hardware tab, click the Driver Signing button, and choose the Ignore ratio button. After the unattended installations are complete, return to the default settings.

Chapter 3

Managing Windows 2000 Professional

These are the areas that are generally testable on the MCSE Professional 2000 examination:

1. Implement, manage, and troubleshoot input and output (I/O) devices.

2. Update device drivers.

3. Manage and troubleshoot driver signing.

4. Monitor and configure multiple processing units.

5. Configure and troubleshoot fax support.

6. Configure and troubleshoot desktop settings.

7. Configure support for multiple languages or multiple locations.

8. Configure and troubleshoot accessibility services.

Managing Windows 2000 Professional

Introduction

This chapter is the longest for a reason. It has many screen shots that are absolutely necessary to learn in order to prepare for the exam. There is a lot of critical information here, so read and reread this chapter.

The first topic we'll discuss is the Control Panel. In this section we will highlight some utilities that you may see on the examination. You will receive some valuable information about the Accessibility Options. Pay special attention to what the ToggleKeys and StickyKeys options are used for, and take a close look at how accessibility features can be turned off automatically.

Next, you will be shown how to gain access to the Computer Management Utility and become familiar with what this utility is used for. We will also briefly cover subsections of the Computer Management Utility in this section.

Next, we will discuss the benefits of the Microsoft Management Console (MMC). The MMC is one of the primary administrative tools in Windows 2000 Professional. There are four modes and each offers different types of access to the MMC. You will learn that you can access the MMC by typing "mmc" in the Run command line.

Two different types of Registry editors are shipped with Windows 2000 Professional—REGEDIT and REGEDT32. You will become familiar with the characteristics of each. The most important characteristic about REGEDIT is that it cannot be used in read-only mode.

The Device Manager is the main tool that you use to configure hardware for your computer. You will learn how to access Device Manager and the Troubleshooter Wizard. You will also learn how to troubleshoot certain hardware devices using Device Manager, as well as how to update a device driver. You should also be aware that the best place to get a current device driver is the manufacturer's web site.

We will then take a look at how to configure the video adapter. The most important aspect of the configuration process is that the Adapter tab has a Properties button, which will bring up a dialog box that enables you to change drivers and resources. You will then discover that the Monitor tab enables you to change the video's refresh frequency.

Driver Signing is a special driver certification process developed by Microsoft to certify that drivers are authorized for use on your computer. You will learn how to access the Driver Signing utility. There are three options that you must learn how to set. You must know what each option does for the Driver Signing process. You will then discover that there is a command line utility, "signverif", which will allow you to check whether a driver is a signed driver.

You must know how to enable support for multiple processors and, in the section after that, must learn how to configure the computer for multiple languages. In this same general area you will learn how to configure a computer to permit users to send and receive faxes.

Finally, we will instruct you on how to use the System Information utility to troubleshoot your computer's current configuration. You will not be able to correct problems through this utility. You probably will have to use Device Manager for this.

THE CONTROL PANEL

The Control Panel should be your primary tool for configuring your computer. We will not list each of the items located in the Control Panel. Instead, we will highlight the important items that you need to know in order to prepare for the examination.

The first item to discuss is the Accessibility Options applet. This utility adjusts the appearance and behavior of Windows 2000 to enhance accessibility for vision-impaired, hearing-impaired, and mobility-impaired users. You do not require additional hardware or software to configure these functions. They are built into the Windows 2000 Professional operating system.

Accessibility Options

You can find the Accessibility Options applet in the Control Panel. In the following list of Accessibility Options tabs we have listed the most common features.

Keyboard tab. This tab is used to configure special features such as StickyKeys, FilterKeys, and ToggleKeys. Table 3-1 lists the most common Accessibility Options that can be configured.

Table 3-1: Accessibility Options

Option	Description
*ToggleKeys	Is used if you want to hear tones when pressing the CAPS LOCK, NUM LOCK, and SCROLL LOCK keys
*StickyKeys	Is used if you want to use SHIFT, CTRL, or ALT keys by pressing one key at a time.

Sound tab. The Sound tab enables users to activate the SoundSentry that displays a visual warning when the computer emits a sound. Also on this tab is the ShowSounds option, which will display captions for speech and sound on the computer.

General tab. This tab enables the SerialKey feature that permits users to employ a substitute device instead of a keyboard or mouse. Now, for the important part of this tab. Notice in Figure 3-1 that there is a "Turn off accessibility features after idle for:" checkbox. ***If this checkbox is selected, the accessibility features will be turned off after a predetermined time. If you do not want to turn off this feature, then the checkbox must be unchecked.***

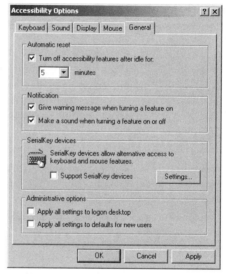

Figure 3-1: Accessibility Options, General Tab

EXAM TIP: Become familiar with all the features that are included in the Accessibility Options feature. In particular, know that the General tab is used to turn on or off the accessibility features through the "Turn off accessibility features after idle for" checkbox.

There are other icons listed in the Control Panel. Table 3-2 provides a good representation of the most used icons and gives descriptions of their use.

Table 3-2: Other Icons in the Control Panel

Icon	Description
Add/Remove Hardware	Used to install and remove hardware on your computer. This utility is normally used for older legacy devices (non-PnP).
Add/Remove Programs	Used to install and remove programs or to add or remove Windows 2000 components.
Display	Used to configure the computer's display (monitor). This is where the display's drivers are loaded.
Folder Options	Used to configure folder properties and offline files and folders.
Regional Options	Used to set regional options, which includes numbers, currency, time, date, and input locales.
Scheduled Tasks	Used to configure tasks to be run at specific times.

EXAM TIP: Know what ToggleKeys and StickyKeys are used for.

THE COMPUTER MANAGEMENT UTILITY

The Computer Management utility enables you to use a single utility to manage the following items. This utility can be accessed by right-clicking the My Computer icon located on the desktop and *selecting the Manage option*.

System Tools – Many useful tools are located here, such as Event Viewer, System Information, Performance Logs and Alerts, Shared Folders, Device Manager, and Local Users and Groups. So many useful utilities located in one place! Figure 3-2 gives you a good representation of the System Tools.

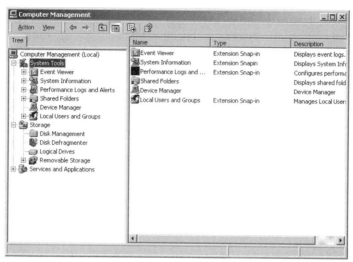

Figure 3-2: System Tools

Storage – As the name implies, this utility is used to manage the computer's storage devices. The tools located here are Disk Management, Disk Defragmenter, Removable Storage, and Logical Drives.

Services and Applications – Many utilities are located here also, such as DHCP, DNS, Indexing Service, WMI Control, Telephony, Services, and IIS.

EXAM TIP: Know how to gain access to the Computer Management utility—right-click on the My Computer Icon and select Manage. You may have to perform some simulated tasks from this utility for the exam and you must know what is located here.

THE MICROSOFT MANAGEMENT CONSOLE

The Microsoft Management Console (MMC) is one of the primary administrative tools in Windows 2000 Professional. It starts out by default as a blank utility. You have to select the snap-ins (administrative tools) that you will access frequently and add them to the console. The MMC allows you to customize the tools you need to accomplish certain tasks. The MMC was designed to provide a standardized appearance for all the snap-ins you wish to use. MMC snap-ins can be saved and shared with other administrators. You can access the MMC by *typing "mmc"* in the Run dialog box. The MMC can be configured with the permissions listed in Table 3-3.

Table 3-3: MMC Permissions

Option	Description
Author Mode	Users have full use of all the MMC functions.
User Mode-full access	Users have full access to window management commands, but they cannot add or remove snap-ins.
User Mode-limited access, multiple window	Users can create new windows, but they can only access the portion of the console tree that was visible when the console was last saved.
User Mode-limited access, single window	Users can only access the portion of the console tree that was visible when the console was last saved. They cannot create new windows.

EXAM TIP: You must know all the modes listed in Table 3-3 and what type of permissions each will provide. In particular, know the two modes preceded by the "*". You must also be aware that you can access the MMC by typing "mmc" in the Run dialog box. Finally, know that MMC is one of the primary administrative tools in Windows 2000 Professional.

How to Add a Snap-in to the MMC

First, select Console>Add/Remove Snap-in. This will open a dialog box. Click the Add button to open the Add Standalone Snap-in dialog box. Identify the snap-in you want to add to the console and click the Add button. Then, click the Close button followed by the Finish button. After you have added the snap-ins to the MMC, you can save them by selecting Console>Save As and entering a name for the console. By default, custom consoles are saved with an .msc extension.

THE REGISTRY EDITOR

The Registry Editor is used to make changes to the Registry. This tool is to be used only when absolutely necessary and only when Microsoft instructs you to make changes there. We would recommend that you back up the Registry before you make any changes to it. Normally, you would use the Control Panel applets to make safe changes to the Registry. There are two different Registry Editor utilities in Windows 2000 Professional:

- *REGEDT32* – This is the primary Registry Editor used in Windows 2000 Professional. You can edit the entire Registry with this utility. To access this utility you would type "REGEDT32 in the Run dialog box.

- *REGEDIT* – The only reason this utility is included with Windows 2000 Professional is because it offers better search capabilities than the REGEDT32 tool. This utility does not have all the editing features that REGEDT32 has. For example, *REGEDIT cannot be used in Read-only mode*. Access this utility by typing "REGEDIT" in the Run dialog box.

EXAM TIP: Be familiar with the two different Registry Editors used in Windows 2000 Professional. Most importantly, know that REGEDIT cannot be used in Read-only mode.

HOW TO INSTALL HARDWARE

Plug-and-Play Devices

Plug-and-Play devices are just as their name implies. These devices are automatically recognized and configured by the system without any help from the user. Resources are also automatically allocated and the correct driver is loaded for the device. If you have a Plug-and-Play device that is approved by Microsoft, then you should never have to make any configuration settings for it.

Legacy Hardware

What is legacy hardware? It is an older hardware device that does not support Plug-and-Play. You should not see too many of these devices any more. If you are unfortunate enough to have to install legacy hardware in your computer, it must be configured manually through the Device Manager.

The Device Manager, depicted in Figure 3-3, can be accessed by right-clicking the My Computer icon and selecting the Manage option. This will bring up the Computer Management Console. Now, select *System Tools and then Device Manager*. In the right pane, double-click on the category of the device you want to configure. Then, double-click the actual device. A Properties dialog box will appear next, as shown in Figure 3-4.

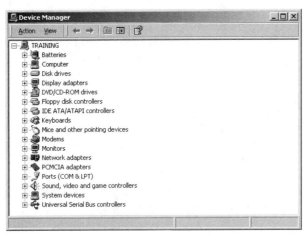

Figure 3-3: Device Manager Utility

Most devices have a General tab, as illustrated in the figure. This tab lists the device type and manufacturer. It also includes a Device status panel that tells you whether the device is working properly or not. There is also a *Troubleshooter button* that you can use when you are having device problems. At the bottom of the screen is an area where you can enable or disable a device.

Figure 3-4: Device Manager, General Tab

There is also a Properties tab, illustrated in Figure 3-5. The appearance and functions associated with this tab will differ according to the device you are reviewing.

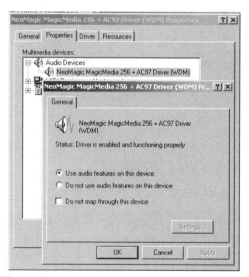

Figure 3-5: Device Manager, Properties Tab

Finally, the Driver tab is shown in Figure 3-6. This tab includes Driver Provider, Driver Date, Driver Version, and the Digital Signer. Most important are the buttons at the bottom. One is for Driver Details. The other two are for *uninstalling a driver and updating a driver.*

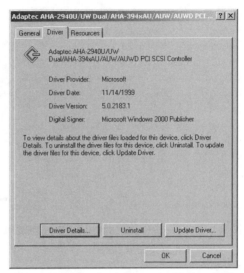

Figure 3-6: Device Manager, Driver Tab

EXAM TIP: Know that Device Manager can be accessed by right-clicking the My Computer icon and selecting the Manage option. This will bring up the Computer Management Console. From this point, select System Tools and then Device Manager. Also, be aware that the Troubleshooter button is located on the General tab on the Device Properties dialog box. Finally, know that you can uninstall and update a driver on the Driver tab of the Device Properties dialog box.

To correct a conflict between two devices (one legacy and one Plug-and-Play), simply edit the CMOS settings for the legacy device and this will tell Windows that it cannot use this IRQ. The other device will automatically be configured with other resource settings.

EXAM TIP: Know how to correct a resource conflict between two devices.

You are responsible for an older computer that has Windows 2000 Professional installed. Some time ago, you installed a non-Plug-and-Play ISA modem that was set up to use IRQ 5. Yesterday you added a newer PCI modem and rebooted the system. You want to make sure that the new modem, which is Plug-and-Play compatible, was configured properly. You decide to review the device's setting in the Device Manager. To your surprise, you find that there is an IRQ conflict between the two modems. It appears that both modems are using IRQ 5. How can you recover from this problem?

Challenge #1

HARDWARE DEVICES

Configuring Hardware with Device Manager

You can use the Device Manager to delete device drivers for devices that have been removed from the system, or that have received updated drivers.

You should already know the path to the Device Manager. Locate the network adapter card that is currently installed in the computer by expanding the Network Adapters item. Then, locate the NIC card and right-click on it to make the Device Properties dialog box appear. Then, select the Driver tab, depicted in Figure 3-7. Finally, click the Uninstall button and the driver will be deleted.

Figure 3-7: NIC Card Drivers Tab

Challenge #2

You were just hired yesterday, and today you are given the task of replacing the network adapter card on one of your Windows 2000 Professional computers. After you replace the card, you notice that the new card uses a different driver than the old network adapter card. What utility should you use to remove the device driver for the original card?

Go to the Ports (COM & LPT) node, expand it and right-click on the Communications Port (COM1) entry. Select the Properties entry and click the Resources tab, as shown in Figure 3-8. Place a check in the "Use automatic settings" box.

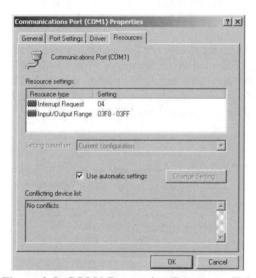

Figure 3-8: COM1 Properties, Resources Tab

Anytime you have a built-in device on the motherboard, the operating system will default to the built-in device. Here is how you can overcome this—disable the integrated device (i.e., sound card) in Device Manager, as shown in Figure 3-9. Install the new sound card in the computer and let Windows 2000 Professional automatically detect it during the next boot of the computer.

Figure 3-9: Disabling an Integrated Device in Device Manager

EXAM TIP: Know how to disable a device that is built into the motherboard.

John has been your network technician for years and he has decided to upgrade the built-in sound card on his Windows 2000 Professional machine. His machine is currently being used for important company financial documents and cannot be offline for very long. On his first attempt to install a new sound card that is listed on the HCL, he is unsuccessful. You are called in to assist. How can you configure the computer to use the new sound card?

When you see a red X on a device in the Device Manager, as illustrated in Figure 3-10, it means that someone has disabled the device. To re-enable the device: right-click on the device, select Properties, and on the General tab of the device's Properties page, select the Use This Device (enable) option under the Device usage section of the page.

Figure 3-10: Example of a Disabled PCI Modem

EXAM TIP: Know that a red X on a device means that it was disabled by someone as well as the correct procedures to re-enable the device.

You can use the Device Manager to check the system for hardware changes. Right-click on the computer's name in Device Manager (right panel) and select "Scan for hardware changes". We have provided an example in Figure 3-11.

Figure 3-11: Scanning for Hardware Changes

EXAM TIP: Be familiar with the various Device Manager processes and be aware that they work on any Windows 2000 computer. Remember to use the Device Manager, right-click on the computer's name, and select "Scan for hardware changes". You really need to become familiar with the Device Manager. You can expect at least three questions on the exam about devices failing.

Using Control Panel to Configure Hardware

Video Adapters – You can change the settings for your video adapter by using the Display Properties dialog box. You can access these settings by right-clicking in an empty area of the desktop and selecting Properties from the pop-up menu, or you can access the Display Properties dialog box from the Display icon located in the Control Panel.

After you have located the Display Properties dialog box, go to the Settings tab, shown in Figure 3-12. This tab enables you to change the Colors options for your video adapter and set its resolution. If you must make more advanced changes you should click on the ***Advanced button on the Settings tab***. This brings up a screen that has five tabs. The two tabs that you really need to concentrate on are the Adapter and Monitor tabs.

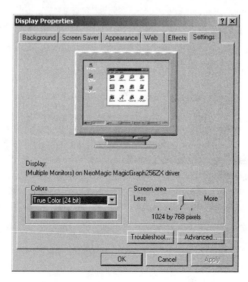

Figure 3-12: Display Properties Dialog Box, Settings Tab

The Adapter tab, shown in Figure 3-13, has a Properties button that will bring up the *same adapter properties that you would see in Device Manager.* Here you can update drivers or change the resources used by the adapter.

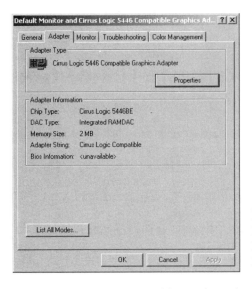

Figure 3-13: Display Properties Dialog Box, Adapter Tab

The Monitor tab, depicted in Figure 3-14, enables you to change the *Refresh Frequency* of the adapter. If the refresh rate is too low, the monitor will flicker.

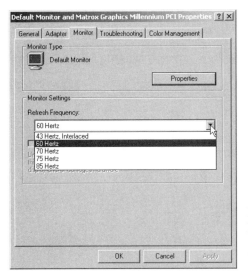

Figure 3-14: Display Properties Dialog Box, Monitor Tab

SUPPORTING MULTIPLE MONITORS

Windows 2000 Professional has a new feature that enables you to extend your desktop over a *maximum of 10 monitors*. Using all 10 monitors would permit you to have a different application on each monitor and to perform different operations at the same time. To enable multiple-display support, a separate video card must be installed for each monitor. *The only adapter cards that can be used for multiple-monitor operations are Peripheral Connection Interface (PCI) or Accelerated Graphics Port (AGP) adapters.* If you have a different type of card installed, you will not be able to use the multiple-display feature. It is common to find video display cards that are built into the motherboard. If you choose to include these in a multiple-display operation, then the motherboard chipset must use the AGP or PCI standard. *If it does not support this standard, the motherboard video display card must be disabled in Device Manager or, in some cases, even uninstalled.*

If the built-in video display card supports multiple-display operations you must install Windows 2000 Professional before the second card is installed. If you try to install a second video display card before the operating system has been installed, the Windows 2000 Professional Setup program will try to disable the built-in adapter.

Initiating the multiple-display support is easy. Simply turn off the computer and install the additional video adapter cards (don't forget to attach a monitor to each card). Turn on the computer, and provided the cards are Plug-and-Play compatible, they will be automatically configured. Next, enable multiple-display support in the Display Properties page. To access the Display Properties dialog box, right-click an empty area on the desktop and select Properties, then select the Settings tab, as shown in Figure 3-15.

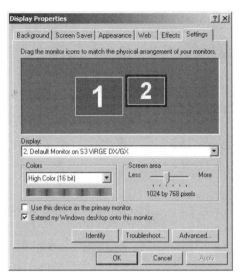

Figure 3-15: Display Properties Dialog Box, Settings Tab

After the Display Properties dialog box opens, select the monitor that will be the additional display in your multiple-display configuration and click in the "Extend my Windows desktop onto this monitor" checkbox. You can see this checkbox in Figure 3-15 near the bottom of the screen. You must perform these steps for each video adapter installed.

EXAM TIP: Learn how to enable your computer for multiple-monitor support, using up to 10 monitors. Be aware that the only adapter cards that can be used are Peripheral Connection Interface (PCI) or Accelerated Graphics Port (AGP) adapters. Also, know how to enable this support when you have a built-in video adapter card.

DEVICE DRIVERS

Updating Drivers

A device driver is programming code that enables the device to operate with your computer. The following procedure can be used to update a device driver through the Device Manager.

Go to the Device Manager and in the right panel locate the device whose driver you want to update. After you double-click the device, it will bring up the device Properties dialog box. Click the Driver tab, shown in Figure 3-16, and then click the Update Driver button. *After you click this tab the Upgrade Device Driver Wizard will start.* Simply follow the rest of the wizard's instructions and the driver will be updated.

Just one more word on device drivers—check Microsoft's Hardware Compatibility List (HCL) first to ensure that the device that you wish to install is listed. After you check the HCL and verify that the device is supported the *best place to obtain a current device driver for it is the manufacturer's web site.*

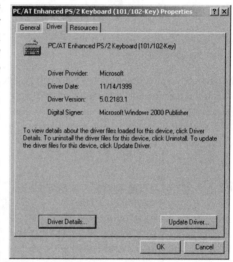

Figure 3-16: Driver Tab

EXAM TIP: Not only should you know how to access the Device Manager, but you must also know how to update a device driver. Also be aware that the best place to obtain a current device driver is the manufacturer's web site.

Driver Signing

Remember that drivers are pieces of programming code that allow your hardware to operate with an operating system. In the past poorly written drivers caused problems with the Windows operating system. Since then, Microsoft has introduced a system called Driver Signing, which guarantees that a driver is properly tested prior to release.

If you wish to enable Driver Signing on your computer, you must use the Driver Signing Options dialog box. You can reach this feature by right-clicking My Computer, selecting Properties, and then clicking the Hardware tab in the System Properties dialog box, depicted in Figure 3-17. On the Hardware tab, *click the Driver Signing option in the Device Manager section*. This will bring up the Driver Signing Options dialog box. The options you can choose when implementing Driver Signing are as follows:

> *Ignore* – This option enables Windows 2000 to install all drivers whether they are signed or not. You will not be prompted with a message about driver signing.

> *Warn* – This option tells Windows 2000 to display a warning message before installing an unsigned driver. The user can choose to continue with the installation or cancel it. This is the default setting.

> *Block* – This option tells Windows 2000 to prevent the installation of any unsigned driver. A message will be displayed, but you will not have the option to continue with the installation.

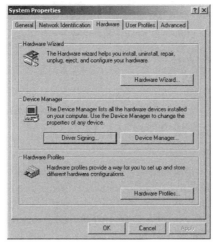

Figure 3-17: System Properties Dialog Box, Hardware Tab

NOTE: At the bottom of the Driver Signing Options dialog box is a checkbox that enables you to "Apply setting as system default", as illustrated in Figure 3-18. This means that the Driver Signing setting that you select will be applied to all users who log on to the computer. You may ask, How can I tell if the driver is Signed prior to installation? The answer is that you can use the command-line utility "signverif". This will tell you whether Microsoft has approved this driver through the Driver Signing program. To use this utility the Warn option must be selected prior to running the utility. You have to be *logged on as the Administrator* to change any Driver Signing options and to select the "Apply setting as system default" check box.

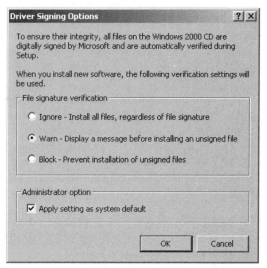

Figure 3-18: Driver Signing Dialog Box

EXAM TIP: Be able to access the Driver Signing Options dialog box. Also, know what each of the Driver Signing options will do...pay particular attention to whether a message is displayed and whether you are allowed to install the driver. Know that the "Apply setting as system default" checkbox will apply the Driver Signing option to all users of the computer. Finally, be aware that the command-line utility "signverif" will enable you to check whether a driver is a signed driver.

SYSTEM INFORMATION UTILITY

The System Information utility, shown in Figure 3-19, can be used to gather and *display information about the computer's current configuration*. This information is useful when you are troubleshooting your computer. This utility is comprised of these categories: System Summary, Hardware Resources, Components, Software Environment, and Internet Explorer 5. It can be accessed through the

Computer Management Console. Remember how to get there? *Right-click the My Computer icon and select Manage.*

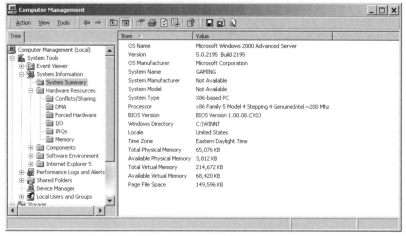

Figure 3-19: System Information Utility

EXAM TIP: Know that you can use the System Information utility to troubleshoot your computer's current configuration. However, you will not be able to correct problems through this utility. Instead, you will have to use Device Manager to make corrections. Also, know how to get to the System Information utility.

CONFIGURING LAPTOP HARDWARE

Laptops are a normal part of corporate life. They are used at work and taken out of the office, either for business, travel, or working at home. Laptops have limited power supplies and therefore Windows 2000 Professional has included Power Options with laptops in mind. This feature can be accessed through the Control Panel's Power Options icon. There may be four or five tabs located on the Power Options Properties dialog box depending on which services have been enabled on the computer. These tabs include: Power Schemes, Advanced, Hibernate, APM*, and UPS. *The APM tab only appears on those systems where the Advanced Power Management feature has been enabled.* The only tabs we will discuss are the Power Schemes, Hibernate, and APM tabs.

Power Schemes

The Power Schemes tab is shown in Figure 3-20. *This tab is used to configure when the monitor and hard drives are turned off automatically.* If you have not used the computer for a predetermined amount of time, these items will be turned off to conserve power. After all, a laptop on a business trip is no good with a dead battery.

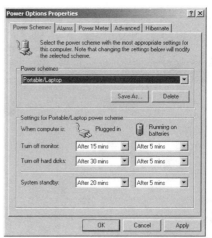

Figure 3-20: Power Options Properties, Power Schemes Tab

Hibernate

The Hibernate tab can be used to ensure that any data stored in RAM (memory) is also saved to the hard disk. With this support enabled you will not lose any valuable documents when the computer is shut down. The Hibernate tab is shown in Figure 3-21. Notice the *"Enable hiberate support"* check box in the middle of the screen. *One important item to consider is that after this checkbox is selected, you have to use the Power Schemes tab to select the amount of time the computer will wait before it hibernates.*

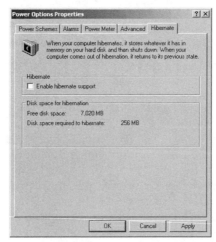

Figure 3-21: Power Options Properties, Hibernate Tab

Chapter 3

APM

The Advanced Power Management (APM) tab gives you the ability to configure your laptop to conserve power consumption. *Your BIOS must support the Advanced Configuration and Power Interface (ACPI) to be able to use the APM feature.* You can tell if your BIOS does not support the ACPI standard, because if it does not, you won't have an APM tab. Notice the *"Enable Advanced Power Management support"* checkbox in Figure 3-22.

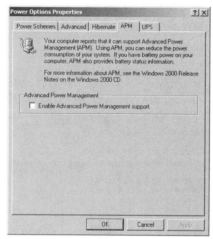

Figure 3-22: Power Options Properties, APM Tab

EXAM TIP: You can expect at least one or two questions from the Power Options utility area. Concentrate on the highlighted area.

A user approaches you explaining that they are having a problem with their company laptop. It appears that the computer will not shut down properly. It gets to the shutdown screen and stays there. Even the on/off switch will not permit him to shut the computer down. What can you do to shut down the laptop properly?

Challenge #7

CONFIGURING MULTIPLE-PROCESSOR SUPPORT

Windows 2000 Professional can support up to two processors if your computer system has this feature. This means that you may have to upgrade your BIOS to provide multiple-processor support. *To enable multiple-processor support you use the Device Manager utility with the Upgrade Device Driver Wizard.* After the driver has been installed, the Task Manager utility can be used to define processes with a particular processor. This is called "processor affinity". You will learn more about this later in this book.

EXAM TIP: Know that if your computer's BIOS provides multiple-processor support, you only need to upgrade the device driver to enable two processors.

MANAGING FAX SUPPORT

For fax support you must have a device connected to the computer that is capable of sending faxes (i.e., a fax modem). Fax support must be configured when an Administrator logs on to the system by using the Fax icon in the Control Panel. After double-clicking the Fax icon, the Fax Properties dialog box will appear. Select the Advanced Options tab and then select the Open Fax Service Management Console button, shown in Figure 3-23.

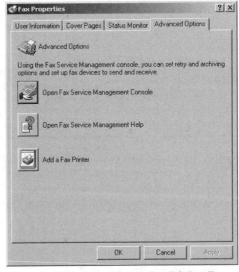

Figure 3-23: Fax Properties Dialog Box, Advanced Options

After the Open Fax Service Management Console button has been clicked, a Fax Service Management window will appear. Click the Devices option in the left pane and then double-click the fax device to be configured. A fax device Properties dialog box will appear, as shown in Figure 3-24. This is an important screen, so pay attention. *Notice that there are two checkboxes here: "Enable send" and "Enable receive".* These check boxes must be configured according to the features you desire.

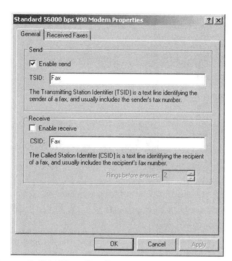

Figure 3-24: Fax Device Properties Dialog Box

EXAM TIP: In order to enable a user to send and receive faxes, you must be logged on as the Administrator and the feature must be enabled in the fax device's Properties dialog box, as shown in Figure 3-24.

CONFIGURING WINDOWS 2000 SERVICES

A service in Windows 2000 Professional is usually associated with a process that performs tasks in the operating system. Services can be managed with the Services utility, as shown in Figure 3-25. This utility can be accessed in many ways. However, we will give you only one of them—through the Services icon in the Administrative Tools folder.

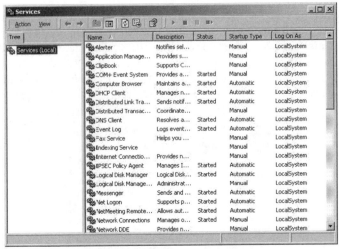

Figure 3-25: Services Window

Review each service that is listed in the right-hand pane of the Services window. If you want to configure a certain service's properties, you should double-click the service. This will bring up the service's Properties dialog box. We will not explain all the tabs shown, only the Log On tab, shown in Figure 3-26. Notice that this tab enables you to use a "Local System account" or to specify a particular account with the "This account" option. The *"This account" option is important because you must select the correct account to start the service or it may affect whether the service is properly performed.*

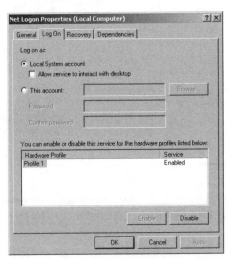

Figure 3-26: Service Properties Dialog Box, Log On Tab

ENABLING MULTIPLE LANGUAGES AND REGIONAL SETTINGS

You can enable your computer to provide support for different languages. This support enables you to edit documents in different languages. You can also provide support for different language interfaces. Windows 2000 Professional can be configured to permit a user to view, edit, and print documents in a different language. However, a localized version, such as the English version, cannot support multi-language user interfaces. A Multi-language version must be installed to provide this support.

A Multi-language version can be installed that has most of the common languages. When a specific language is installed, it contains the fonts and files that enable the monitor to display that language. If you wish to provide support for a particular language after the operating system has been installed, you can *use the Regional options in the Control Panel*. You can also use the Muisetup.exe executable file if you wish. Each language will require 45 MB of disk space.

After a localized version, such as German, has been installed using the Regional options, you will see a new icon on the taskbar that shows the current locale and keyboard inputs in use. *You can switch to a different language by clicking the icon on the taskbar and selecting the language you wish to use.*

Jordan is the software manager of a Windows 2000 network in Germany. All of the computers have the German localized edition of Windows 2000 Professional installed. The company has hired three Americans and now must permit these users to create, view, and edit documents in English from the company's existing computers. What can Jordan do to provide support of the English language?

Challenge #8

EXAM TIP: Know that to enable a language for a computer you must use the Regional options in the Control Panel. Next, know that you can switch to a different language by clicking the icon on the taskbar and then selecting the language that you want to use.

Review Questions

1. You are the administrator of a Windows 2000 network. A new user arrives that is hearing impaired. You want to configure the computer to emit sounds when certain locking keys are pressed on the keyboard. You are on a shoestring budget and must enable this feature without the use of additional hardware or software. Which of the following settings in the Accessibility options of the Control Panel would you use?
   a. StickyKeys
   b. SerialKeys
   c. ToggleKeys
   d. SoundKeys

2. You are new on the job and have just become familiar with the MMC snap-in. Now you have to provide access to this snap-in to a coworker. You wish the coworker to have full access to the MMC, but not be allowed to add or remove snap-ins. Which of the following would be the best option?
   a. Management mode
   b. User mode, full access
   c. User mode, limited access
   d. Author mode

3. You are trying to make some configuration changes to your Windows 2000 Professional computer and must use a Registry editing tool. You are aware that making changes in the Registry is dangerous and would like to use a tool with a Read-only option to avoid making any accidental changes to the computer. Which of the following is the best tool to use?
   a. REGEDIT
   b. REGEDT32
   c. EDITREG
   d. REGISTEREDIT

4. You are responsible for an older computer that has Windows 2000 Professional installed. Some time ago, you installed a non-Plug-and-Play ISA modem that was set up to use IRQ 5. Yesterday you added a newer PCI modem and rebooted the system. You want to make sure that the new modem, which is Plug-and-Play compatible, was configured properly. You decide to review the device's settings in Device Manager. To your surprise, you find an IRQ conflict between the two modems. It appears that both modems are using IRQ 5. Which of the following procedures will fix this problem?

   a. Configure Device Manager to change the IRQ for the original modem to IRQ 9.
   b. Configure Device Manager to change the IRQ for the original modem to IRQ 10.
   c. Change the CMOS settings on the computer to reserve IRQ 5 for non-Plug-and-Play devices.
   d. Change the CMOS settings on the computer to reserve IRQ 10 for non-Plug-and-Play devices.

5. You were just hired yesterday and today you are given a project to replace the network adapter card on one of your Windows 2000 Professional computers. After you replace the card, you notice that the new card uses a different driver than the old network adapter card. Which of the following is the best utility to use to make sure that the device driver for the old card is deleted from the hard disk?

   a. Add/Remove Programs
   b. Device Manager
   c. Network and Dial-Up Connections
   d. Add/Remove Hardware wizard

6. Tommy has installed a new network adapter in one of your Windows 2000 Professional computers. This computer has some mission-critical information and must permit users to connect immediately. The computer, however, appears to be unable to communicate with any of the users on the network. You must confirm that the network card was installed properly. Which of the following utilities should be used to check the card's configuration?

   a. NT Diagnostics
   b. System Information
   c. Device Manager
   d. System Management Console

7. Jim is the senior network engineer and he is having problems with a Windows Professional computer. The only change that he made was the installation of a new modem yesterday. Jim uses Device Manager and notices that an incorrect driver has been installed for the modem. He tries to use the Phone and Modem Options in the Control Panel to remove the driver, but he is unsuccessful. Each time he tries to remove the modem using this method the computer freezes. Jim must install the correct modem driver as quickly as possible. Which of the following methods will enable him to correct this problem?

   a. Use the Add/Remove Hardware wizard to uninstall the modem. Restart the computer.
   b. Shut down the computer, remove the modem card, and restart the computer. Shut down the computer again, insert the modem card, and restart the computer.
   c. Delete all references to modems in the Registry.
   d. Run the Modem troubleshooter and remove the modem when prompted. Restart the computer.

8. John has been your network technician for years and he has decided to upgrade the built-in sound card on his motherboard. The Windows 2000 Professional computer is currently being used for important company financial documents and cannot be off line for very long. He installed a new sound card that is listed on the HCL. He is unsuccessful with his first attempt to install the new card. You are called in to assist. Which of the following processes must be performed to enable the computer to use the new sound card and to make certain that the correct device drivers are installed? (Select three.)

   a. Install the new sound card into the computer.
   b. Disable the integrated sound card in Device Manager.
   c. Let Windows 2000 automatically detect the new sound card during the next boot of the computer after the sound card is installed.
   d. Disable the new sound card in the CMOS.

9. You have just upgraded a Windows 98 computer to Windows 2000 Professional. Next, you decide to install a USB scanner while the system remains powered on. How can the computer be forced to properly search for and detect the newly installed scanner?
   a. Restart the computer.
   b. Log off and back on to the computer.
   c. Right-click on the computer's name in Device Manager and select "Scan for hardware changes".
   d. This is not possible since Windows 2000 Professional does not support adding hardware while the computer is on.

10. Shara is responsible for ensuring that all the Windows 2000 network computers have the proper device drivers installed. She has just installed a new driver for the network interface card and is concerned that the driver be the most current and approved by Microsoft. Which of the following features will automatically tell her whether the driver has passed Microsoft's driver certification process?
    a. Event Logs
    b. Driver Signing
    c. Device Manager
    d. Service Pack Slipstreaming

11. A user installs a new video adapter on one of your Windows 2000 Professional computers. One hour later, you receive a call from a user who reports that the computer will not boot up. You have identified that the problem was caused by the installation of an unsigned device driver. You must make sure that this does not happen again and that the solution will be applied to all users on the computer. Which of the following options must be used in the Driver Signing Options dialog box to guarantee that users will be prevented from installing any unsigned device drivers? (Select two answers.)
    a. Set File Signature Verification to Block.
    b. Set File Signature Verification to Ignore.
    c. Set File Signature Verification to Warn.
    d. Select the Apply settings as system default checkbox.

12. Charles is the network administrator of a Windows 2000 network configured as a workgroup. The workgroup has two file servers and 25 Windows 2000 Professional client computers. You must configure all the computers to prevent any unsigned drivers from being installed in the workgroup. Which of the following actions will ensure that no unsigned drivers are installed?
    a. Configure a group policy for the domain that ignores all unsigned drivers.
    b. Configure a group policy for the default domain controller to block all unsigned drivers.
    c. Configure the two file servers and the 25 Windows 2000 Professional client computers to block unsigned drivers.
    d. Do nothing; this is the default setting.

13. Fran has been ordered to install a new network interface card in one of the network's Windows 2000 Professional computers. She wants to make sure that the new card is configured properly. The card has been installed and she needs to use a utility that will show the computer's current configuration. Which of the following is the best selection for viewing the current configuration?
    a. NT Diagnostics
    b. System Configuration Manager
    c. System Information
    d. System Diagnostics

14. A user approaches you explaining that they are having a problem with their laptop. It appears that the computer will not shut down properly. It gets to the shutdown screen and stays there. The on/off switch will not allow you to shut the computer down. Which of the following should you perform to enable the laptop to shut down properly?
    a. Enable APM in Control Panel, Power options.
    b. Disable APM in the BIOS.
    c. Enable hibernate in Control Panel, Power options.
    d. Pull out the battery and then shut down.

1. **c.** ToggleKeys are used if you want to hear tones when pressing the CAPS LOCK, NUM LOCK, and SCROLL LOCK keys. StickyKeys is used if you want to use the SHIFT, CTRL, or ALT keys by pressing one key at a time. SerialKeys and SoundKeys do not exist.

2. **b.** User mode, full access allows users full access to window management commands, but they cannot add or remove snap-ins. The User mode, limited access allows users to create new windows, but they can access only the areas of the console tree that were visible when the console was last saved. Author mode allows use of all the MMC functions. There is no such mode as Management mode.

3. **b.** REGEDT32 is the primary utility that you should use in Windows 2000. It offers full editing of the Registry and the option of using the utility in Read-only mode. REGEDIT is a Registry editing program that is used with Windows 2000 because it has better search capabilities than REGEDT32. REGEDIT does, however, lack the Read-only mode seen in REGEDT32. c. and d. are just made up.

4. **c.** Edit the CMOS (setup) settings on the non-Plug-and-Play device because the Plug-and-Play modem can be configured automatically by Windows 2000 Professional.

5. **b.** You would install the device in Device Manager and this would result in the driver being deleted from the hard drive. The Add/Remove Programs utility is used to manage programs, not hardware. Network and Dial-Up Connections is used to configure settings for the NIC card and will not allow you to delete drivers. The Add/Remove Hardware Wizard is used to remove hardware, but in this case Device Manager is used.

6. **c.** Device Manager is the best place to make sure that hardware is installed properly. If the device has a yellow "!" on it, there is a problem with the device. The NT Diagnostics utility was used in Windows NT and is not available in Windows 2000 Professional. System Information will provide useful information, but not enough to tell you whether the NIC is installed properly. There is no such utility as System Management Console.

7. **a.** The safest way to uninstall hardware is using the Add/Remove Hardware Wizard. Then restart the computer and start again. We recommend that you never use the Registry to perform any task unless you really know what you are doing. The Modem troubleshooter will not prompt you to remove the modem.

8. **a, b, c.** First the new sound card must be installed on the computer in order to work. Then you must disable the integrated sound card in Device Manager or it may conflict with the newly installed sound card. After you disable the sound card that is located on the motherboard, Windows 2000 will automatically detect the new sound card with no problem.

9. **c.** In Device Manager, right-click on the domain controller's name and select "Scan for hardware changes". But as a general rule, as soon as you plug the USB device into the USB port Windows should detect it. Restarting your computer is not the best solution in this case, since the device is a USB scanner and the computer is turned on. Logging off and back on will not enable the computer to detect the device.

10. **b.** Driver Signing is a new feature where Microsoft has certified which drivers are approved for installation. The Driver Signing utility will warn, ignore, or block a user trying to install a driver. Event Logs will not inform you if a driver is certified by Microsoft. Device Manager is used to install device drivers, but it is not used to certify if a driver is approved for installation by Microsoft. Service pack slipstreaming is a new process that will allow you to install applications and not be required to reinstall the service pack. Reinstalling service packs was very common in Windows NT 4.0.

11. **a, d.** Because you want to prevent users from installing any unsigned device driver, you must use the Block option. Ignore and Warn will allow the user to install the driver. Finally, you must select the "Apply setting as system default" checkbox to make this the default option for all users of this computer.

12. **c.** In order to prevent any user from installing unsigned drivers you must configure each computer manually. You cannot configure a group policy because you do not have a domain controller.

13. **c.** The System Information utility is used to collect and display information about the computer's current configuration. This information can be used to troubleshoot your computer's configuration. NT Diagnostics was used in Windows NT 4.0 and cannot be found in Windows 2000 Professional.

14. **a.** If the laptop's BIOS supports Advanced Power Management (APM) then you can enable APM with the Power options located in the Control Panel. Enabling Hibernate will not allow the laptop to shut down properly. Pulling out the battery will allow the laptop to shut down, but this is not the preferred method.

Challenge Solutions

1. The best solution to this problem is to edit the CMOS (Setup) settings on the computer to reserve IRQ 5 for the non-plug-and-play device. This will force the automatic configuration (Plug-and-Play) of the other modem, thereby removing the conflict.

2. Because we are in the Device Manager section we will use that utility. You should already know the path to Device Manager. In the right-hand panel, locate the network adapter card that is currently installed in the computer by expanding the Network Adapters item. Then locate the NIC card and right-click to make the Device Properties dialog box appear. Then select the Driver tab. Finally, click the Uninstall button and the driver will be deleted.

3. The solution should be simple to you now. Use Device Manager, go to the CD-ROM device, and right-click and select properties. Then go to the Resources tab and place a check in the "Use automatic Settings" box.

4. Anytime you have a built-in device located on the motherboard, the operating system defaults to the built-in device. Here is how you can correct this problem: Disable the integrated sound card in Device Manager. Install the new sound card on the computer. Let Windows 2000 Professional automatically detect the new sound card during the next boot of the computer after the sound card is installed.

5. When you see the red X, it means that someone has disabled the device. Here is how you re-enable the modem: Right-click on the modem, select Properties, and on the General tab of the modem's Properties page select Use This Device (enable) under the Device usage section of the page.

6. Right-click on the computer's name in Device Manager (right panel) and select "Scan for hardware changes".

7. Because we are in the APM section, that should be the solution. If the laptop's BIOS supports APM, enable the APM feature in the Power options applet of the Control Panel. This should allow the computer to shut down properly.

8. Instruct Jordan to use Regional options in Control Panel to add input locales and keyboard layout Input Method Editors (IME) for English. because the company is using a German localized edition of Windows 2000 Professional, support for the English language must first be installed. After it is installed the taskbar can be used to select the English language.

Users and Groups

These are the areas that are generally testable on the MCSE Server 2000 examination:

1. Implement, configure, manage, and troubleshoot local user accounts.

2. Implement, configure, manage, and troubleshoot local user authentication.

   - Configure and troubleshoot local user accounts.
   - Configure and troubleshoot domain user accounts.

Introduction

This chapter includes some subject matter that is normally covered in Windows 2000 Server. However, we feel it is necessary to include this information since it will help you pass the Professional exam. After all, Windows 2000 Professional is most commonly installed in a domain environment and you must be able to troubleshoot this operating system in an environment that you are likely to be working in.

In this chapter you will learn that domain user and group accounts are created using the Active Directory Users and Computers utility. Local user and group accounts are created using the Local Users and Groups utility.

Afterward, we will move on to cover default built-in accounts. You will learn that the Administrator account has full control over the computer. Conversely, the guest account is disabled by default for security reasons.

Next, we will discuss why Active Directory user and group accounts must be created on Windows 2000 Servers. You will learn that a security group is used to assign permissions to resources and a distribution group is used for e-mail distribution.

The Backup Operators group does not need explicit permissions for files to be able to back up the file system. Power Users is a group whose members can create users and groups, but can only manage users and groups they create.

You will also discover that when you have a Windows 2000 Professional computer that is not part of a domain, you must use the Local Users and Groups utility to create a user account. You must be logged in as an Administrator or as a member of the Power Users group to create a user account. The user name must be distinguishable from all the user names and groups on the local computer. If the username is not unique, you will not be able to log on to the computer. Finally, know that in order to create a new user account you must right-click the Users folder in the Local Users and Groups utility and select the New User option.

For the exam you must also know some information about the Active Directory Users and Computers utility. We will focus on the options associated with the Account tab of the user Properties dialog box. Finally, you will learn that logon hours can only be implemented on an Active Directory user account, and not on a local user account. Logon options can be accessed through the Active Directory Users and Computers utility.

LOCAL AND ACTIVE DIRECTORY USER AND GROUP ACCOUNTS

The Active Directory is a directory service that enables you to manage the network from a single location. It is designed so that you can create user and group accounts for domain users. Active Directory can only be implemented on a Windows 2000 Server acting as a domain controller. The utility used to create these accounts is the *Active Directory Users and Computers utility.*

Local user and group accounts can be created on a Windows 2000 Professional computer configured in a workgroup. This means that user and group accounts only apply to that computer. The utility used to create these accounts is the *Local Users and Groups utility.*

EXAM TIP: Know that domain user and group accounts are created using the Active Directory Users and Computers utility. Also, know that local user and group accounts are created using the Local Users and Groups utility. It is important to know that local user and group accounts are configured on a Windows 2000 Professional computer in a workgroup environment.

BUILT-IN USER ACCOUNTS

When you install Windows 2000 Professional, several built-in user accounts are created by default. In Table 4-1 we have listed only the important built-in user accounts.

Table 4-1: Built-in User Accounts

User Account	Description
Administrator	This account has *full control* over the computer.
Guest	This account provides users access to a computer even if they do not have a user name and password. This account is *disabled by default* for security reasons.
Initial user	This account is only created in a workgroup environment and is a member of the Administrator group.

NOTE: All of these accounts are created on local computer environments. This means that the computer is a member of a workgroup and not a domain. One account is not usually listed in any charts: It is the Initial User account that belongs to the person that installed the operating system. The *Administrator and Initial User* are part of the Administrators group, by default.

EXAM TIP: You must know that the Administrator account has full control over the computer. The guest account is disabled by default for security reasons. Finally, know that the Initial User account is the person that installed the operating system and that the Administrator and Initial User accounts are part of the Administrators group by default.

GROUP ACCOUNTS

Local Group Accounts

Local group accounts created on a Windows 2000 Professional computer are for that computer only. The user and group accounts are stored in a local database.

Active Directory Group Accounts

Active Directory group accounts are group accounts that apply to entire networks (sometimes called domain group accounts). They must be stored on a *domain controller*. There are two different types of groups: security groups and distribution groups. The *security group* is important because it is a grouping of users that can be given access to specific resources, such as assigning permissions. A *distribution group* cannot be used to assign permissions and is usually used for e-mail distribution. The following are the different scopes of groups.

- *Domain local groups* – This group type is used to assign permissions to resources. It can contain user accounts, universal groups, and global groups from any domain in the tree or forest. It can also contain other domain local groups from its own local domain.

- *Global groups* – This group type is used to organize users for network-wide access to resources. It can contain user and global groups from the local domain.

- *Universal groups* – This group type is used to organize users according to the global catalog. The global catalog is a listing that contains information about every object in the Active Directory. The universal group may contain users from anywhere in the domain tree or forest, other universal groups, and global groups.

EXAM TIP: Establishing Domain Local Groups is the most efficient method of setting up groups for a single domain network. This group type is best suited for accessing resources in a single domain.

EXAM TIP: Know that Active Directory user and group accounts must be created on a domain controller. Also, be aware that a Security group is used to assign permissions to resources. A distribution group is used for e-mail distribution. Finally, know that domain local groups are used when dealing with a single domain structure.

Built-in Group Accounts

Table 4-2 describes the default built-in group accounts that are important to know when taking the examination:

Table 4-2: Built-in Group Accounts

Group	Description
Administrators	This group has Full Control rights and privileges. It occurs in local and domain environments.
Backup Operators	This group has rights to back up and restore the file system, but only through the Backup utility. This group *does not need explicit permissions* to the files in order to back up the file system. This group occurs in the local and domain environments.
Guests	This group is used to provide users that do not have a username and password access to resources. This group occurs in the local and domain environments.
Power Users	This group has more rights than normal users, but not as many rights as the Administrators. They can create users and groups, but they can *only manage users and groups they create*. This group can also create shares and printers. Local group only.
Users	When a user account is created it automatically becomes a member of this group. This group is useful when you want to apply a permission to all the users that will work with the computer.

EXAM TIP: Know that the Backup Operators group does not need explicit permissions to the files to back up the file system. Power Users is a group whose members can create users and groups, but can only manage users and groups that they have created.

USING THE WINDOWS SECURITY DIALOG BOX

You must present a valid user name and password to locally log on to a Windows 2000 Professional computer. If the correct information is not entered at the logon prompt, you will not be able to use any of the operating system's features. By using the Local Users and Groups utility, you can create user accounts that will enable certain users to log on to that computer. In order to reach the logon prompt, you must press the CTRL+ALT+DELETE key combination. When the correct credentials are entered at the logon prompt, the user is given an access token that tells the computer what permissions they have to its resources. This access token looks at the user account and group account memberships to determine what type of access the user will have.

The Windows Security dialog box, depicted in Figure 4-1, has many buttons located near the bottom of the screen. This box shows information about the current user that is logged on along with the date and time they logged on to the computer. This feature enables you to shut down or log off the computer. The Lock Computer button will lock the computer with the current user logged on. *When this button is used the applications continue running.* To return the computer to normal operation, the password of the user that locked the computer must be entered correctly. The Task Manager utility can be accessed from this location. Finally, users can change their passwords from this screen.

Figure 4-1: Windows Security Dialog Box

LOCAL USER ACCOUNTS

Local user accounts are accounts that are created and managed on a Windows 2000 Professional computer installed in a workgroup. These accounts cannot be used in the Active Directory (domain structure).

You create local user accounts and groups with the Local Users and Groups utility. This utility can be accessed in the *Computer Management utility,* or through the MMC as a snap-in. Make certain that you remember how to get to the Computer Management utility. Right-click the My Computer icon and select Manage to open the Computer Management console. Then expand the System Tools folder to expose the Local Users and Groups utility.

EXAM TIP: Remember that you get to the Local Users and Groups utility in the Computer Management console by right-clicking the My Computer icon, and then selecting the Manage option. This opens up the Computer Management utility. Then, expand the Systems Tools folder.

You must use the *Local Users and Groups utility* to create user accounts when the computer is configured in a workgroup and is not part of a domain. In this case, you cannot use the Active Directory Users and Computers utility.

Let's say that you are the administrator of a Windows 2000 Professional computer that is not part of a domain. You are having problems creating a user account for a new employee. You need to create a new user account, but are not sure of which utility to use. Determine which utility you will use.

Challenge #1

EXAM TIP: Know that if you have a Windows 2000 Professional computer that is not part of a domain, you must use the Local Users and Groups utility to create a user account.

New User Accounts

To create user accounts, you must be logged in as an *Administrator, or as a member of the Power Users group.* In Windows 2000, user names must be between 1–20 characters. *The user name must be distinguishable from all the user names in the local computer. *To create a new user account, you should right-click the Users folder and then select the New User option.* Figure 4-2 depicts the New User dialog box.

Figure 4-2: New User Account Dialog Box

The *Username is the only required field.* The rest are optional. The password can be up to 14 characters and is case sensitive.

Disabled User Accounts

If a user leaves the organization, you have two options—delete the account or disable the account. If you disable the account and a new user arrives who requires the same privileges and access as the other user, you can simply rename the account to the new user and change the password. If you delete the account, you cannot undelete it. Even if you create a new account with the same name, it will not be the same user account. To delete a user account, go to the Users folder and, in the right panel, highlight the user account to be deleted and select Delete. You will be prompted whether you want to delete this account. Select the Yes option to delete the account. The Administrator and Guest accounts cannot be deleted.

For security purposes, we recommend that you simply disable a user account instead of removing it. A disabled account cannot be used by a hacker to log on to a network. You may also want to disable a user account for your department heads or a user that takes a vacation and will not be accessing the network. Disabling a user account for a position that will be filled by someone else will enable you to rename that account to another user with the permissions and rights already established. This will reduce the network administrator's workload. You should also disable a user's account immediately after you receive word that they have been fired. This will stop any unhappy former employee from causing problems with your network. You can disable a user account by checking the *"**Account is disabled**" checkbox.

EXAM TIP: Know that when you create a new user account, the only required field is the User name field. Also, know that you should disable a user account rather than delete it when you know the position will be refilled by another person. This will save time administering user accounts. Finally, know how to disable a user account on the General tab by checking the "Account is disabled" checkbox.

"Disable" the account, rename it, then change its password, and the new user can start working immediately with the same network permissions that the old user had. Figure 4-3 shows a user account Properties dialog box on the General tab. Notice that the highlighted checkbox labeled "Account is disabled".

Figure 4-3: User Account Dialog Box, General Tab

Challenge #2

Let's say that you are the administrator of a small Windows 2000 network. Your friend was fired today and you are told that network security is a primary concern. A replacement is expected to arrive in a few weeks. What is the proper way to handle the user account of your former coworker?

You should change a user's password when they can't remember it. After you change the password, the user can once again log on as normal. You can change the password by right-clicking the user account and selecting the "Change Password" option. This is will produce the Change Password dialog box depicted in Figure 4-4.

Figure 4-4: Changing a Password

LOCAL USER PROPERTIES

You can manage a user account through the user Properties dialog box. This box is accessed by highlighting the user account, right-clicking it, and selecting the Properties option from the pop-up menu. Figure 4-5 illustrates the General tab of this dialog box.

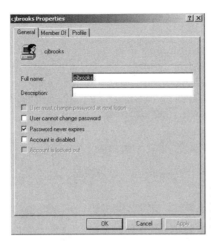

Figure 4-5: User
Properties Dialog
Box, General Tab

EXAM TIP: Know how to get to the user Properties dialog box and definitely know all the options that are located on the Account tab.

Let's say that you want to force a user to change their password. What checkbox would you select? Well, you must use the account's Properties, General tab and check the "User must change password at next login" checkbox. Notice that there are other important security features on this screen, such as *"User cannot change password", "Password never expires" and "Account is disabled".*

EXAM TIP: Know how to change a user's group membership by using the Member Of tab on the user Properties dialog box.

The user Properties dialog box can also be used to change a user's group membership. You can use the Member Of tab, shown in Figure 4-6, to make these changes. If you want to add a user to a group, click the Add button and select the desired group. If you want to remove an individual from a group, click the group to be deleted and press the Remove button.

Figure 4-6: User
Properties
Dialog Box,
Member Of Tab

The user profile, logon script, and home folder are set up using the Profile tab of the user Properties dialog box, depicted in Figure 4-7. In the figure, closely examine at the User profile section—in particular the Profile path. The default location for the user profile is the boot partition (usually \WINNT) and the Documents and Settings folder. The path will be: *WINNT\Documents and Settings.*

EXAM TIP: Know that the local path to a user profile is WINNT\Documents and Settings.

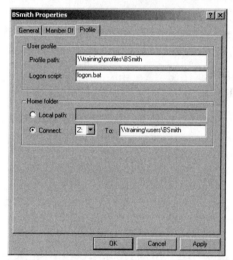

Figure 4-7: User Properties Dialog Box, Profile Tab

The user profile, highlighted in Figure 4-8, is an important topic on the exam. The first thing you need to do here is set up a *shared network folder for the individual.* This will be accomplished on a domain controller. Then, enter the path to the shared network folder from the *Profile tab* in the Properties dialog box of the user account. Here is an example:

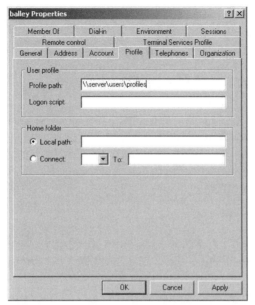

Figure 4-8: Active Directory User Properties Dialog Box, Profile Tab

The figure illustrates the Active Directory being used to create a roaming user profile. Roaming user profiles enable a user to log on to the network from any network computer and still use their user account settings. A roaming profile cannot be created on a Windows 2000 Professional computer: It must be created on a Windows 2000 Server configured in a domain. *In order to establish a roaming user profile, you must create a shared folder on a Windows 2000 Server and use the Active Directory user Properties dialog box, with the Profile tab pointing to the shared folder.*

Let's say that you are an administrator who is new to the networking environment and are given the task of administering the company's largest Windows 2000 domain. This domain currently has a DNS server and uses Active Directory. Your network has a native Windows 2000 network consisting of three Windows 2000 Servers and 50 Windows 2000 Professional client computers. You want to create roaming user profiles to enable users to log on from any computer in the network and receive their personal profile. What steps must you take to accomplish this task?

Challenge #3

Active Directory User Accounts

In Windows 2000 you manage Active Directory user accounts with the Active Directory Users and Computers utility, which is identified in Figure 4-9. This utility is accessed through the *Administrative Tools applet*. The path is *Start/Programs/Administrative Tools/Active Directory Users and Computers*. Note that Active Directory user accounts are considered to be domain accounts and can only be accessed in the Active Directory.

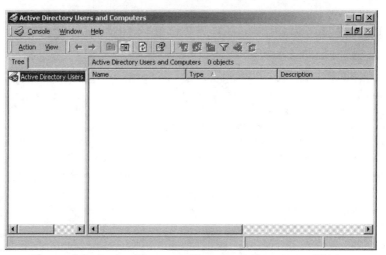

Figure 4-9: Active Directory Users and Computers Utility

The process for creating user accounts with the Active Directory Users and Computers utility is nearly the same as that used with the Local Users and Groups utility. However, this utility provides an entry for a domain path and a user logon name for pre-Windows 2000 clients.

After the user account has been created it can be managed by double-clicking the user account and selecting the tab on the user Properties dialog box that you wish to make changes on. There are 12 tabs including: General, Address, Account, Profile, Telephones, Organization, Member Of, Dial-In, Environment, Sessions, Remote Control, and Terminal Services Profile. We don't need to explain each of these tabs. In this section, we will only explain the most important tabs.

The first is the Account tab, shown in Figure 4-10. This tab is essential to learn for the test. The Account tab can be accessed in the user Properties dialog box. On this tab, you can change the logon name (user name) and Account options, such as User must change password at next logon and other password options. Finally, there is an Account expires section, which by default is set to Never. You could use this option for a temporary user where you want the account to expire after a certain date. The radio button to use in that case is the "End of" button at the bottom of the screen. Take a close look at the Logon Hours button; we will be talking about this tab in the next paragraph. As a side-note, examine the Log On To button. Briefly, this button gives you the option to select the computers that this user will be allowed to logon to.

EXAM TIP: Memorize all the features offered on the Account tab along with the information in the previous paragraph.

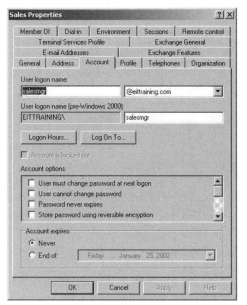

Figure 4-10: User Dialog Box, Account Tab

NOTE: The logon hours can only be set on an Active Directory user account and *NOT on a local user account.* This is an important point to remember.

Now, for an important feature that you will probably see on the exam: the *Logon Hours dialog box, depicted in Figure 4-11.* This feature enables you to restrict when users can log on to the network, and is often used when backups are being performed. The default setting is that users are allowed to log on 24 hours a day, every day. The blue portion shows when a user is authorized to log on and the white portion shows when they cannot log on. To set whether a user can log on or not, just select the boxes that you wish to consider and hit either the "Logon Permitted" or "Logon Denied" radio button.

EXAM TIP: Know that the Logon Hours function can only be implemented on an Active Directory user account and not on a local user account. Also, know how to access the Logon Hours option, using the Active Directory Users and Computer utility—right-click the user Account, select Properties, select the Account tab, and finally press the Logon Hours button.

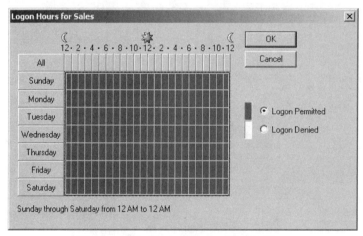

Figure 4-11: Logon Hours Dialog Box

The next tab that is essential to master for the test is the *Dial-in tab, shown in Figure 4-12.* This tab is used to provide Remote Access Permission (Dial-in or VPN). Notice the Allow access and Deny access radio buttons under the first section? These are very important to remember. There are also Callback Options which will call back a user if configured for that feature.

EXAM TIP: Know that the Dial-in tab of the user Properties dialog box is used to provide Remote Access.

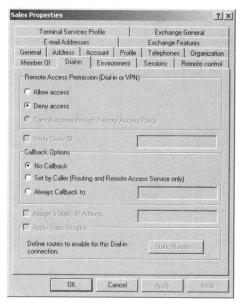

Figure 4-12: User Dialog Box, Dial-in Tab

MANAGING GROUPS

A good administrator will not assign permissions to a user, but will instead assign the users to a group and assign permissions to the group. This procedure will permit the administrator to save time when assigning permissions to all the users on the network. Can you imagine assigning individual permissions to 10,000 users!

Creating local and domain groups is the same procedure except that you use different utilities. Another difference is that local groups are created by right-clicking the Groups folder and then selecting New Group. To create a Domain Group, you must right-click the Users folder and then select New followed by the Group option.

In order to create a group you must be logged on as an Administrator, or as a member of the Power Users group. Remember, the members of the Power Users group can only manage the groups that they create. A good rule to follow is that if a built-in group can be used then it should be used instead of creating a new group. This is because built-in groups are already set up with the appropriate permissions—you only have to add a user to the group.

Remember that group names must be distinguishable from other groups or user names in the computer (or domain, if it is an Active Directory environment). A group name can be up to 256 characters long. The only required entry in the Group dialog box is the group name. It is easy to add a user to a group that you have just created. Just click the Add button and select the user to be added. To remove a user from a group, use the Remove button.

EXAM TIP: Read the previous paragraphs on groups and memorize all the information that you can. There is much useful, testable information in them.

Renaming groups is easy in Windows 2000 Professional. You would normally rename a group if the existing name does not express the current duties of the group. You could not rename groups in Window NT 4.0. Renaming a group does not change its members or permissions. To rename a group, right-click the group and choose the Rename option as shown in Figure 4-13.

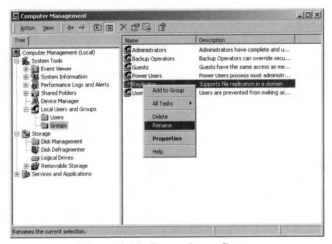

Figure 4-13: Renaming a Group

Deleting groups is also easy. You would only delete a group if you knew that you would not need this group again. After the group has been deleted all permissions and user assignments are lost. The only good thing is that the individual user accounts assigned to this group will not be lost. If you want to delete a group, right-click the desired group and select the Delete option. You will be prompted whether you really want to delete this group. You should select the Yes option.

One difference between Local and Active Directory Groups is that the Group dialog box for Active Directory Groups permits you to select the Group scope and Group type, as illustrated in Figure 4-14.

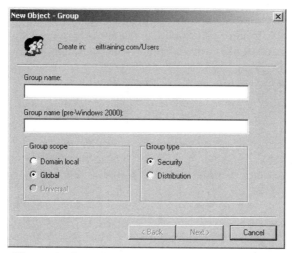

Figure 4-14: Active Directory Group Dialog Box

GENERAL DETAILS OF ACTIVE DIRECTORY

The Active Directory is not usually covered by most Windows 2000 Professional textbooks. However, it is necessary to understand Active Directory to answer many possible exam questions. First, the Active Directory is a database that stores all the information pertaining to a network in one location. With Windows NT 4.0, each server had individual databases located on each machine that only pertained to those computers.

The Active Directory includes organizational structures such as containers, domains, and organizational units (OUs). A container is used to define the structure of a network. Domains and OUs are substructures that are usually placed into containers. A domain is a group of objects that share security and account information. Each domain must have a domain controller, which maintains a complete domain database. Each domain can contain many OUs, which are used to logically organize a domain. Think of an OU as a logical structure for group users, groups, security policies, computers, printers, file shares, and other objects that mirror your physical network structure. One main point to remember when it comes to OUs is that *OUs cannot be moved from one domain to another domain.*

EXAM TIP: Know that you cannot move OUs from one domain to another domain.

Domains can be connected with other domains to create domain trees and domain forests. A domain tree is an organization of domains in a single, contiguous namespace. Domains in a domain tree have trust relationships that enable users of one domain to access resources in another domain. A domain forest is a group of domain trees that are not part of a contiguous namespace. These structures are usually created when a company merges with another company. Domain forests can have trusts established with other forests to allow users to share resources.

In the Active Directory structure, the domain controllers must periodically update the network with any changes to their databases. The domain controllers replicate the data to each other to ensure that the Active Directory is constantly up-to-date on all machines.

Review Questions

1. Tanya is new to the networking environment and is given the task of administering a large Windows 2000 domain. This domain currently has a DNS server available and uses Active Directory. Her network has a native Windows 2000 network consisting of three Windows 2000 Servers and 50 Windows 2000 Professional client computers. She wants to create roaming user profiles to enable users to log on from any computer on the network and receive their personal profile. Which of the following processes will enable Tanya to create roaming user profiles?
   a. Create a read-only folder on a server.
   b. From the Profile tab in the Properties dialog box of each user account, enter the path to a read-only folder.
   c. Create a shared folder on a server.
   d. From the Profile tab in the Properties dialog box of each user account, enter the path to a shared folder.

2. Jerald is managing user accounts and is having trouble locating a user's local profile on a Windows 2000 Professional computer. Which of the following is by default the proper location for a user's local profile?
   a. Boot partition\username
   b. Boot partition\Winnt\profiles
   c. WINNT\Documents and settings
   d. Boot partition\Winnt

3.	You are the administrator of a Windows 2000 Professional computer configured in a workgroup. Which of the following accounts are members of the Administrators local group by default? (Select all that apply.)
a. Replicator
b. Initial User
c. Administrator
d. Backup Operators

4.	Tommy is a member of the Backup Operators group and has some questions about his backup duties. He first asks if he must be given explicit NTFS permissions to a file in order to back up and restore it. Which of the following best answers his question?
a. Yes
b. No
c. If the computers have Logon locally rights
d. If the computers have been promoted to domain administrators

5.	You are a member of the IT department of your company. Your user account has just been added to Power Users group. You are not sure what permissions now apply to you. You are wondering whether you can now access all files, regardless of whether you have been granted permission or not. Which of the following is the best answer?
a. Yes
b. No
c. If their effective permissions allow
d. If they also belong to the Administrators group

6.	You are the administrator of a small Windows 2000 network. Your friend was fired today and you are told that network security is a primary concern. A replacement is expected to arrive within a few weeks. Which of the following is the proper way to handle the user account of your former coworker?
a. Lock out the account.
b. Delete the account.
c. Disable the account.
d. Apply a policy to the account.

7. In order to create a share on a Windows 2000 Professional computer that is configured in a workgroup, a user must be a member of one of which two groups? (Select two.)
   a. Everyone
   b. Power Users
   c. Administrators
   d. Supervisor

8. Nicole has Administrator rights to assist you with administering a Windows 2000 Professional computer configured in a workgroup. Her primary duties are creating backups and setting up user accounts. She is constantly reviewing other users' documents. You want her to have fewer rights and still be able to perform her duties. What rights should you give?
   a. Full Administrator rights
   b. Power User and Backup Operators
   c. Server Operators privileges
   d. Normal users rights

9. You are the local administrator of a Windows 2000 Professional computer configured in a workgroup. The user who normally uses this computer is leaving the company and another employee will be assuming her position. The new user must be given the same permissions as the old user and you want to minimize your administrative workload. Finally, the old user must have no access to any resource. Which of the following provides the correct way to achieve your goals?
   a. Rename the user account and change the password.
   b. Copy the old account to the new account and then delete the old account.
   c. Copy the old user profile to the new user account.
   d. Delete the old account. Create a new account and place it in all the groups that the old account was in. Manually reassign all the user-specific rights and permissions from the old account to the new account.

10. You must come up with a naming convention policy for creating user names on your Windows 2000 Professional computer. Which requirements must be followed to create a new user account? (Select all that apply.)
    a. The user name cannot exceed 20 characters.
    b. The user name must be unique.
    c. The user name cannot consist solely of either periods or spaces.
    d. The user name must be at least 8 characters in length.

11. Keith is responsible for creating users and groups on a Windows 2000 Professional computer that is configured in a workgroup. He must create some new user accounts and groups on this computer but he is not sure of all the rules. Which of the following statements are true? (Select all that apply.)
   a. If you rename a user account it will retain all of its properties.
   b. If you rename a group it will retain all of its properties.
   c. If you delete a user account and then create another one with the same name, it will retain all of the properties of the original account.
   d. If you delete a group and then create another one with the same name, it will have all of the properties of the original group.

12. You are the local user accounts manager for a Windows 2000 Professional computer that is configured in a workgroup. You have an assistant to help you administer the user accounts on this computer. Your assistant creates eight new user accounts and you want him to be able to manage those accounts, but no other user account on the computer. Which of the following groups should he be assigned to?
   a. Printer Operators
   b. Administrators
   c. Backup Operators
   d. Power Users

13. You are the local administrator for a Windows 2000 Professional computer that is configured in a workgroup. You know that you can change a user's password with the Local Users and Groups utility. But you are not sure how a normal user can change their password on this computer. Which of the following provides the most correct answer?
   a. Through the Local Users and Groups utility
   b. Using the Change Password button in the Windows Security dialog box
   c. Through the Computers and Users utility
   d. Using the Change Password button in the System Tools dialog box

14. You are the local administrator of a Windows 2000 Professional computer that is configured in a workgroup. One of the users is always locking the computer. This computer has many applications that are always running and you want to know what happens to those applications when the user locks the computer. Which of the following is the correct answer?

    a. The computer is locked. Applications continue to run.

    b. The computer is locked. Applications stop.

    c. The computer is locked and must be rebooted to start the applications.

    d. The computer is automatically rebooted when unlocked.

Answers and Explanations

1. **c, d.** Create a shared folder on the server and then go to the user accounts Properties dialog box, use the Profile tab, and enter the path to the shared folder.

2. **c.** WINNT\Documents and Settings is the default location for user profiles.

3. **b, c.** The Replicator group is not part of the Administrators group by default and the administrator would in most cases not include this account. The Initial User is part of the default Administrators local group, by default. The initial user is the person that installed the operating system.

4. **a.** Usually, the most logical answer is correct. Backup Operators can back up files even if they are not given permissions to the files. However, they can only access the files with the Backup utility. Logon locally rights has no bearing on whether the files are backed up or not. Most backups are actually performed by pulling data across the network. Domain administrators can perform backups and many other tasks. But, it is not practical to have Backup Operators with domain administrators' full access privileges.

5. **b.** Power Users cannot access any NTFS resources that they have not been given permissions to. "No" is the right answer. Power Users cannot access any NTFS resources that they have not been given permissions to. If the Power Users belonged to the Administrators Group, you would have too many individuals with Full permissions on your network to do anything they want.

6. **c.** By disabling the account you provide network security and are able to rename that account with the new employee's name. Locking out an account is only useful if a hacker is trying to get into the network. After a predetermined amount of time the account will reset and become active again. Applying a policy will not allow you to disable an account

7. **b, c.** Of course members of the Administrators group can create shares on a Windows 2000 professional computer. Power Users can also create shares on a Windows 2000 Professional computer. There is no such default group as the Supervisor. The Everyone group by default cannot create shares.

8. **b.** Putting her in the Power Users and Backup Operators groups will limit her privileges and at the same time allow her to do her work. Giving her Administrator rights would give her full privileges to do as she wishes on the network. Server Operator privileges are only configured on a server. Normal users rights will not allow her to do any of her duties.

9. **a.** Simply rename the user account for the new employee and change the password. Copying the old account to a new account will not reduce your workload. Nor will copying the old user profile to the new user account. Answer d. will work, but you shouldn't go through the entire process when you can just rename the old user account.

10. **a, b, c.** For this question these are the correct answers. The username can be up to 20 characters in length. The user name must be distinguishable from any other user names and groups on the Windows Professional computer. A user name cannot consist solely of either periods or spaces. However, the user name can contain spaces and periods.

11. **a, b.** If you rename a user account or group it will retain all of its properties, such as permissions. When a user account is created, it is given a Special ID that is used when assigning properties and will not change if it is renamed. When a user account or group is deleted and another one is created with the same name, it will change the Special ID that is used when assigning permissions.

12. **d.** Power Users was designed to take care of groups of users and not have the rights to manage any other users. Backup Operators cannot manage these eight users. Administrators can manage these eight users and all the other users on the network. Printer Operators do not have rights to configure any options for these eight users.

13. **b.** The local user would use the Change Password button in the Windows Security dialog box. This box appears when the user presses the CTRL + ALT + DEL key combination. The local user does not have permission to access the Local Users and Groups utility. There is no Change Password button in the Systems Tools dialog box.

14. **a.** Locking the computer will not stop any applications that are currently running on it. When a user locks a computer, it is usually a temporary solution used to stop other users from accessing their data. The user that locks the computer must use their password to unlock the computer.

Challenge Solutions

1. You must use the Local Users and Groups utility. The key to this question is that the computer is configured in a workgroup and is not part of a domain, so you cannot use the Active Directory Users and Computers utility. Don't be fooled by this possible question.

2. Save yourself some work and "Disable" the account. When the new employee arrives for work, just rename the account, then change the password, and the new user can immediately start working with the same network permissions that the old user had. Figure 4-3 shows the user account Properties dialog box on the General tab. Notice the highlighted checkbox labeled "Account is disabled".

3. The first thing you do is set up a shared network folder for the individual. This will be accomplished on a domain controller. Then, from the Profile tab in the Properties dialog box of the user account, simply enter the path to the shared network folder.

Chapter 5

User and Hardware Profiles

These are the areas that are generally testable on the MCSE Server 2000 examination:

1. Configure and manage user profiles.

2 Manage hardware profiles.

Introduction

This chapter is short, but contains six problems that provide important information for when you take the examination.

You will first learn what a local user profile is. It is basically the individual user settings that a user configures on a computer. These settings are placed in a folder under the path C:\Documents and Settings folder, by default. Local profiles are only used when a user logs on locally to a Windows 2000 Professional computer.

Another type of profile is a roaming profile. It is the same as a local profile except that it is located on a Windows 2000 Server and is specifically configured as a roaming profile. You will be shown the proper steps for setting up a roaming profile and given some real-world problems to help you understand the process.

Next, you will learn how to create a mandatory user profile by renaming the NTUSER.DAT file and giving it a *.MAN extension*. You must be logged in with Administrator privileges to enable mandatory profiles. Mandatory profiles can be used only with roaming profiles. You will learn that once a user logs on to the network, they can make changes to the mandatory profile, but they will not be saved to the mandatory profile.

Finally, you will learn how to configure a hardware profile. A hardware profile is most often used in laptop computers.

DEFINING A USER PROFILE

What is a user profile? It is the personal user settings configured for each user of a computer. Some examples of these personal settings are: wallpaper selections, desktop settings, shortcuts, mapped network drives, screen appearance, accessibility options, mouse and keyboard preferences, and other items. Basically, any time a user configures a personal setting on the computer, it becomes part of their user profile.

HOW TO CREATE A USER PROFILE

User profiles are a good idea when you have more than one user that can log on to a Windows 2000 Professional computer and you want to maintain separate user settings for each user. When a user logs on to the computer, their user profile is loaded and will display the preferences that were in effect during the last successful Windows session. Anytime a user makes a change to their desktop environment and logs off, the changes are saved to their user profile. *User profiles are stored in the C:\Documents and Settings folder, by default.* This means that user profiles are used for the local computer, by default. If the user logs into a domain and needs to have their user profile loaded from any network computer, you should use a roaming profile to configure the user account.

The first time a new user logs on to a local computer, they will receive the default user profile. They can then make personal preference changes, which will create a user profile specifically for them. *The folder that stores the user profile is actually given the same name as the user's logon name.* This folder contains a file called NTUSER.DAT, which holds user data and is used to interface with the Registry.

Challenge #1

Danny has configured a user's computer with accessibility options set for the impaired user. They are saved to a network shared folder. The company hires a new employee that can use the same profile. What action can Danny perform to enable the new employee to use the same profile?

Enabling Roaming Profiles

As mentioned earlier, a roaming profile enables a user to log on to the network from any network computer and receive their personal user profile. In order for roaming profiles to operate properly, the network must be set up in a domain environment and a Windows 2000 Server must be configured to enable roaming profiles. The steps to follow are:

1. A profile must be created to be used as the roaming profile.

2. A folder must be created on a Windows 2000 Server and must then be shared.

3. The profile must be copied to the shared folder.

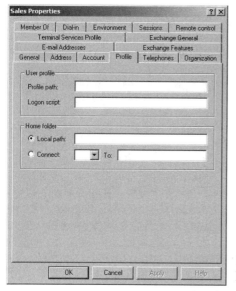

4. After the profile has been copied, you must use the Active Directory Users and Computers utility's user's Properties dialog box to establish a path to the profile. The path must lead to the folder that was created to hold the profile on the server. This is best shown in Figure 5-1.

Figure 5-1: Enabling Roaming Profiles

Tina works at a Windows 2000 Professional computer. Sometimes she is required to work at a Windows NT 4.0 Workstation computer located in a different office. She tries to print a document from this computer but she cannot locate her printer. What should you do to enable Tina to print from any network computer?

Toby is the network engineer for a large Windows 2000 network. The network consists of two Windows 2000 Servers and 50 Windows 2000 Professional computers. Both of the servers use Active Directory. Each user account is configured to use roaming profiles. Many users are complaining of a very slow logon process. He knows that the My Documents folder is a portion of the user's profile. He knows the reason why the logon process appears to be considerably slower: The users are storing large documents into the My Documents folder. He must now come up with a procedure to stop the My Documents folder from being downloaded to the user's desktop, thereby keeping it on the server. What should Toby do?

Enabling Mandatory Profiles

Some companies demand that all their users have the same desktop settings, so they often implement mandatory profiles. When this type of profile is established, the user preference settings are automatically downloaded to the user when they log on to the network. *After a user logs on they can make changes to their environment, but those settings will be lost when they log off and log back on to the network. You must be logged on as an Administrator to establish a mandatory profile. A mandatory profile is created when the NTUSER.DAT file is renamed to NTUSER.MAN.* Remember, this file is in a shared folder located on the network server. *Mandatory profiles can be used only with roaming profiles.* They cannot be implemented for local users. A local user is one who logs on to a Windows 2000 Professional computer that is configured in a workgroup. If the network clients are running Windows NT 4.0 or Windows 2000, the profile file name does not need to be included in the path to the mandatory profile. The system automatically knows to look for the .MAN file extension.

Challenge #4

Kevin is the administrator of a Windows 2000 network. The network contains 100 Windows 2000 Professional computer and two Windows 2000 Servers. He has been asked to configure a mandatory user profile for all the network users. The mandatory profile that he creates sets the monitor resolution to 1024 x 768 with 16-bit color. Fifty percent of the computers on the network have display adapters that support VGA, while the others support SVGA. After he creates the profile, users report that when they log on at certain computers and try to use a custom bitmap, the monitor becomes distorted and the colors are wrong. He must fix this problem to enable all the users to view a custom bitmap from any of the network computers. What can Kevin do to correct this problem?

Challenge #5

You have a new employee and you have enabled a roaming profile to ensure that he receives the same desktop settings at every network computer. He is not aware that the company has a policy that enforces backgrounds on the desktop. The new user logs on successfully and makes some changes to his desktop. He logs off and takes a break. When he returns and logs back on he receives the original desktop settings. He does not like the appearance of his desktop and complains to you. Why can't the new employee retain his desired desktop settings?

Challenge #6

George is the user profile manager for a Windows 2000 network. The network consists of two Windows 2000 Servers and 1000 Professional computers. He wants to implement a mandatory profile for a user named Ralph. George creates a user account for Ralph and configures the account as a roaming profile. He is not certain of the steps he must perform now to establish user settings for the new user account and make them mandatory for Ralph. What actions can George perform to create a desktop environment for Ralph and then make it a mandatory profile?

EXAM TIP: Know how to create a mandatory user profile by renaming the NTUSER.DAT file and giving it a *.MAN extension. Be aware that you must be logged in with Administrator privileges to enable mandatory profiles. Mandatory profiles can be used only with roaming profiles. Finally, know that after a user logs on to the network, they can make changes to the mandatory profile, but they will not be saved to the mandatory profile.

HARDWARE PROFILES

Hardware profiles are most often used in laptop computers. This is because when the laptop is used in the office, it is probably being used a docking station to provide the network connection. However, when the computer is used at home, a network connection is not normally used, which will cause error messages when the computer is started up. These error messages are eliminated when you create one hardware profile for work and another profile for home use. Hardware profiles are created using the System Properties dialog box, which is accessed through the System icon located in the Control Panel. You must then click the Hardware tab followed by the Hardware profile button.

As you examine Figure 5-2, notice that that you can see all the hardware profiles configured for this computer. If you have more than one hardware profile configured, you will be given hardware profile selection options at system startup. You should be aware that if you have only one profile you will not see these options at startup and you cannot delete this profile. At least one hardware profile must be present in order for the system to boot up properly. The default hardware profile that was created when you first installed Windows 2000 Professional is called Profile 1.

Figure 5-2: Hardware Profiles Dialog Box

EXAM TIP: Know that hardware profiles are generally used for laptop computers where one hardware configuration will be used at work with a docking station and another hardware configuration will be used at home without a docking station.

1. You are the network manager for a Windows 2000 network. Your network has 50 Windows 2000 Professional computers configured as peers. Most of your users want to be able to log on to any computer and receive their personal desktop settings. Which of the following is the correct choice for doing this using the least amount of administrative effort?
    a. Create all user account on all computers and creates a roaming profile.
    b. Create all users in a workgroup.
    c. Put all users in a domain and create user accounts.
    d. Put them in a domain and create a roaming profile and user account for each user.

2. Danny has configured a user's computer with accessibility options set for the impaired user. These options are saved to a network shared folder. The company hires a new employee who needs to use the same profile. Which of the following actions can Danny perform to enable the new employee to use the same profile?
    a. Log on as a different user.
    b. Copy the options to a floppy and then to the local account.
    c. Copy the options directly to C:\Documents and Settings\(username).
    d. You can't do this. You must manually set up an accessibility option.

3. Kevin is the administrator for a Windows 2000 network. The network contains 100 Windows 2000 Professional computer and 2 Windows 2000 Servers. He has been asked to configure a mandatory user profile for all the network users. The mandatory profile that he creates sets the monitor resolution to 1024 x 768 with 16-bit color. Fifty percent of the computers on the network have display adapters that support VGA while the others support SVGA. After he creates the profile, users report that when they log on at certain computers and try to use a custom bitmap, the monitor becomes distorted and the colors are wrong. He must fix this problem to permit all the users to view this custom bitmap from any network computer. Which of the following is the correct solution?
    a. Configure a roaming user profile for each user in the accounting group.
    b. Configure a separate user profile for each user in the accounting group.
    c. Change the custom bitmap to a 16-color bitmap that has 640x480 resolution, and reconfigure the mandatory user profile.
    d. Reinstall the appropriate WDM-compliant drivers for the computers that do not display the custom bitmap correctly.

4. You want to configure all the users of a Windows 2000 Professional computer with the capability to store personal files in a particular location. You are not sure of the proper term for this folder. Which of the following is the correct term?
   a. Home folder
   b. Locked folder
   c. User folder
   d. Personal private folder

5. Tina works at a Windows 2000 Professional computer. Sometimes she is required to work at a Windows NT 4.0 Workstation computer in a different office. She tries to print a document from this computer, but she cannot locate her printer. Which of the following will enable Tina to print from any network computer?
   a. Create a mandatory profile.
   b. Create a roaming profile.
   c. Create a read-only folder on a server.
   d. From the Profile tab in the Properties dialog box of the user accounts, enter the path to a read-only folder.

6. You wish to implement roaming profiles for all the users on the network. Some of the users dial in to the network and you want to minimize their logon time. Which of the following would be the most correct solution?
   a. Use the GPO to redirect "Documents and Settings" to a network share rather than on to the local machine.
   b. Configure the server for RRAS
   c. Change the extension on the policy from .pol to .man.
   d. Add more RAM to the RRAS server

7. You are the administrator of a small Windows 2000 network that is growing each day. You decide that you want to implement roaming profiles and to change the location of a user's roaming profile from C:\Documents and Settings to a network share \\Svr1\users\<users name>. Which of the following is the best way to implement roaming profiles on your network?
   a. On the server, configure user Properties and enter the path as
      \\Svr1\users\<users name>
   b. On the Windows 2000 Professional computer, configure user Properties and enter the path as \\Svr1\users\<users name>
   c. On the server, copy the profile to C:\Documents and Settings
   d. On the Windows 2000 Professional computer, copy the profile to C:\Documents and Settings.

8. Terry is the user profile manager for a Windows 2000 network. This network consists of three Windows 2000 Servers and 200 Windows Professional computers. Two of the network servers are configured to use Active Directory. He wants to implement roaming user profiles to permit any user to log on to the network from any computer and receive their personal profile. He knows that he must perform this task on a Windows 2000 Server. Which of the following steps will Terry use to enable roaming user profiles? (Select two answers.)
   a. Create a read-only folder on a server.
   b. From the Profile tab in the Properties dialog box of the user accounts, enter the path to a read-only folder.
   c. Create a shared folder on a server.
   d. From the Profile tab in the Properties dialog box of the user accounts, enter the path to a shared folder.

9. Toby is the network engineer for a large Windows 2000 network. The network consists of two Windows 2000 Servers and 50 Windows 2000 Professional computers. Both of the servers use Active Directory. Each user account is configured to use roaming profiles. He knows that the My Documents folder is a portion of each user's profile. Many users are complaining of a very slow logon process. The reason that the logon process is considerably slower is that the users are storing large documents into the My Documents folder. He must now come up with a procedure to stop the My Documents folder from being downloaded to the user's desktop, thereby remaining on the server. Which of the following is the correct procedure?
   a. Configure the Desktop folder to be available offline through the Offline Files. Configure the folder to be synchronized when users log on or log off.
   b. Change the roaming profile from a personal roaming profile to a mandatory roaming profile by changing the name of the ntuser.dat file to ntuser.man.
   c. Set a disk quota on the My Documents folder on each user's desktop. Set a maximum limit on the amount of data that a user can save to that folder and check the box to "Redirect excess data to network server". Enter a UNC path with the location of the network share that you would like the data to be redirected to.
   d. Create an empty folder on the network server. Share this folder out and configure it as a DFS root share. Configure the My Documents folder for each user to be a DFS link.
   e. Enable Folder Redirection through Group Policies and configure the My Documents folder to be redirected to a share on the centralized server.

10. Roy is a new employee and you have enabled a roaming profile to ensure that he receives the same desktop settings at any network computer. He is not aware that the company has a policy that enforces backgrounds on the desktop. Roger logs on and successfully makes some changes to his desktop. He logs off and takes a break. When he returns and logs back on, he receives the original desktop settings. He does not like the appearance of his desktop and complains to you. Which of the following best explains why Roy cannot retain his desired desktop settings?

   a. Roy does not have the appropriate permission to the bitmap file for the background he wishes to use. You must have at least Read permission to the file containing the background you wish to use.

   b. Roy is not a member of the Power Users group. In order to make permanent changes to user settings, you must be a member of this group.

   c. Roy's account has been configured with a mandatory profile. In this case, the user can still modify the desktop, but the changes are not saved when the user logs off.

   d. Roy's account is a member of the Guest Users group. Members of the Guest Users group automatically have their changes discarded upon logoff.

11. George is the user profile manager for a Windows 2000 network. The network consists of two Windows 2000 Servers and 1000 Professional computers. He wants to implement a mandatory profile for a user named Ralph. George creates a user account for Ralph and configures the account as a roaming profile. He is not sure of what steps he must perform now to establish settings for the new user account and make them mandatory. Which of the following are the most correct choices? (Select two answers.)

   a. Log on as Ralph and configure the appropriate desktop environment settings.

   b. Log on as Administrator and configure the appropriate desktop environment settings.

   c. Log on as Ralph and rename the Ntuser.dat file in C:\Documents and Settings\Ralph to Ntuser.man.

   d. Log on as Administrator and rename the Ntuser.dat file in C:\Documents and Settings\Ralph to Ntuser.man.

12. You are the systems administrator for a large Windows 2000 network. A user named Sally must have a roaming profile that will enable her to log on to any network computer and receive her profile settings. After you set up the roaming profile she logs in on a Windows NT 4.0 computer and does not receive any of her profile settings. Which of the following is the most likely reason the roaming profile not operating properly?
    a. Windows 2000 profiles don't roam to an NT 4.0 machine.
    b. The profile path is wrong.
    c. The Ntuser.dat file is locked open on the NT Workstation.
    d. She must use the mandatory profile.

13. Sammy is the current network administrator for a small Windows 2000 network. He has just enabled a roaming profile on a Windows 2000 Server. The company likes the profile so much that they direct him to make it mandatory. Sammy knows that the Ntuser.dat file must have its extension changed, but he is not sure of the proper one to use. Which of the following is the correct extension?
    a. .pol
    b. .pwl
    c. .man
    d. .cfg

Answers and Explanations

1. **d.** The only way to realistically implement roaming profiles on a network is to install a Windows 2000 Server and create user accounts configured as roaming profiles.

2. **c.** This location is where the local profiles reside. Copying the options to a floppy and then to the local account will not update the profile. Logging on as a different user will not solve your problem

3. **c.** The monitor distortion occurs on the computers that only support VGA. In order to enable all the network users to use this custom bitmap, you must change the mandatory user profile to use a lower resolution of 640x480.

4. **a.** You would store private files in your home folder.

5. **b.** Creating a roaming profile ensures any user can log on to any computer on the network and receive their personal profile, which includes printer settings.

6. **a.** Using a network share rather than the local machine will increase the speed of the logon. Changing the extension from .pol to .man will not provide the desired results. Adding more RAM to the RRAS server will not increase the speed of your logon.

7. **a.** The key to this question is that a Windows 2000 Server must be configured for roaming profiles. This is accomplished in the user Properties dialog box on the Profile tab by entering the path to the profile.

8. **c, d.** To start the process, you must share a folder on the server. The Profile tab of the Properties dialog box of the user account is where you enter the path to the shared network folder. Creating a read-only folder on the server will not provide roaming profiles.

9. **e.** Redirecting the folder to the share on the centralized server will accomplish the results you require. Configuring offline features will not speed up the authentication of the user's logon. Changing the profiles to mandatory will not speed up the logon process. Disk quotas do not allow a "Redirect excess data to network server" checkbox. Creating a DFS root share will not speed up the logon process.

10. **c.** It is obvious that the company enforces each users' desktop settings by using a mandatory profile that reloads each time a user logs on to the network. Once a user logs on, they can make changes to the desktop, but the changes will be lost at the next logon.

11. **a, d.** First, you must log on as Ralph and configure the appropriate desktop environment settings. If you log on as the Administrator, the desktop settings would be in the Administrator profile and not Ralph's. Then the Administrator must log off from the user account, then log back on with the Administrator account and rename the Ntuser.dat file to Ntuser.man. Only an Administrator has permissions to create a mandatory profile. The Editor does not have permissions to rename the Ntuser.dat file to Ntuser.man. The .man extension is what makes the profile mandatory.

12. **b.** The path to the profile is wrong. The default location to user profiles is C:\Documents and Settings. Check the location of the user profiles by right-clicking the user account Properties and review the Profile Path text box. Windows 2000 user profiles are compatible with Windows NT 4.0, but the path to the location of each share for the profiles is different. The roaming profiles have individual profiles for each user, and the Ntuser.dat file locking up would not cause a problem for the user. Mandatory profiles do not necessarily make the profile roaming. In fact you must have a roaming profile established to configure a mandatory profile.

13. **c.** The NTUSER.DAT file must be renamed to Ntuser.man.

Challenge Solutions

1. You must copy the configured user profile to the new user's profile. This is accomplished by copying it to the C:\Documents and Settings folder in the new user's folder.

2. Create a roaming profile. This will ensure that any user can log on to any computer on the network and receive their personal profile, which includes printer settings.

3. Enable Folder Redirection through Group Policies and configure the My Documents folder to be redirected to a share on the centralized server. (We haven't covered Group Policies; this chapter covers profiles ; We will cover Group Policies later in this book.)

4. The answer is simple: Change the mandatory user profile to allow a lower resolution of 640 x 480. This way, the users that have computers that only support VGA can properly view the custom bitmap. Remember, when you configure a mandatory profile it is mandatory that each network user have the settings located in the profile.

5. Roy's account has been configured with a mandatory profile. In this case, the user can still modify the desktop, but the changes are not saved when the user logs off. Yes, it is obvious that the company enforces each users' desktop setting by using a mandatory profile that reloads each time a user logs on to the network. Once a user logs on, they can make changes to the desktop, but they will be lost at the next log on.

6. First, the administrator must log on as Ralph, and configure the appropriate desktop environment settings, then log on as Administrator and rename the Ntuser.dat file in *C:\Documents and Settings\Editor to Ntuser.man*. Yes, first you must log on as Ralph and configure the appropriate desktop environment settings. If you logged on as the Administrator, the desktop settings would be in the Administrator's profile and not Ralph's. Then the administrator must log off from the user account, then log back on with the Administrator account and rename the Ntuser.dat file to Ntuser.man. Only an Administrator has permissions to create a mandatory profile. Ralph does not have permissions to rename the Ntuser.dat file to Ntuser.man. The .man extension is what makes the profile mandatory.

Chapter

Disk Management

These are the areas that are generally testable on the MCSE Server 2000 examination:

1. Configure, manage, and troubleshoot file compression.

2. Configure and manage file systems.

   • Convert from one file system to another file system.

   • Configure file systems by using NTFS, FAT32, or FAT.

3. Implement, manage, and troubleshoot disk devices

   • Install, configure, and manage DVD and CD-ROM devices.

   • Monitor and configure disks.

   • Monitor, configure, and troubleshoot volumes.

   • Monitor and configure removable media, such as tape devices.

4. Encrypt data on a hard disk by using the Encrypting File System (EFS).

Introduction

This chapter is loaded with a lot of testable information. If there is a chapter that you need to read and reread, this is the one. You can expect many questions taken from this chapter.

Windows 2000 Professional supports these file systems—FAT16, FAT32, and NTFS. You will be presented with the characteristics of each file system. When you select a file system, you must select one that will enable you to obtain the results you desire. We are positive that you will format your partitions and volumes with NTFS except in some very specific situations. After a file system has been converted to NTFS it cannot be converted back to the old file system without the possibility of losing data. The command to convert partitions to NTFS is: CONVERT c: /fs:ntfs.

You will learn that there are two types of disk storage supported by Windows 2000 Professional. One is basic storage and the other is dynamic storage. Basic storage is used to support older operating systems and can support up to four partitions. Dynamic storage is a new feature with Windows 2000 Professional that enables you to create volumes instead of partitions. Three different types of dynamic volume are supported in Windows 2000 Professional: simple volumes, spanned volumes, and striped volumes. The Disk Management utility is used to manage both basic and dynamic storage.

You will be shown that the only way to recover from a failed dynamic volume in Windows 2000 Professional is from tape backup.

The next section covers how to apply disk quotas on your computer. Finally, we will show you how to compress and encrypt files and folders. You will find that you cannot compress and encrypt a file at the same time.

CONFIGURING FILE SYSTEMS

A file system is a method of storing data on your hard drives. As you discovered in Chapter 1, Windows 2000 Professional supports FAT16, FAT32, and NTFS file systems. You would normally use FAT16 and FAT32 if you wanted to dual-boot your computer with an older operating system such as DOS, Windows 95, or Windows 98. Selecting the correct file system to support both operating systems is necessary to ensure that both operating systems can recognize the file system. Table 6-1 defines the attributes of each file system and the operating system supported by each. We have listed the most important file systems and operating systems.

Table 6-1: File System Attributes

ITEM Operating System Support	FAT16 Most	FAT32 Win95, Win98, Win2000	NTFS WinNT and Win2000
Compression	No	No	Yes
Long Filenames	Yes	Yes	Yes
Quotas	No	No	Yes
Encryption	No	No	Yes
Local File Security	No	No	Yes
Maximum Volume Size	2 GB	32 GB	2 TB

NOTE: The maximum volume size for each is as follows: FAT16: 2 GB, FAT32: 32 GB, and NTFS: 2 TB. *FAT32 only supports volume sizes up to 32 GB.*

EXAM TIP: Memorize the contents of Table 6-1. You must know that if you choose a certain file system, some particular feature may not be supported. For example, if you want to enable compression, disk quotas, encryption, or local file security on a computer, you must use the NTFS file system.

Challenge #1

Tommy is the primary network administrator for your Windows 2000 network. He has been asked to install the Windows 2000 Professional operating system on a new computer on a FAT 32 partition. He installs the new computer and uses the Disk Management utility to view the partition. He is surprised to see that the entire hard drive cannot be used. Why did this happen?

Based on Table 6-1 above, you may want to convert FAT16 and FAT32 file systems to NTFS. Be careful because this is a one-way process. *After you convert to NTFS you cannot convert back to the old file system without the possibility of*

losing data. This is a very important fact to remember when taking the exam. They will try to fool you into converting back to the old file system. Don't fall for this trick!

There is a command-line utility in Windows 2000 Professional to convert file system partitions to NTFS. The command is: CONVERT. Here is what it would look like if you typed it at the command prompt. (Notice that [drive:] reflects the partition you will be converting.)

*CONVERT [drive:] /fs:ntfs

NOTE: Sometimes, the conversion will not take place immediately. Don't worry. The next time you reboot the conversion will take place automatically. This delay usually occurs when the partition you are converting contains the system files or the page file.

> **EXAM TIP:** Know that once a file system is converted to NTFS it cannot be converted back to the old file system without the possibility of losing data. Also, know that the command to convert partitions to NTFS is: CONVERT c: /fs:ntfs.

DISK STORAGE

Two types of disk storage are supported by Windows 2000 Professional. One is basic storage and the other is dynamic storage. Basic storage is used to support older operating systems and can support up to *four partitions*. Dynamic storage is a new feature with Windows 2000 Professional that allows you to create volumes instead of partitions. We will now go into more detail on each storage system.

Basic Storage

Basic storage is used with the older operating systems prior to Windows 2000 Professional. It is comprised of primary and extended partitions. Partitions are logical management structures created to enable you to efficiently organize your hard drive space. When the first partition is created on a particular hard drive it becomes the primary partition. As stated earlier, each physical hard drive can have up to four partitions. After a partition has been established, the next step is to format the partition with the file system of your choice and then install the operating system. Partitioning a hard drive enables you to install different file systems, and even different operating systems on each partition.

Basic disks have some limitations. If you create two partitions and want to use the extra space on the second partition because the first partition is full, this cannot be done unless you delete a partition.

Dynamic Storage

Dynamic storage enables you to divide physical disks into dynamic volumes. *Dynamic volumes can only be used by Windows 2000* and cannot contain partitions or logical drives. What this means is that once you decide to use dynamic volumes, you cannot combine them with basic storage partitions. Three different types of dynamic volume are supported in Windows 2000: simple volumes, spanned volumes, and striped volumes. When you first install Windows 2000, or performed an upgrade from Windows NT 4.0, you are using basic storage. The utility used to upgrade to Dynamic Disks is the Disk Management utility. It is covered later in this chapter. The next sections will describe the features of the three different types of dynamic volumes.

> **Challenge #2**
>
> Jennifer has a computer with Windows 2000 Professional installed on it. It is configured to use Dynamic Disks. She wants to install other operating systems to use in a dual-boot fashion. Because her job involves testing different operating systems, she would like to install as many different operating systems as possible. How many different operating systems can be used in this situation?

Dynamic Volume Types

Dynamic volume types include:

- *Simple volumes* – The name almost describes the type of volume. A simple volume contains drive space from a single dynamic drive. This type of drive is used when your single hard drive has enough disk space to hold your entire volume. *And, of course, because it is comprised of a single hard drive, the system and boot partitions are located on simple volumes.*

- *Spanned volumes* – This type of volume can be made up of the disk space of between ***two and 32 dynamic drives**. Spanned volumes are normally used when you are running out of disk space and want to dynamically extend the volume with space from an additional hard drive. Data on these volumes is written sequentially on each disk before going to the next physical drive. ***One important point to note is that you do not need to allocate the same amount of space to the volume set from each physical hard drive.** In simple terms, this means that you can use a 600 MB partition from one physical drive with ar 500 MB partition from a different physical drive. ***This type of volume does increase the read/write performance, as do the following volumes. A big disadvantage of this type of volume is that if any drive in the spanned volume set fails, all data may be lost.**

- *Striped volumes* – This type of volume stores data in equal stripes on between ***two and 32 dynamic drives**. You use this type of volume when you want to combine the space of several physical drives into a single volume and ***increase disk performance**. The increased performance occurs because the data is written in stripes on different disks, and the speed is increased because each physical disk has its own read/write head. ***This type of volume does not provide any fault tolerance. This means that if any drive in the volume set fails, all data may be lost. The free space used in a striped volume must be equal in size on all drives.**

EXAM TIP: There is so much testable information in the previous paragraphs that we will not repeat each item. This is a major area for the exam and you can expect most of this information to be hit hard. We have highlighted the areas that you must know. Primarily, know the pros and cons of each type of dynamic volume.

Charles is the current administrator of an important Windows 2000 Professional computer on his Windows 2000 network. This computer has an application installed that gets numerous hits from network clients and it is getting slower in returning query data. His disk drive configuration is basic disks and he believes that Dynamic Disks will boost his computer's performance. He currently has two hard disks of 2 GB each and plans to add 3 GB hard disk. He wants to use a disk configuration that will provide the fastest client access to the hard drives. Which type of Dynamic Disk is the best possible choice?

Challenge #3

Challenge #4

Kevin is learning how to manipulate disk drives on his Windows 2000 Professional computer. Currently his computer has a basic disk configuration with two primary partitions and one extended partition. The extended partition has two logical drives, and one of these drives (drive F) has been formatted with the NTFS file system. Drive F is used to store home folders for your network users. Many users have been saving documents to their home folders and he is running out of disk space. He has another disk drive with 10 GB of unallocated space that can be used for the home folders. What can Kevin do to increase the amount of storage available in the logical drive?

Challenge #5

Jake has just been promoted to assistant administrator for your large Windows 2000 network. His primary responsibility is the management of the disk drives on each of the network computers. You ask him to set up a striped volume on one of the Windows 2000 Professional computers. The computer currently has five 5 GB drives that can be used to set up the new configuration. He has asked you how much space would be available to store data on the striped volume. What is the answer?

DISK MANAGEMENT UTILITY

The Disk Management utility, shown in Figure 6-1, is used to manage basic and dynamic storage disks. You must be *logged on with Administrative* privileges to have access to all the options in this utility. This utility can be accessed most directly by right-clicking on the My Computer icon, selecting Manage, and expanding the Computer Management utility. Then, expand the Storage folder and click the Disk Management folder. This utility can also be added to the MMC as a snap-in or it can be accessed through the Administrative Tools folder. Finally, the Disk Management utility can also be accessed by typing *"Diskmgmt.msc"* at the Run command prompt.

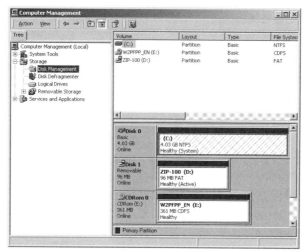

Figure 6-1: Disk Management Utility

NOTE: Notice the information in the right pane of the screen. You can extract a lot of information about your disk from this screen.

Some of the tasks that can be performed using the Disk Management utility include adding a new disk, creating and deleting partitions and volumes, *upgrading basic disks to Dynamic Disks*, and viewing disk and volume properties.

Upgrade to Dynamic Disks

Remember that when you *upgrade basic disks to Dynamic Disks, this is a one-way process and if you try to convert back to basic disks, your data may be lost.* To upgrade, you must access the Disk Management utility, right-click the drive to be upgraded, and select the Upgrade to Dynamic Disk option, as shown in Figure 6-2. After you select this option, you must reboot the system and the disk will become a Dynamic Disk.

EXAM TIP: Remember that you must be logged on with Administrative privileges to have access to all the features in Disk Management. Know how to access the Disk Management utility—especially by using the DISKMGMT.MSC command at the Run command prompt. Know that this utility can be used to upgrade basic disks to Dynamic Disks and that the conversion is a one-way process.

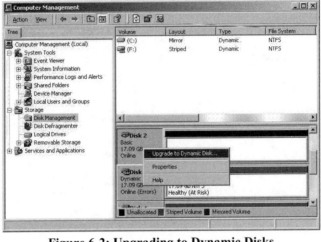

Figure 6-2: Upgrading to Dynamic Disks

- *Creating extended volumes* – An extended volume is created when you take a single simple volume and add disk space to the volume from free space on the same physical hard drive. *To create an extended volume, the simple volume must be formatted with NTFS.* You cannot extend volumes that were originally created as basic disk partitions and then converted to a Dynamic Disk. *Also, the system or boot partition cannot be extended.* After the volume has been extended, no portion of the volume can be deleted without losing data on the entire set.

- *Adding a new disk* – Adding a new disk is a simple process if your computer supports hot swapping. Hot swapping is adding or removing the disk while the computer is still running. Just add the drive, access the Disk Management utility, select Action, and then choose the *Rescan Disks option.* If your system does not support hot swapping, you will have to shut down the system, then add the drive and restart the computer. By default the new drive will be configured as a Dynamic Disk.

Challenge #6

Jon Paul is the administrator of a very small Windows network. One of his Windows 2000 Professional computers is configured with a spanned volume that consists of three physical hard drives. This computer is a newer model that supports hot swapping. The information on this computer is critical and he backs up the data daily. One day one of the disks fails and he replaces the failed disk with a new unpartitioned disk. His company needs to access the information on this computer and this prompts him to recover the spanned volume and the data as quickly as possible. How can he solve this problem?

DISK FAILURE RECOVERY

Currently, Windows 2000 Professional does not provide disk fault tolerance. Windows 2000 Server does provide disk fault tolerance in the form of mirrored and RAID-5 volumes. Unfortunately, Windows 2000 Professional does not support these two types of Dynamic Disks. The only way to recover from a disk failure is by using the tape backup to restore the data.

DATA COMPRESSION

Data compression is the storage of data in a format that uses less disk space. Compression must take place on an NTFS partition. Compression takes place in files and folders independently. This means that you can have compressed files in an uncompressed folder and uncompressed files in a compressed folder. A compressed file cannot be detected by the user when it is accessed. As you open a compressed file, it is uncompressed automatically, and it will automatically be compressed again when the file is closed. *Since compression can only take place on an NTFS partition, if you move the file or folder to a FAT partition, it will automatically uncompress the file or folder. You will also lose the compression attribute if the file or folder is moved or copied to a floppy disk. This is because a floppy cannot be formatted with NTFS. Finally, you cannot both compress and encrypt a file at the same time.* We will discuss encryption later in this chapter.

The compression feature is accessed in Windows Explorer using the path—Start, Programs, Accessories, Windows Explorer, or by simply right-clicking the My Computer icon and selecting Explore. This feature is shown in Figure 6-3. In Explorer, locate the file or folder you want to compress, right-click on it, and select the Properties option. In the Properties dialog box, click the Advanced button on the General tab. *On the Advanced Attributes dialog box, check the "Compress contents to save disk space" checkbox. To uncompress a file or folder, just remove the check in the checkbox.*

Figure 6-3: Compressing a File or Folder

NOTE: When you compress a folder that contains files, a Confirm Attribute Changes dialog box will appear. You must decide whether you want to compress only this folder or if you want to compress the subfolders and files located in the folder.

When you copy or add a file into a compressed folder in the same partition, the file is compressed automatically (inherits folder attributes). If you move a file across partitions into a compressed folder, the file is compressed automatically (inherits folder attributes). If you move a file within the same partition to a compressed folder the file retains its original state (compressed or not compressed). If you move a file from a different NTFS drive into a compressed folder, it is also compressed. However, if you move a file from the same NTFS drive into a compressed folder, the file retains its original state, either compressed or uncompressed.

Challenge #7

You have just established a shared folder on the fastest Windows 2000 Professional computer in your network. This folder will be accessed by users from the Fort Walton Beach office. You add some subfolders, including one called Destin2, which is compressed. You have to move some files from another folder called Sales into the Destin2 folder. While you are moving the file, you have to make sure that the files are compressed when you move them, but you do not want to compress the remaining subfolders in the Sales folder. What action should you take to successfully move the files?

To help you visualize these relationships review Table 6-2.

Table 6-2: Compressed File and Folder Attributes

Action	Location	Result
Copy/Add	Same partition	Inherits folder attributes of folder being copied into
Copy/Add	Different partition	Retains its own attributes
Move	Same partition	Retains its own attributes
Move	Different partition	Inherits folder attributes of folder being moved into

EXAM TIP: Know how to compress a file or folder with Windows Explorer. Be aware that compression can only occur on an NTFS volume. Finally, memorize the information in Table 6-2 and know what happens to a compressed file when you copy or move it.

George is your network's newest Windows 2000 Professional expert. He is currently working on a Windows 2000 Professional computer that has an NTFS volume with compression enabled. He has a 2 MB bitmap in a compressed folder that he would like to copy to a floppy disk. This bitmap is 1 MB in its compressed state. When he tries to copy the file, he receives this message: "Insufficient disk space". What can George do to copy the bitmap to a floppy drive disk?

Challenge #8

DISK QUOTAS

Managing Disk Quotas

Employees often try to download large files that are maintained on the company computer. Administrators need a way to control the amount of disk space any one user can utilize. In Windows 2000 this is accomplished with disk quotas. *To use this feature, the volume must be formatted with NTFS. Disk quotas can be specified for all users or on a per-user basis.* We will begin by looking at how to specify disk quotas for all users.

First, some things to consider before you use disk quotas:

- Disk quotas can only take place on an NTFS partition.

- Disk quotas are based on the actual file size and not on the compressed size.

- Disk quotas are applied at the volume level only.

- Disk quotas are based on file and folder ownership. If a users creates, copies, or takes ownership of a file, they receive the credit for the disk space used.

- Disk quotas do not apply to members of the Administrators group.

- You must be logged on as Administrator to establish quota limits.

Disk quotas are configured using the Volume Properties dialog box. The volume Properties dialog box can be accessed by right-clicking the drive letter in Windows Explorer and selecting the Properties option. When the volume Properties dialog box appears, click the Quota tab, as shown in Figure 6-4. Disk quotas are disabled by default. Therefore, if you wish to enable this feature, you must do so manually.

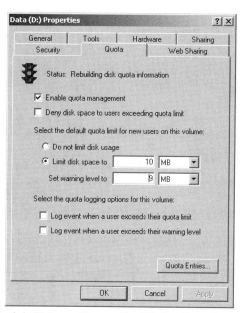

Figure 6-4: Volume Properties Dialog Box, Quota Tab

As you examine Figure 6-4, you should notice the four setting options listed in Table 6-3.

Table 6-3: Quota Options

Option	Description
Enable quota management	Determines whether disk quotas are used or not.
Deny disk space to users exceeding the quota limit	Is used to deny any additional disk space to users who exceed their disk quota limit. If they try to exceed their limit, they will receive an "out of disk space" error message.
Select the default quota limit for new users on this volume	Is used to set quota limits for new users. With this option you can choose Do not limit disk usage, or Limit disk space to. The Limit disk space to radio button enables you to set a usage point that will warn the user.
Select the quota logging options for this volume	Is used to log whether a user exceeds their quota limit or exceeds their warning levels.

NOTE: *When you enable quotas for users, you must be aware that any current users who have created files on the volume will not be affected by quota limits.* That is why it is a good idea to initiate quotas for your users when the Windows 2000 Professional operating system is initially installed.

In Figure 6-4, we saw how to set quotas for all users. Now, we will examine how to set quotas for individual users. Setting individual quotas limits enables you to specify single users that you want to have unlimited disk space, while establishing limits for other users. This feature can also be used to set lower warning levels for users that constantly exceed their disk space. Because the default quota limits established for all users apply only to new users, you would establish quota limits individually for the current users. Here is how you establish individual quota limits:

On the Quota tab of the volume Properties, as illustrated in Figure 6-4, you will notice a "Quota Entries..." button. When the dialog box appears, simply double-click the users and modify the disk quota entries, shown in Figure 6-5.

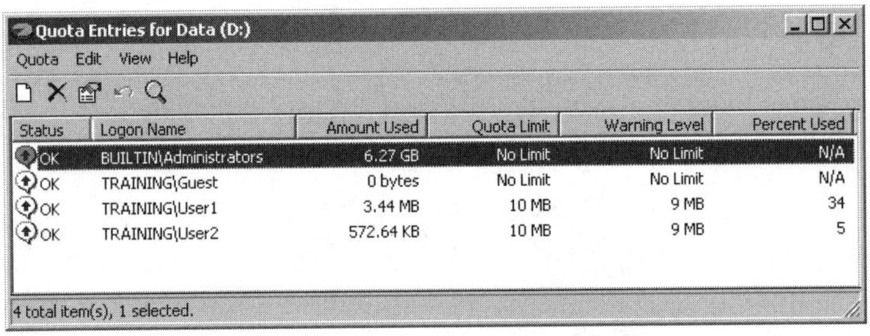

Figure 6-5: Quota Entries Dialog Box

To monitor disk quotas on your computer, you must use the Quota Entries dialog box. Remember, you get to this location by clicking the *Quota Entries button* in the Quota tab of the volume Properties dialog box. Here are some entries you could see depending on the status of the particular user's status.

- A green arrow indicates OK.

- A yellow triangle indicates the warning level has been exceeded.

- A red circle indicates the quota level has been exceeded.

EXAM TIP: It is likely that you will receive at least three questions on disk quotas. Review this section carefully.

DATA ENCRYPTION WITH EFS

Encrypting and Decrypting Folders and Files

Encrypting data on your computer is accomplished using the Encrypting File System (EFS). EFS enables users to provide greater security by encrypting their files. *EFS can only be used on an NTFS partition*. Encrypted files can only be accessed by a user with the correct password or the proper key. If a user does not have either, they will be denied access. Even users with Full Control NTFS permissions cannot access the files without the key. *To encrypt a file, you must access Windows Explorer*, then right-click the file and select Properties. Then, on the General tab, click the Advanced button and check the "Encrypt contents to secure data" checkbox. This is illustrated in Figure 6-6. *To decrypt the file, simply uncheck this option.*

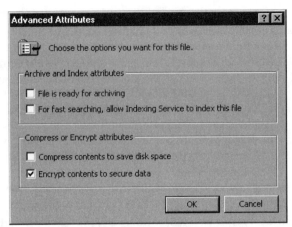

Figure 6-6: Encrypting a File or Folder

This is important! A user only needs *Write permissions to the file or folder to encrypt a file.*

If you don't want to encrypt the file in Explorer, you can use the CIPHER command line feature. *The command is CIPHER /[command parameter] [filename],* which could appear as: *CIPHER /e myfile.* The command parameters you need to know are listed in Table 6-4.

Table 6-4: CIPHER Command Parameters

Parameter	Description
/e	Used to encrypt a file
/d	Used to decrypt a file

If a user encrypts a file and then leaves the company, you must be able to recover the encrypted file. You can do this by *using the Recovery Agent to access the encrypted files. The default Recovery Agent is the Administrator.* The exact process calls for the Administrator to log on and use the Windows Backup utility. The backed up file is then restored on the computer where the Recovery Agent is located. Next, access Windows Explorer, right-click the file, and then in the General tab, click the Advanced button. On the Advanced tab, clear the "Encrypt contents to secure data" checkbox and the file will no longer be encrypted. One thing to consider is that you are decrypting the backup file and the original file is still encrypted.

EXAM TIP: File encryption is another favorite topic that can be expected on the exam. This is another important section to review and put into your memory banks.

TROUBLESHOOTING DISK DEVICES AND VOLUMES

The Check Disk Utility

The Check Disk utility is used to check hard disks for bad sectors, attempt to fix file system errors, and scan for/recover bad sectors. You should run this utility occasionally to prevent your system from crashing. You can access this utility in Computer Management, expand the Storage folder to see the Disk Management utility, then right-click the partition and choose the Properties option. Click the Tools tab of the volume Properties dialog box, shown in Figure 6-7, and then click the Check Now button.

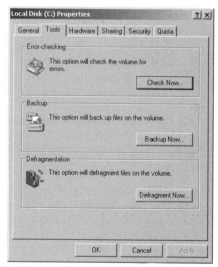

Figure 6-7: Using the Check Disk Utility

NOTE: *If you try to perform a Check Disk of the partition that contains the system or boot partition, the disk check cannot be accomplished because the system cannot gain exclusive access to the partition. The disk check will occur the next time the system is restarted.*

Review Questions

1. Tommy is the primary network administrator for your Windows 2000 network. He is asked to install a new computer with Windows 2000 Professional that is to be installed on a FAT 32 partition. He installs the new computer and uses the Disk Management utility to view the partition. He is surprised to see that the all of the hard drive cannot be used. Which of the following explains why this problem occurred?
    a. FAT32 supports partition sizes up to 2 GB.
    b. FAT32 supports partition sizes up to 32 GB.
    c. FAT32 supports partition sizes up to 32 MB.
    d. FAT32 supports partitions of unlimited size.

2. Jerald is concerned about the maintenance and configuration of the hard drives on his Windows 2000 Professional computer. His current configuration is three basic disks. He has heard a lot about Dynamic Disks and would like to make the conversion. Which Windows 2000 utility will enable him to convert basic disks to Dynamic Disks?
    a. Disk Manager
    b. Disk Management
    c. Disk Administrator
    d. Local Disks and Volumes

3. Jerry is new to the Windows 2000 environment and he needs more information about the Encrypting File System (EFS). In particular, he needs to know that which of the following are capable of encrypting a file or folder in Windows 2000 Professional? (Select two answers.)
    a. Windows Explorer
    b. Cipher.exe
    c. Crypto.exe
    d. System Tools

4. Charles is the current administrator of an important Windows 2000 Professional computer for your Windows 2000 network. This computer has an application installed that gets numerous hits from network clients and it is getting slower in returning query data. His disk drive configuration is established as basic disks and he believes that Dynamic Disks will boost his computer's performance. He currently has two hard disks of 2 GB each and plans to add a 3 GB hard disk. He wants to use a disk configuration that will provide the fastest client access to the hard drives. Which of the following Dynamic Disk types should he use?
    a. Spanned volume
    b. Striped volume
    c. RAID-5 volume
    d. Simple volume

5. Kevin is learning how to manipulate disk drives on his Windows 2000 Professional computer. Currently his machine has a basic disk configuration with two primary partitions and one extended partition. The extended partition has 2 logical drives and one of these drives (drive F) has been formatted with the NTFS file system. Drive F is used to store data folders for your network users. Many users have been saving documents to their data folders and he is running out of disk space. He has another disk drive with 10 GB of unallocated space that can be used for the home folders. Which of the following is the best possible solution to your disk space problem?
    a. Convert both disks to Dynamic Disks, and extend the spanned volume that was the original logical drive, drive F, by using that volume and unallocated space from the second disk drive.
    b. Create a new partition or volume on the second disk drive. Create a new folder on drive G. Mount the new partition or volume to that folder.
    c. Extend drive G by creating a volume set using the logical drive and unallocated space from the second disk drive.
    d. Create a new partition or volume on the second disk drive and mount it to the folder in which home directories reside.

6. Jake has just been promoted to assistant administrator for your large Windows 2000 network. His primary responsibility is the management of the disk drives on each of the network computers. You ask him to set up a striped volume on one of the Windows 2000 Professional computers. The computer currently has five 5 GB drives to use to set up the new configuration. He asks you how much space would be available on the striped volume to store data. Which of the following is the best possible answer?
   a. 20 GB because one disk is used for parity
   b. 15 GB because two disks are used for fault tolerance
   c. 30 GB
   d. 25 GB

7. James is the administrator of a Windows 2000 network. One of his Windows 2000 Professional computers has a system partition formatted with NTFS. He wants to convert this partition back to a FAT partition. Which of the following will enable James to convert the NTFS partition to a FAT partition without any loss of data?
   a. Use the Convert.exe command.
   b. Use the convert C:/fs:FAT command.
   c. FAT.exe
   d. It cannot be done.

8. You are responsible for a Windows 2000 Professional computer that is running out of disk space. You know that you can temporarily solve the problem by compressing all of the largest files. Which of the following reflects the correct path to compress a file or folder?
   a. Select a file or folder from within Windows Explorer/Properties/General Tab/Advanced.
   b. Select a file or folder from within Disk Management and click the Compression button.
   c. Select a file or folder from within the Backup Utility and click the Compression button.
   d. Select a file or folder from within Network Neighborhood and click the Compression button.

9. You have just established a shared folder on the fastest Windows 2000 Professional computer in your network. This folder will be accessed by users from the Fort Walton Beach office. You add some subfolders to the shared folder. The Destin2 folder, which is compressed, is one of the subfolders that was added to the shared folder. You must move some files from another folder called Sales into the Destin2 folder. While you are moving the file, you have to make certain that the files are compressed, but you do not want to compress the remaining subfolders in the Sales folder. Which of the following actions should you take to successfully move the files?
   a. Move each of the files from Sales to Destin2.
   b. Copy the files from Sales to Destin2, and then delete the original files.
   c. Compress Sales, apply changes only to the subfolder to be moved, and then move the files from Sales to Destin2.
   d. Encrypt Destin2, move the files from Research to Sales, and then decrypt Sales.

10. You are the network engineer responsible for a particular Windows 2000 Professional computer. This computer is configured with two partitions formatted with the FAT file system. The computer is also used to store very sensitive documents. You must enable encryption of this data to provide an added level of security and ensure that the documents do not fall into the wrong hands.

   Required result: Data should be secure and encrypted. Administrative effort should be minimum. You should have the ability to recover encrypted files in case the file owner leaves your company without information. Other permissions on encrypted files should be unaffected.

   Optional result 1: File-level security is required on the disk where data is stored.

   Suggested solution: Convert the FAT file system to Windows 2000 NTFS file system. Use the Encrypting File System (EFS) to encrypt data.

   Which results will the suggested solution produce?
   a. The suggested solution produces the required result and the optional result.
   b. The suggested solution produces only the required result.
   c. The suggested solution produces only the optional result.
   d. The suggested solution does not produce the required result.

11. You are the network technician for a medium-sized Windows 2000 network. One of your Windows 2000 Professional computers is running out of disk space and you must make sure that the system will not crash if the disk space available reaches zero. You want to implement disk quotas to limit the amount of space network users can use. To start the process you need to know at what level disk quotas are applied. Which of the following levels best reflects the level at which disk quotas are applied?
   a. Volume level
   b. Drive level
   c. Folder level
   d. File level

12. Johnny is a typical Windows 2000 network user. The network administrator has just enabled encryption on Johnny's Windows 2000 Professional computer. He is moving to a different Windows 2000 Professional computer and he needs to move all of his encrypted files to the new computer. The shared folder that will hold the documents is located on a volume that is formatted with NTFS. When the files are moved, what will happen to the encryption?
   a. The encrypted file will automatically be decrypted.
   b. Encrypted files and folders cannot be moved or copied. Decrypt and then move or copy the file or folder.
   c. The encrypted file will remain encrypted on the shared Windows 2000 folder.
   d. The encrypted file will inherit the encryption state of the shared NTFS folder.

13. George is your network's newest Windows 2000 Professional expert. He is currently working on a Windows 2000 Professional computer that has a NTFS volume with compression enabled. He has a 2 MB bitmap in a compressed folder that he would like to copy to a floppy disk. This bitmap is 1 MB in its compressed state. When he tries to copy the file, he receives this message: "Insufficient disk space". Which of the following is the best method for George to copy the bitmap to a floppy drive disk?
   a. Use a third-party compression tool such as PKZIP to compress the file.
   b. Confirm the NTFS volume has compression set to MAX.
   c. Format the target floppy disk with NTFS and then copy the file.
   d. Confirm the disk is HD (High Density).

1. **b.** A FAT32 partition can only support partition sizes up to 32 GB. That is another reason to use NTFS.

2. **b.** This utility can be used to convert basic disks to Dynamic Disks. One word of caution: Once you convert to Dynamic Disks you cannot convert back to basic disks without data loss. The Disk Administrator was used in Windows NT 4.0 and is not available in Windows 2000. There is no such utility as Local Disks and Volumes in Windows 2000 Professional.

3. **a, b.** You can use Windows Explorer. Find the folder you want to encrypt, right-click the file or folder, and select Properties. In the General tab of the Properties dialog box, click the Advanced button, then check the "Encrypt contents to secure data" checkbox, then click OK. You can also use the Cipher.exe command with the following syntax: CIPHER /[command parameter] [filename], for example, CIPHER /e documents. There is no such command as Crypto.exe and you cannot use System Tools to encrypt a folder.

4. **b.** A striped volume stores data in equal stripes between two or more dynamic drives. Since the data is written sequentially in the stripes, you can take advantage of multiple I/O performance and increased speed. Because data is written sequentially, you do not see the performance enhancements with spanned volumes, that you do with striped volumes. If any of the drives in the spanned volume set fails, you lose access to all of the data in the spanned set. RAID-5 is not available with Windows 2000 Professional.

5. **a.** One of the benefits of Dynamic Disks is the ability to extend a spanned volume to increase the size of the volume. You cannot extend basic disks.

6. **d.** You end up with 5 drives at 5 GB each for a total of 25 GB. You do not lose any space for parity because a striped volume does not provide fault tolerance.

7. **d.** You cannot convert an NTFS partition back to a FAT partition without losing data. There is no such utility as FAT.exe. The Convert.exe command can be used only to convert file systems to NTFS.

8. **a.** The Advanced Attributes dialog box will offer an option at the bottom of the page to Compress contents to save disk space. The Backup, Disk Management, and Network Neighborhood utilities cannot be used to compress a file.

9. **c.** When you apply changes to the subfolder and then move the files under the Sales folder to Destin2, the files that are moved will retain their compressed attribute at their new location. Remember that you cannot encrypt and compress a file or folder at the same time.

10. **a.** Because you have converted the disks to the NTFS file system, file security can be obtained. Also, because you are using EFS encryption you will protect of sensitive files and the Recovery Agent (the Administrator) can decrypt and EFS files.

11. **a.** Disk quotas are specified only for NTFS volumes at the volume level, even if the NTFS partition resides on the same physical hard drive.

12. **c.** When an encrypted file is moved to an NTFS folder on a Windows 2000 machine the encryption will remain intact. Remember that the user that encrypted the file is the only person, other than the Recovery Agent, that can access their personal encrypted files.

13. **a.** You must use a third-party compression tool to compress the file and then copy it to the floppy disk. You cannot format a floppy disk with NTFS.

Challenge Solutions

1. Look at Table 6-1 to help you answer this problem. Simply put, FAT32 only supports volume sizes up to 32 GB.

2. Don't let this trick question send you down the wrong path. The only operating system that can recognize Dynamic Disks is Windows 2000.

3. After you review the types of dynamic volumes it should become obvious to you that the striped volume will provide you the fastest disk access. Go back and review the characteristics of each Dynamic Disk if you guessed wrong.

4. First, and foremost, basic disks cannot be extended. Both disks must be converted to Dynamic Disks. Now you can extend the spanned volume that was the original logical drive by using that volume and the unallocated space from the second disk drive.

5. First, take the five drives and multiply by 5 GB and you have a total storage space of 25 GB. In a striped volume you gain tremendous speed and you do not lose any disk space for fault tolerance.

6. Rescan the disks. Remove the spanned volume and create a new spanned volume that includes the new disk. Format the spanned volume. Use Windows Backup to restore the data. The key to solving this problem is to rescan the disks because your computer supports hot swapping. Then, because a spanned volume has no fault tolerance, it must be removed and a new spanned volume created. Then restore the data from backup.

7.   Compress the Sales folder, apply the changes to the subfolder to be moved only, and then move the files from Sales to the Destin2 folder. The key to this problem is that you have to make sure the files are compressed when you move them. First, we must assume the folders are on the same partition. When you copy or add a file into a compressed folder, in the same partition, the file is compressed automatically (inherits folder attributes). If you move a file across partitions into a compressed folder, the file is compressed automatically (inherits folder attributes). If you move a file within the same partition to a compressed folder the file retains its original state (compressed or not compressed). If you move a file from a different NTFS drive into a compressed folder, it is also compressed. However, if you move a file from the same NTFS drive into a compressed folder, the file retains its original state, either compressed or uncompressed.

8.   You must use a third-party compression tool such as PKZIP to compress the file, then copy the file to disk. One note of importance is that a floppy disk cannot be formatted in NTFS. You may also receive a message that will give you the option to copy a compressed file to a network share or a floppy disk. Choose the network share because it is formatted with NTFS. A floppy disk cannot be formatted with NTFS and the third-party compression tool is not listed in the answer.

9.   Because the "deny space to users who exceed their limit" has been enabled, the only way to enable Tony to save this file is to remove files from his home folder until the total uncompressed file size is less than 100 MB.

Chapter 7

Local Computer Security

These are the areas that are generally testable on the MCSE Server 2000 examination:

1. Implement, configure, manage, and troubleshoot policies in a Windows 2000 environment.

    *   Implement, configure, manage, and troubleshoot local policies in a Windows 2000 environment.

    *   Implement, configure, manage, and troubleshoot system policies in a Windows 2000 environment.

2. Implement, configure, manage, and troubleshoot auditing.

3. Implement, configure, manage, and troubleshoot account policies.

4. Implement, configure, manage, and troubleshoot security by using the Security Configuration and Analysis tool.

Introduction

In this chapter you will learn that the local policies are managed by the Local Computer Group Policy utility and that domain group policies are managed by the Domain Controller Security Policy snap-in. You will also find that by default domain policies override the settings of a local computer group policy. You can access the Group Policy snap-in through the MMC, or by using the Administrative Tools utility.

You will learn the different policies that can be applied to a system. The first is password policies which enable the administrator to define passwords for your network. In particular, you will learn that the Enforce Password History feature can be used to force a user to select a different password. This particular policy enables you to determine how many previous passwords will be used to filter the password. Another type of policy that can be configured is the Account Lockout Policy. This type of policy is used to increase security by defining the number of times a person can unsuccessfully log in before the account is locked out. You will also see how Audit Policies are implemented to enable auditing. The secedit command is used to force a security options policy to be updated immediately.

For backward compatibility, Windows 2000 Professional permits you to control users' desktops through system policies. Even though you can still use system policies, it is recommended that you use group policies instead. Know that the POLEDIT command typed into the Run dialog box will enable you to configure system policies.

Next, you will be shown that the Security Configuration and Analysis Tool is used to analyze the local computer's security settings. This utility does not automatically make security changes—you have to make the changes manually.

Finally, you will be given some real-world problems to solve in implementing group policies on your network.

SECURITY SETTINGS

Security is a must for most organizations. If you don't have a good security plan, your network may suffer some unfortunate events. In Windows 2000 security can be managed at the local level using the *Local Computer Group Policy* object. It can be accessed by adding a snap-in to the MMC or by using the Administrative Tools utility.

Security can also be managed at the domain level. ***Domain policies override*** the settings of a local computer group policy. This means that if you implement a local computer policy on a computer and then you implement a domain policy, the domain policy will have priority over the local policy. Domain policies are managed through the Domain Controller Security Policy snap-in to the MMC or by using the Administrative Tools utility. The Active Directory Users and Computers utility is used to manage domain controller security policies for an organization unit.

EXAM TIP: Know that the local policies are managed through the Local Computer Group Policy utility. Finally, know that domain policies override, by default, the settings of a local computer group policy.

ACCOUNT POLICIES

Account policies, shown in Figure 7-1, can be accessed using the Group Policy snap-in. In Group Policy you will notice that you can access the Account Policies folder by expanding the Local Computer Policy option, followed by Computer Configuration, Windows Settings, Security Settings, and then Account Policies. These are used to define password settings and an account lockout policy.

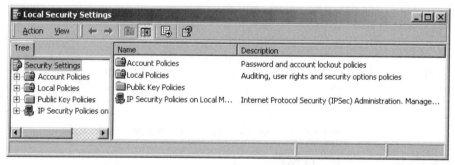

Figure 7-1: Local Group Policy, Account Policies

Password Policies

Password policy is a folder under the Account Policies folder, which enables you to set password policies for the computer, as listed in Table 7-1, but not for individual users. There are many password policy options to choose from, but we have only listed the important ones.

Table 7-1: Password Policies

Policy	Description	Minimum/Maximum
Enforce password history	Used to track all of the user's password histories.	0 / 24 history
Maximum password age	Defines the maximum number of days users can keep a password.	1 / 999 age
Minimum password length	Defines the minimum number of characters a password can have.	0 /14 length
Passwords must meet complexity requirements	Defines password filters.	N/A

NOTE: The Enforce password history policy is used when a user changes their password and, depending on the number used, will not let the individual continue to use the same password. The Maximum password age policy is used for security purposes to force a user to change their password after a predetermined amount of time. The Minimum password length policy is used to specify a password length. If this option is not set, a password is not required. The Passwords must meet complexity requirements policy is used to prevent users from creating simple passwords. The Enforce password history policy can be accessed in the Password Policy folder, as illustrated in Figure 7-2.

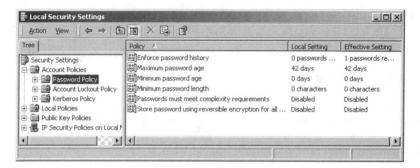

Figure 7-2: Password Policy Folder

EXAM TIP: Definitely know that the Enforce password history policy will force a user to select a different password and that you, the administrator, determine how many previous passwords will be used to filter the new password.

Challenge #1

Denise is the local security officer for your Windows 2000 Professional computer. She has just learned that many users continue to use the same password every time they log on. She has established a policy requiring all users to change their passwords. She must create a new policy that will force all users to cycle through a specific number of unique passwords before being allowed to reuse them. Which of the password policies listed in Table 7-1 will accomplish this task?

Account Lockout Policies

Account lockout policies, as illustrated in Figure 7-3, are used to stop hackers from breaking into your computer. These policies are configured so that after a predetermined number of unsuccessful logon attempts, within a certain number of minutes, the account will be locked for a specific amount of time. Table 7-2 lists all the account lockout policies that are important. You should memorize the contents of this table.

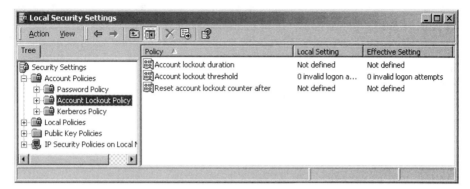

Figure 7-3: Account Lockout Policy Folder

Table 7-2: Account Lockout Policies

Policy	Description	Minimum/Maximum
Account lockout duration	Defines how long the account will be locked if the Account lockout threshold is exceeded.	0 / 99,999
Account lockout threshold	Defines the number of invalid attempts permitted before account is locked out.	0 / 999
Reset account lockout counter after	Defines how long the counter will remember unsuccessful logon attempts.	0 / 99,999

EXAM TIP: Memorize the information in Table 7-2 and become familiar with account lockout policies.

NOTE: The Account lockout threshold policy is disabled by default. Account lockout policies work hand-in-hand with each other. If the Account lockout threshold policy is enabled, the Account lockout duration is set to 30 minutes and the Reset account lockout counter after is set to 5 minutes. One important point to know is that account lockout policies take effect immediately.

Let's say you have users who connect to your Windows 2000 Professional computer remotely. They also require access to other servers on the network. You are concerned about dictionary attacks from the Internet and need to configure an account lockout policy to solve this problem. How would you go about this?

LOCAL POLICIES

Local policies, illustrated in 7-4, are used to control users after they have logged on to the network. They can be used to configure auditing, user rights assignment, and security options.

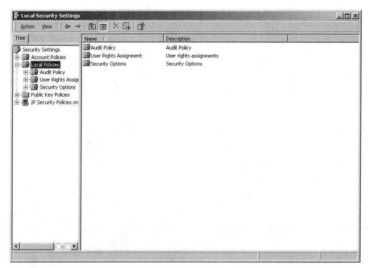

**Figure 7-4:
Local Policies
Folder**

Audit Policies

Audit policies, shown in Figure 7-5, allow the administrator to monitor certain actions that users perform. When you set up an audit policy, you can decide to audit the success or failure of a specific event. Auditing is turned off by default and it must be turned on manually. After auditing policies have been enabled, you can review the results in the Event Viewer utility. Be careful not to turn on too many auditing features, because it will adversely affect system performance. Table 7-3 describes the most important audit policies.

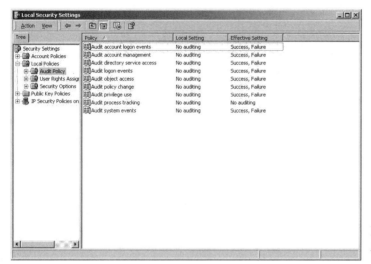

Figure 7-5:
Audit Policy

Table 7-3: Audit Policies

Policy	Description
Audit account logon events	Used to determine when a user logs on, logs off, or makes a network connection.
Audit account management	Used to determine when user and group accounts are created or deleted and management actions.
Audit logon events	Used to audit events related to logon, such as running a logon script or accessing a roaming profile.
Audit object access	Used to audit access to files, folders, and printers.

EXAM TIP: Memorize the information in Table 7-3 on audit policies.

To enable auditing you must enable auditing of the deleted subfolders and files in the property sheet of the share. This is accomplished in Windows Explorer. Figure 7-6 shows a shared folder Properties dialog box. This screen is accessed by selecting the Security tab, then clicking the Advanced button, and selecting the Auditing tab.

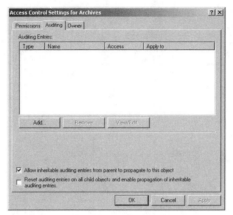

Figure 7-6: Enabling Auditing on a Shared Folder

Toby is the administrator of a Windows 2000 Professional computer and he has to find out who has been deleting files and folders on the computer. He has narrowed down the search and has learned that the folders are being deleted from a particular shared folder that belongs to the IT department. He now must audit the IT department's shared folder for file and subfolder deletion. What steps must he take to activate this security measure?

Challenge #3

User Rights

User rights assignments, listed in Table 7-4, are used to determine the rights a user or group will have on a computer. These rights are not the same as permissions, which are applied to objects such as files and folders. In this section we will mention the most important user rights. The User Rights Assignment policy, illustrated in Figure 7-7, can be accessed by expanding the Local Policies folder to show the User Rights Assignment policy folder.

Table 7-4: User Rights

Right	Description
Access this computer from the network	Used to enable access to the computer from the network.
Back up files and directories	Used to enable access to the system to back up all files and directories. It does not matter whether or not the user has permissions to the files and directories.
Log on locally	Used to enable a user to log on locally at the computer.

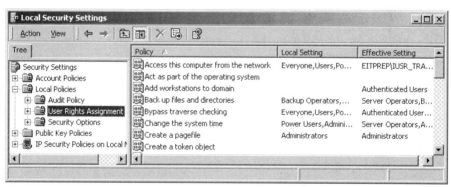

Figure 7-7: User Rights Assignment Policy

Security Options

The security options policies, shown in Figure 7-8, are used to configure security for the computer. These are different from user rights in that user rights are assigned to a user or group, while security options are assigned to a computer. We have highlighted the most common security options in Table 7-5.

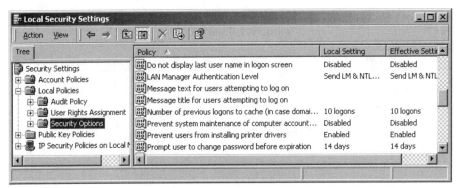

Figure 7-8: Security Options Policy

Table 7-5: Security Options Policy

Security Option	Description
Audit the access of global system objects	Used to permit access to global system objects to be audited.
Disable CTRL+ALT+DEL requirement logon	Used to disable the requirement for the CTRL+ALT+DEL logon.
Do not display last user name in logon screen	Does not allow the last user name to be displayed in the Logon screen at logon.
Message text for users attempting to log on	Enables you to display a test message when users log on.
Prompt user to change password before expiration	Displays a message telling the user to change the password before expiration.
Recovery Console; allow floppy copy and access to all drives and folders	Enables you to copy all files and folders from the system when in the Recovery Console.

NOTE: You must remember that the Recovery Console, by default, does not allow you to copy all files and folders from all drives unless this option is used.

You must understand that group policies may only be updated periodically on the local machine. To force a Security options policy to be updated immediately, type *secedit /refreshpolicy MACHINE_POLICY* at the command prompt. As a side note, if you want to refresh policies under the User Configuration note, type *secedit/refreshpolicy USER_POLICY* at the command prompt.

Assume that you have just implemented a security options policy and have noticed that your changes have not taken effect yet. What should you do?

Challenge #4

Local computer policies can be used to limit a user's activity. As an example, let's say that for security reasons you want to *remove the Logoff option from the Start menu* for a group of computers. You could configure a local computer policy that will not include the Logoff option on the Start menu. This would be much quicker than right-clicking the taskbar, selecting Properties and bring up the Taskbar & Start Menu dialog box, then select the Advanced tab, finally, at the bottom of this screen you will clear the Display Logoff Option.

You are the security manager for five Windows 98 computers configured in a workgroup. You wish to upgrade these computers to Windows 2000 Professional. For security reasons, you want to remove the Run option from the Start menu of these five workgroup computers. You have an inventory program that needs to run continuously. How could you remove this option from the Start menu?

Challenge #5

EXAM TIP: Know that the SECEDIT command is used to force a security options policy to be updated immediately. You must also know the two ways to remove the Logoff option from the Start menu.

Local Computer Security   **175**

SYSTEM POLICIES

System policies can be used to control the computer's system configuration and the user's environment. These policies actually edit the Registry to make changes to the system. System policies can be used to establish policies for a single user, group, or computer. They can also be used for all users and for all computers. System policies were commonly used in Windows NT 4.0. There are many areas in this section to discuss, but the likelihood that it will be on you exam is slim, so we will move on to the next topic. The only item that you may need to know is that *POLEDIT* typed in the Run dialog box is used to configure a system policy.

> **EXAM TIP:** Know that the POLEDIT command typed in the Run dialog box will enable you to configure system policies.

SECURITY CONFIGURATION AND ANALYSIS TOOL

The *Security Configuration and Analysis tool*, depicted in Figure 7-9, is used to analyze the local computer's security settings and provides you with information to make changes to the security settings. This tool is used with security templates that you configure for the way you want the security settings to be and you are given an analysis report. The template is then compared to the system's actual settings. The Security Configuration and Analysis utility can be accessed by adding a snap-in to the MMC.

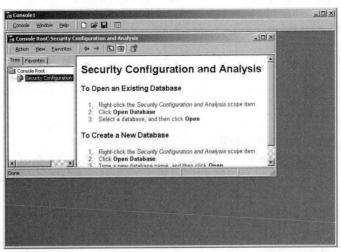

Figure 7-9:
Security
Configuration
and Analysis
Tool

The following process must be used to properly employ this utility.

1. First, use the Security Configuration and Analysis tool to *set a working security database that will be used to perform the security analysis.*

2. Then, *import a security template that reflects the security setting you would like to see on the local computer.*

3. After the template has been compared with the local computer's security settings you will receive the results of the security analysis, which can be viewed in the Security Configuration and Analysis snap-in, under the configured security item.

4. You can then *manually make changes on the local computer based on the security analysis results.*

EXAM TIP: Learn the process for generating a security analysis report and understand what each step accomplishes. Know that the Security Configuration and Analysis tool is used to analyze the local computer's security settings. Also be aware that this utility does not automatically make changes—you must make the changes manually.

NOTE: After the template is applied to the local computer, the results can be reviewed. Each entry will have an "x" or a checkmark. The "x" means that the template and the local computer policy do not match. The checkmark means that they do match. If you want to fix all the entries that have an "x", you must use the Group Policy snap-in.

What types of settings can be used on the security template? You can specify:

- *Account Policy settings* - which are password policies, account lockout policies, and Kerberos policies (on domain controllers).

- *Local Policy settings* - which are audit policies, user right assignments, and security options.

- *Event log settings* - which are applied to Event Viewer Log files.

- *Restricted Groups settings* - which enable you to manage local group membership.

- *Registry settings* - which are used to specify security for local Registry keys.

- *File System settings* - which are used to specify security for the local file sytem.

- *System Service settings* - which are used to specify security for system services and the startup mode for each service.

Ashley is responsible for the security policies of your Windows 2000 Professional computer. Today, she has discovered that someone has been trying to break into her computer. Now she is really concerned with network security and starts the evaluation process by performing a security analysis on the Windows 2000 Professional computer where the security breach occurred. Which Windows 2000 utility can she use to perform a security analysis and obtain assistance to configure the computer's local security settings?

EXAM TIP: Be aware that you use the Security Configuration and Analysis tool to perform a security analysis on a Windows 2000 Professional computer.

APPLYING GROUP POLICIES IN THE DOMAIN ENVIRONMENT

Normally, this section is not covered in the Windows 2000 Professional area. However, we feel that you need to know some basics to understand the entire process.

After you have created a group policy for a group of users on your Windows network, you must be careful of one thing. There is a *"No Override"* option, as seen in Figure 7-10. Selecting this option will prevent parent group policies from affecting the policy of users in a particular group. For example, let's say you create a group policy for an organizational unit called Destin and you do not want the parent domain Florida to override the members of the Destin OU. Just select the "No Override" option and the Destin OU group policy will not be affected by the parent policy. Remember, this option is not enabled by default and must be set manually. As a side note, if you are having problems applying policies to child domains, check to make sure that the "No Override" option has not been selected. If it has been, the policy will not be applied to the child domain.

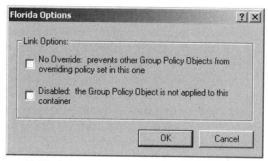

Figure 7-10: No Override Option of the Group Policy

Review Questions

1. Toby is the administrator of a Windows 2000 Professional computer and he has to find out who has been deleting files and folders on his computer. He has narrowed the search and has found that the folders are being deleted from a particular shared folder that belongs to the IT department. He must now audit the IT department's shared folder for file and subfolder deletion. Which of the following steps must he take to enable auditing?

   a. Enable auditing of the Directory Service Access event in Local Policies then enable auditing of the deleted subfolders and files for each folder you wish to audit.

   b. Enable auditing of the deleted subfolders and files in the Security tab of the domain object's property sheet.

   c. Enable Audit Object Access event in Local Policies, then enable auditing of the deleted subfolders and files for each folder you wish to audit.

   d. Enable auditing of the deleted subfolders and files in the property sheet of the share in Explorer.

2. Jerry is in charge of security for a Windows 2000 Professional computer configured in a workgroup. He has made some new changes in security and needs to make sure that those changes are applied immediately. Which of the following command-line utilities could he use to force an immediate update of the new security policies?

   a. Regedit
   b. Updatesec
   c. Secedit
   d. Refreshsec

3. You have been promoted to local administrator for a Windows 2000 Professional computer because your assistant administrator has recently been fired and a replacement is not expected for some time. You have to secure the computer immediately, because someone has been hacking into it. You determine that you must lock out the assistant's user account. The account has been configured for lockout and you are wondering what action to take next to ensure that the lockout will occur immediately. Which of the following actions is the best choice?
    a. Force an Active Directory synchronization.
    b. Disable their access at the network level.
    c. Reboot the computer.
    d. Nothing. The lockout is immediate.

4. Denise is the local security officer for your Windows 2000 Professional computer. She has just learned that many users continue to use the same password every time they log on. She has established a policy requiring all users to change their passwords. She needs to create a new policy that will force all users to cycle through a specific number of unique passwords before being allowed to reuse them. Which of the following will ensure that this new policy will be applied successfully?
    a. Use different passwords
    b. Require C2 authentication
    c. Enforce password history
    d. Passwords are only valid for 30 days.

5. Ashley is responsible for security policies for a Windows 2000 Professional computer. Today, she discovered that someone has been trying to break into the computer. Now she is really concerned with network security and starts her evaluation process by performing a security analysis on the computer that had the security breach. Which of the following utilities can she use to perform a security analysis and obtain assistance to configure the computer's local security settings?
    a. Local Security Manager
    b. Security Configuration and Analysis
    c. Security Manager and Analyzer
    d. Security System Manager

6. John, the chief of network security, uses the Security Configuration and Analysis snap-in on a daily basis. He has just used a security template to analyze a Windows 2000 Professional computer. He is not sure when the template's settings will be implemented on the computer. Which of the following best answers his question?

   a. Immediately
   b. After next logon
   c. Never
   d. After you restart the computer

7. You are the security manager for five Windows 98 computers configured in a workgroup. You wish to upgrade these computers to Windows 2000 Professional. Now, for security reasons, you want to remove the Logoff option from the Start menu for these five workgroup computers. Which of the following will permit you remove this option from the Start menu? (Select two answers.)

   a. On the Advanced tab of the Taskbar & Start Menu dialog box, clear the Display Logoff Option.
   b. On the Advanced tab of the Taskbar & Start Menu dialog box, clear the Administrative Tools Option.
   c. On the General tab of the Taskbar & Start Menu dialog box, clear the Personalized Menus option. Log off and then log on to the computers.
   d. Use a local computer policy that does not include the Logoff option on the Start menu.
   e. Use the User Profiles tab within the properties of My Computer to change the profile from a local profile to a roaming user profile.

8. You are the local administrator for a Windows Professional computer. You want to establish a lockout policy for this computer to prevent hackers. You set the lockout threshold for 3 failed attempts, but you did not set a lockout time. The computer will be locked out after how long?

   a. 5 minutes
   b. 10 minutes
   c. 12 minutes
   d. 30 minutes
   e. It will not lock out.

9. The local security officer for your Windows 2000 Professional computer is concerned about individuals attempting to break into your computer. He decides to configure a policy to audit failed logons. After the policy has been configured and implemented, he notices that there are many occurrences of someone trying to access resources on your network. Now, he has a plan to establish a lockout policy that specifies the number of invalid attempts that will be permitted before the account will be locked out. Which of the following would he most likely use to perform this task?
   a. Account lockout threshold
   b. Account lockout counter
   c. Account lockout specified period
   d. Account lockout duration

10. You are the local administrator for a Windows 2000 Professional computer configured in a workgroup. Someone has been reading certain important files, and you have enabled auditing of object access with a local group policy on a computer. You know that enabling auditing is a two-step process. You use Windows Explorer to specify which files and folders you would like to audit, but you cannot find an option to configure auditing. Which of the following is the most likely reason for this problem?
   a. Auditing of process tracking is not enabled. In order to track system activity such as file access, you must enable process tracking.
   b. Auditing was enabled at the local level. Auditing must be enabled at the domain level to take effect.
   c. The drive that is to be audited was not formatted with NTFS. Drives must be formatted with NTFS to support auditing.
   d. The system has not been restarted. You must restart a system before enabling auditing.

11. You wish to apply specialized local group policies on a Windows 2000 Professional computer. Which of the following are correct statements about computer policies? (Select all that apply.)
   a. Computer configuration policies apply to all users of that computer regardless of user name.
   b. Computer configuration policies are specific to users.
   c. Computer configuration policies apply to guest users only.
   d. Computer configuration policies apply to non-Administrator users.

12. You are the local administrator for a Windows 2000 Professional computer. You are looking for an important Excel project that is due today. You cannot find it and you notice that many important Excel files are missing. You are able to restore the files from backup. Now you want to enable auditing to track all users who access your Excel documents in the future in order to identify the person that is deleting your files. Which two of the following must be performed to meet your goals? (Select two answers.)
    a. Enable the local group policy for auditing object access events that are successful.
    b. Enable the local group policy for auditing object access events that are unsuccessful.
    c. Enable the local group policy for auditing process tracking events that are successful.
    d. Enable the local group policy for auditing process tracking events that are unsuccessful.
    e. Use Windows 2000 Explorer to enable auditing for your files.
    f. Run the diskped-V command and use System Monitor to examine the Logical I/O counter. Restart the computer.

13. You are the administrator of a small workgroup of Windows 2000 Professional computers. Some users have established very small, simple passwords. For security purposes, you would like to force users to establish more complicated passwords when they log on to the computer. Which of the following would be the correct action?
    a. Set account lockout policies.
    b. Implement network security.
    c. Implement Password must meet the complexity requirements of the Installed Password Filters policy.
    d. Set Maximum password age to 5 days.
    e. Set Enforce password history.

1. **d.** Enabling auditing of the deleted subfolders and files located in the shared folder's Properties dialog box while in Explorer will allow you to view these events later in Event Viewer

2. **c.** To verify that changes were applied use, the Secedit command-line utility to force an update of the new security policies. Regedit is used to edit the registry.

3. **d.** When you lock out the account it normally takes place immediately. But if the former employee is currently logged on to the network the lockout will not occur until they log off and log back on to the network. Rebooting the computer will not make the lockout take effect immediately. It is not necessary to force an Active Directory synchronization.

4. **c.** Using the Enforce password history will force the user to cycle through a predetermined number of passwords before the user can use the same password.

5. **b.** The Security Configuration and Analysis utility is used to check the security of a computer's local settings. Take notice that this tool is only used to analyze the security policies of the local security settings. You must use the results of this utility to manually change the local security settings.

6. **c.** The templates don't actually make the changes. They only identify problem areas for you to correct through the use of policies. When the template analyzes the computer it will mark a policy with an "x" or a checkmark. The "x" means that the template and the policy do not match. The checkmark means that they do match.

7. **a,d.** First you could right-click the taskbar and select Properties. This will bring up the Taskbar & Start Menu dialog box. Then select the Advanced tab, and finally, at the bottom of this screen, clear the Display Logoff Option. The second way is to configure a local computer policy that will not include the Logoff option on the Start menu.

8. **d.** This is the default time for an account lockout.

9. **a.** The Account lockout threshold policy specifies the number of invalid attempts allowed before the account is locked out. The Account lockout duration specifies how long the account will remain locked if the account lockout threshold is exceeded.

10. **c.** The drive that is to be audited was not formatted with NTFS. Drives must be formatted with NTFS to support auditing. Enabling the process tracking is not the correct answer. In this case it appears that the partition is not formatted with NTFS. Auditing can be enabled at the local level for the auditing process to work. Restarting the system will not enable auditing.

11. **a.** Computer configuration policies apply to all users of a particular computer regardless of user name. Computer configuration policies apply to all users including administrators.

12. **a, e.** The first step of the two-step process is to configure a local group policy to audit object access that is successful. When access is successful it means that someone has gained access to the resource on your computer and therefore has the capability to delete files. The second step of the process is to use Windows Explorer to audit the files you wish to monitor.

13. **c.** To increase network security, you will implement Password must meet the complexity requirements of the Installed Password Filters policy. You do this by setting a password policy. Account lockout policies will only create more work for you because if you set up lockout policies, then you will have to reset the account. Setting the Maximum password age to 5 days will not solve the problem. Setting Enforce password history will only ensure that users will not use the same simple password within a given time frame.

Challenge Solutions

1. Use the Enforce password history policy to force the user to change their password. It will not allow the user to use the same password, depending on the number you have selected. The Enforce password history can be accessed in the Password Policy folder, as illustrated in Figure 7-2.

2. Since the users will be accessing resources throughout the domain, the best choice would be to edit the Default Domain Policy group policy object to enforce the lockout feature you desire.

3. To answer this question you must know that if you want to enable auditing you must enable auditing of the deleted subfolders and files in the property sheet of the share while in Windows Explorer. Figure 7-6 shows a shared folder Properties dialog box, after selecting the Security tab, then clicking the Advanced button, and then using the Auditing tab.

4. You must understand that group policies may only be updated periodically on the local machine. To force the security options policy to be updated immediately, type secedit/refreshpolicy MACHINE_POLICY at the command prompt. As a side note, if you want to refresh policies under the User Configuration note, type secedit/refreshpolicy USER_POLICY at the command prompt.

5. First you could right-click the taskbar select Properties. This will bring up the Taskbar & Start Menu dialog box. Then select the Advanced tab, and finally, at the bottom of this screen clear the Display Logoff Option. The second way is to configure a local computer policy that will not include the Run option on the Start menu.

6. The tool to use is the Security Configuration and Analysis tool.

Chapter 8

Accessing Files and Folders

These are the areas that are generally testable on the MCSE Server 2000 examination:

1. Monitor, manage, and troubleshoot access to files and folders.

   - Control access to files and folders by using permissions.

   - Optimize access to files and folders.

2. Manage and troubleshoot access to shared folders.

   - Control access to shared folders using permissions.

3. Connect to shared resources on a Microsoft network.

4. Manage and troubleshoot the use and synchronization of offline files.

Accessing Files and Folders

The first part of this chapter will show you how to enable the Offline Files feature on your computer. You will find that this is a two-step process. First, the computer must be enabled to use offline files, and then you must identify the files that will be made available offline.

Also in this chapter you will discover that there are two ways to control access to files and folders. One way is through NTFS permissions. These permissions are used to provide local file-level security. NTFS permissions are cumulative, which means that if you are a member of multiple groups, the least restrictive permission is your effective permission. Another way to control access is with share permissions. This type of permission actually controls access to a particular resource over the network.

You will learn how to apply NTFS permissions to a resource and what types of permissions to give to an individual or group. In addition, you will be shown how to apply Share permissions to a resource. Then you will learn how to determine someone's effective permissions when NTFS permissions are combined with share permissions.

Finally, you will learn how to use the Shared Folder utility to create shares and to monitor access to shares.

MANAGING OFFLINE FOLDERS

Pay particular attention to this section because you may receive at least two possible questions in this area. Offline files and folders is a new feature to Windows 2000 Professional that enables client computers to store a copy of a network file or folder. With this feature, when the client cannot connect to the computer that stores a file or folder, the client still has access to it and there is no loss of productivity. You can access the Offline Files option in Windows Explorer. After Windows Explorer has been opened, click the Tools entry in the menu bar and select the Folder Options option. This will bring up the Folder Options dialog box. Select the Offline Files tab, as illustrated in Figure 8-1.

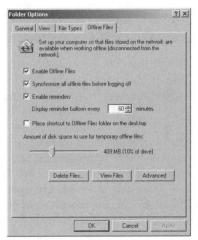

Figure 8-1: Folder Options Dialog Box, Offline Files Tab

Offline files are generally employed by users who use their laptop computers at work and then take them home or on trips. Offline files enable users to perform their work even when they are not at work, or when the shared file or folder is not available. Offline files are copies of network shared files or folders (stored on a different network computer) that are also located on the local computer. In order to use the Offline Files feature, you must have a Windows computer (it does not have to be Windows 2000) to store the shared version of the file or folder. Then, there must be a Windows 2000 Professional client computer configured to use the Offline Files feature. The following paragraphs define the four-step process used to enable this feature.

The Offline Files process starts with the computer that will store the shared file or folder. *The file or folder must be shared and proper permissions given to the users that will access this share.*

After the file or folder has been shared, the client computer can be configured to use offline files and folders. In order for this arrangement to operate properly the client computer must be able to connect to the network so that it can access the shared file or folder. Look again at the Offline Files tab, shown in Figure 8-1. *Notice the "Enable Offline Files" checkbox.* This checkbox is checked by default. This means that offline access is enabled by default, and if you don't want to use this feature you must remove the checkmark. Also, notice that the "Synchronize all offline files before logging off" checkbox is selected by default. This enables the automatic synchronization of the offline files during the logoff process. It makes sure that all the changes you made during your logon session are saved to the network share. If you do not have the automatic synchronization checkbox checked, you will have to perform a manual synchronization of files and folders.

Next you must make files and folders available for offline access. *This is accomplished on the local computer using Windows Explorer by right-clicking the files or folders and selecting the "Make Available Offline" option from the menu.* Doing so brings up the Offline Files Wizard that takes you through the enabling process. During this process you are given the option to synchronize manually or automatically—automatically is the default. If subfolders are involved, you will be prompted whether they should also be made available offline. After you click the "Finish" button, the offline files and folders will be synchronized (copied) to the local computer. You can tell that they are offline files and folders by the icon just below the folder. It looks like two arrows, one going up and one going down.

Finally, you must configure how your local computer will react to the loss of network connectivity. To perform this task, you must use the Folder Options dialog box, on the Offline Files tab, shown in Figure 8-1. Notice the "Advanced" button near the middle right of the screen. After you click this button it will bring up the Offline Files – Advanced Settings dialog box, as shown in Figure 8-2. There are two options here: They are "Notify me and begin working offline" (the default setting) and "Never allow my computer to go offline".

Figure 8-2: Offline Files – Advanced Settings Dialog Box

If you are trying to enable the Offline Files feature and you are not given the "Make Available Offline" option on the remote folder's right-click action menu, you must make sure all the following items are configured properly:

- ***Is the local computer configured to use offline files and folders?*** Refer to Figure 8-1 again. The "Enable Offline Files" checkbox should be enabled by default. However, someone may have removed the checkmark. If this checkbox is not checked, then you will not be given the "Make Available Offline" option when you right-click the file or folder.

- ***Is the folder on the other computer shared and are you given the appropriate share permissions to access it?*** The folder is not shared if you do not see the hand icon below the folder.

Offline Caching

Offline caching is used to specify how folders are cached when the folder is offline. *If this option is not enabled, it will save network bandwidth by not allowing the caching of offline files.* This option can be configured when the share is first established, or later using the folder Properties dialog box. The dialog box is accessed by right-clicking the folder and selecting the Properties option. Then you should select the Sharing tab, shown in Figure 8-3.

Figure 8-3: Folder Properties Dialog Box, Sharing Tab

Notice in Figure 8-3 that there is a button called "Caching". After you click this button, you will be given the option to allow caching with the "Allow Caching" checkbox. If you check it, caching will be activated.

You are the administrator of a Windows 2000 network. You have a Windows 2000 Professional computer and you need to share an important document with other users. Because the document is very sensitive, you do not want the other users to use offline caching. What would you use to configure this option?

EXAM TIP: This area is hit hard on the exam. You may receive three or four questions from this section. You must know all the steps used to establish offline files and how to identify problems with the process. Examine the four Challenges. Read them carefully and know the reason for the problem in each. Finally, know that disabling offline caching will save valuable network bandwidth.

MANAGING LOCAL ACCESS

There are two ways to access files and folders. One is through local access and the other is through network access. Local access can only be managed on a partition formatted with NTFS. It enables you to control who can access a file or folder with NTFS permissions. This means that you can control access after an individual logs on to a network. Network access is a resource that can be accessed over the network by sharing it. Network access is not as secure as local access because it does not allow file-level security.

Using NTFS Permissions

NTFS permissions enable you to control local file security. NTFS permissions are given to users and groups and the permissions are cumulative, depending on the access given to each group. This means that if a user belongs to three groups, such as Marketing—Read, Accounting—Write, and Support—Full Control, the user's effective NTFS permission will be Full Control. To calculate how this works, you first add all the permissions, and the least restrictive is the effective permission. However, if an individual is denied access, this denial overrides any other permission assigned. This means that if you are given Full Control access through a group membership, but another group denies access to the same file, then you will be denied access to the file. Here are the different levels of NTFS permissions:

- Full Control permissions
- Modify permissions
- Read & Execute permissions
- List Folder Contents permissions
- Write permissions
- Read permissions

Controlling access to resources with these permissions can only be accomplished locally and cannot be applied to a network share. In order for someone to access a file or folder, they must be logged on to the computer where the resource is located. If you are concerned with security, take note that the Everyone group, by default, has Full Control permission to the NTFS partition. To make your network more secure, you should remove this permission immediately and only give access to those who must have access to a particular resource.

Applying NTFS Permissions

You can set NTFS permissions in Windows Explorer. Simply right-click the desired file and select the Properties option. A Properties dialog box will appear. Notice that there is a Security tab, shown in Figure 8-4. This tab is not present when a partition is formatted with FAT. This is because FAT does not provide for local security. This tab is used to provide access to a user or group. As a side note, you must be logged on as Administrator to manage NTFS Permissions.

NOTE: *NTFS permissions can only be applied to files and folders for local security. NTFS permissions cannot be applied to shares.* As you will see later, this is accomplished with shared permissions (also called network permissions). NTFS permissions also cannot be applied to printers.

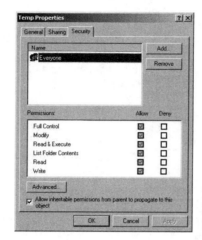

Figure 8-4: File Properties Dialog Box, Security Tab

NOTE: To give access to a user or group, you simply use the Add button and select the user or group you wish to provide access to. Then, in the Permissions section select the level of access to be given. Using the Advanced button will provide you with a more detailed list of permissions. Finally, notice the "Allow inheritable permissions from parent to propagate to this object" checkbox. We will examine this option in the next section.

Inherited Permissions

By default, permissions are given by the parent folder to any files and subfolders located within it. Refer to the *"**Allow inheritable permissions from parent to propagate to this object**"* checkbox. This is checked by default and needs to be unchecked if you wish to apply different permissions to subfolders and files located within a parent folder. After you uncheck this option, you will be given a choice to copy the permissions, or remove the permissions inherited from the parent folder.

> **Challenge #5**
>
> Jimmy is the local administrator for a Windows 2000 Professional computer configured with a single, large partition that has been formatted with NTFS. He has just created an NTFS share on a parent folder that has three subfolders. After the NTFS permissions are applied to the parent folder, what permissions will, by default, be applied to the subfolders?

Effective Permissions

Effective Permissions are a little tricky. As we stated before, NTFS permissions are cumulative based on the permissions given to the user account and their group accounts. First, add all the accesses given to each account and subtract all permissions that have been denied.

Mr. Jones is the new IT Department head and informs you that he would like to make a few changes. He wants to use a Windows 2000 Professional computer that is not currently being used, to create a local share. The computer has one large hard drive that is already formatted with NTFS. The share created is called "Tech" and will be accessed by the employees that use this computer. You have decided to set the following NTFS permissions on the Tech folder:

    Admin: Full Control
    IT: Read
    Finance: Write
    Joe: Read

Joe wants to access the Tech folder and asks you what his permissions to the folder will be. Joe belongs to the global group Support. Support is a member of the domain local groups Admin, Finance, and IT. What is Joe's effective permission to the Tech folder?

You are administering a Windows 2000 Professional computer and want to create a folder that users can access locally. The partition where the folder will reside is formatted with NTFS. You create a folder called DUTIES and must determine which permissions will be given to particular groups in your network. The following are the NTFS permissions that you have applied:

    Authenticated Users: Read & Execute, Write
    IT: Full Control
    Jack: Deny, Write

IT is a local group. Jack is a member of the group IT. What is Jack's effective permission(s) for the folder?

Copying or Moving NTFS Files

Sometimes you may need to copy or move a file that is located on an NTFS partition. Table 8-1 should help you understand the results of these actions.

Table 8-1: Copying or Moving NTFS Files

Action	Location	Result
Copy	Same Partition	Inherits NTFS permissions of folder being copied into.
Copy	Different Partition	Inherits NTFS permissions of folder being copied into.
Move	Same Volume	Retains the original NTFS permissions.
Move	Different Partition	Inherits NTFS permissions of folder being moved into.

NOTE: If you copy or move a file or folder from an NTFS partition to a FAT partition, no NTFS permissions are retained.

EXAM TIP: You must be able to apply NTFS permissions to files and folders and then be able to determine the effective permission for someone who is a member of multiple groups. Be aware that NTFS permissions are used for local file-level security and cannot be applied to a share. Finally, you must know what happens to NTFS permissions when a file or folder is copied or moved. Remember that all the Challenges we have given should be treated as **EXAM TIPS**.

Applied Network Access

Applied network access is also called shared access. It is referred to as network access because users access the shared folder over the network. Sharing a folder is accomplished through Windows Explorer. Simply right-click the folder, select Properties, and on the Sharing tab, illustrated in Figure 8-5, click the "Share this folder" radio button. Shared folders are identified with a hand icon under the folder. If you want to stop sharing a folder, just select the "Do not share this folder" radio button.

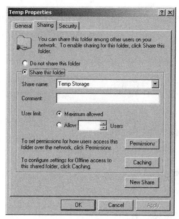

Figure 8-5: Folder Properties Dialog Box, Sharing Tab

Shared Folder Permissions

To set up share permissions on a folder, use the Permissions button on the Sharing tab of the folder Properties dialog box. Clicking this button brings up the shared folder Permissions dialog box, depicted in Figure 8-6. Share permissions are used to provide access to a resource on one computer to an individual or group working from another computer.

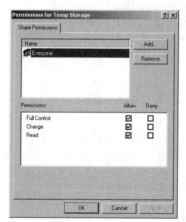

Figure 8-6: Shared Folder Permissions Dialog Box

Share permissions can only be applied at the folder level—not the file level as seen in NTFS permissions. You can only give the following permissions to a shared folder: Full

Control, Change, and Read. When you create the share, by default, the Everyone group is given Full Control permissions. *One thing to note is that if you establish a shared folder, there is no way to block access to files and subfolders.*

Shared Folders Utility

As mentioned earlier, you can create a shared folder in Windows Explorer, or by using the Shared Folders utility. The Shared Folders utility, shown in Figure 8-7, can be accessed through the Computer Management console by expanding the System Tools folder. *This utility lists all the shared folders that are currently enabled on the computer, which is the quickest way to view these shared folders.*

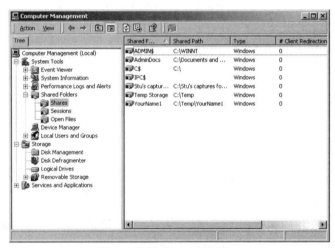

Figure 8-7: Shared Folder

To create a new share, right-click the Shares folder and select the New File Share option from the menu. Follow the screens to finish creating the share. You can also stop sharing a folder by right-clicking it in the right pane and selecting the Stop Sharing option. *The Shared Folders utility can also be used to view all the users who are currently accessing a shared folder.* It can also be used to disconnect users from the share, as well as to view all the files that are currently open.

NOTE: Shared permissions are cumulative. This means that if you are a member of multiple groups, the least restrictive permission will be your effective permission. Take note that after you add all the permissions, you must subtract any denied permissions.

You are administering a Windows 2000 Professional computer and want to create a shared folder that users will utilize over the network. One point to note is that the partition in which the folder will reside in is formatted with FAT16. You establish a folder called WORK and must determine what permissions will be given to particular groups in your network. The following are the share permissions that you have applied:

Tom	Read
Accounting	Change
IT	Full Control
Marketing	Read

The user account Tom is assigned to the global group Support. Support is a member of Accounting and Marketing groups. The user account Tom is also assigned to the global group Clerks. Clerks is a member of the IT group. Based on the permissions assigned to this folder, what are Tom's effective permissions for the folder called WORK when accessed over the network?

Accessing Shared Folders

Users can access shared folders in three different ways. The first one is through the My Network Places applet (located on the desktop). Double-click this icon and then click the Add Network Place option. A wizard will take you through the steps. The next way is by mapping a network drive, as illustrated in Figure 8-8. This is accomplished in Windows Explorer by selecting Tools and then the Map Network Drive option. As you go through the process, make sure the "Reconnect at logon" checkbox is checked. This will save the connection and automatically connect each time you log on.

Figure 8-8: Mapping a Network Drive

Finally, you can use the NET USE command to map a drive at the command prompt. The syntax to use is:

NET USE x: \\computername\sharename

NOTE: The "x" represents the drive letter.

Combining NTFS and Shared (Network Access) Permissions

NTFS permissions and shared permissions work hand-in-hand. When they are combined, the **most restrictive** access is used to determine the access a user will have to the resource. For example, let's say that you are a member of the IT group with Read NTFS permissions. The folder is a shared folder. In addition, you are a member of the Finance group with Write shared access. You would only have Read access because the NTFS permission is the most restrictive.

John is the administrator of a large Windows 2000 network. He has a Windows 2000 Professional computer named "PRO1" that is used by 10 company users. He creates a shared folder called "Users" on PRO1, which is formatted with the NTFS file system. The Users folder contains over 500 files. At this time, 10 users are connected to this computer and accessing files. He establishes permissions to the Users folder as:

Users Share Permissions: Users: Change
Users NTFS Permissions: Users: Full Control

John has just noticed that one of his coworkers has placed five very sensitive files in the Users shared folder. If this information is changed the company could lose business. Because users have the ability to make changes to these files, John must protect the five files in the Users folder from being changed in any way. He has to consider the effect that this will have on his users and the company's image. John's final actions also must have the smallest effect on the other network users connected to different files on the server. What two actions should John take?

Challenge #11

If a user is logged on locally to the computer and directly accesses a folder, only the NTFS permissions will apply. This means that if a user accesses a resource located on a different network computer, both share and NTFS permissions apply. However, if the folder is accessed locally, the share permissions do not apply. This is an important topic to understand.

EXAM TIP: You must know how to set up a shared folder. Then you must know which shared permissions can be applied to the folder and how being a member of multiple groups will affect the effective permission to the folder. Finally, you must be aware that the Shared Folder utility enables you not only to share folders, but also to see who is accessing a shared folder and disconnect them from the share, if you have a need to.

Review Questions

1. Brian is the new administrator for your small, but busy, Windows 2000 network. He is concerned about file security and wants to reduce the risk of other people gaining access to network resources. He plans to use a Windows 2000 Professional computer, which has one partition formatted with the NTFS file system, to start the process. He wants to establish a shared resource, but is not sure of what types of resources can have NTFS permissions applied to them. Which of the following would qualify for NTFS permissions? (Select two answers.)
   a. Files
   b. Shares
   c. Folders
   d. Printers

2. Jim is the local administrator for a Windows 2000 Professional computer configured with a single, large partition that is formatted with NTFS. He has just created an NTFS share on a parent folder that has three subfolders. After the NTFS permissions are applied to the parent folder, what permissions will, by default, be applied to the subfolders?
   a. Full Control
   b. Read
   c. The same permissions that are applied to the parent folder
   d. Change

3. Mike is an expert at assigning NTFS permissions to resources. For example, he creates a parent folder called "Sales" on a Windows 2000 Professional computer. Now, he must assign permissions to this parent folder to a group of users called the "Salesman". He elects to grant read permission to the Salesman group for the parent folder. He also creates individual subfolders that each salesman will use to store personal documents. He knows that each salesman must have full control of their personal folder, but he is unsure how to proceed. Which of the following will allow him to perform the task successfully?
    a. Assign Full Control permission for each user to the Sales folder. The user will automatically have full control over their own folder.
    b. Prevent permission inheritance on each user folder and assign that user Full Control permissions to their folder.
    c. Deny access to the user folder for everyone except the user it is intended for.
    d. You will not be able to make changes to the child objects of the Sales folder.

4. Mr. Jones is the new IT Department head and informs you that he would like to make a few changes. He wants to use a Windows 2000 Professional computer that is not currently being utilized, to create a local share. The computer has one large hard drive that is already formatted with NTFS. The share created is called "Tech" and will be accessed by the employees who use this computer locally. You have determined to set the following NTFS permissions on the Tech folder:

    Admin: Full Control
    IT: Read
    Finance: Write
    Joe: Read

    Joe wants to access the Tech folder and asks you what his permissions to the folder are. Joe belongs to the global group Support. Support is a member of the domain local groups Admin, Finance, and IT. What is Joe's effective permission to the Tech folder?
    a. Access is denied.
    b. Change
    c. Full Control
    d. Read

5. You are administering a Windows 2000 Professional computer and want to create a shared folder that users will utilize over the network. The partition where the folder will reside is formatted with FAT16. You establish a folder called WORK and must determine what permissions will be given to particular groups in your network. The following are the share permissions that you have applied:

Tom:	Read
Accounting:	Change
IT:	Full Control
Marketing:	Read

The user account Tom is assigned to the global group Support. Support is a member of Accounting and Marketing groups. The user account Tom is also assigned to the global group Clerks. Clerks is a member of the IT group. Based on the permissions assigned to this folder, what are Tom's effective permissions for the folder called WORK when it is accessed over the network?
a. No Access
b. Change
c. Full Control
d. Read

6. Jerry is monitoring a Windows 2000 Professional computer and wants to add some files to a shared folder called "Data". He is worried because there may be users connected to the shared folder and he needs to identify those users so he can disconnect them from the share. Which of the following utilities can he use?
a. Server Manager
b. File Manager
c. Windows Explorer
d. Shared Folder

7. You are the administrator of a Windows 2000 network. You have a Windows 2000 Professional computer where you need to share an important document with other users. Because the document is very sensitive, you do not want the other users to use offline caching. Which of the following would you use to configure this option?
a. Assign special permissions.
b. Select shared folder Properties, caching button, deselect "Allow Caching".
c. Delete the special permission allowing caching.
d. Use REGEDIT and remove Allow caching.

8. You are responsible for maintaining a Windows 2000 Professional computer. Today, you are administering a shared folder called "Users" on the computer. The Users folder has NTFS permissions granted to the following local groups: IT, Sales, Managers. Each group has Full Control access to the Users folder. You have made a mistake and now want to restrict the Sales group from making any change to the Users folder. You are not sure which NTFS permission will enable users of the Sales group to read, but not change the data in the Users folder. Which of the following NTFS permissions must be granted to the Sales group?
   a. Read
   b. Write
   c. Change
   d. Full

9. You are the administrator for a small Windows 2000 network. You are currently working on a Windows 2000 Professional laptop. You have redirected a user's My Documents folder to his home folder. Now you must make sure that the user can access all the files in the My Documents folder even when they are not connected to the network. Which of the following actions must be performed? (Select two answers.)
   a. Use Windows Explorer to enable Offline Files.
   b. Use Windows Explorer to configure the properties of your home folder to be available offline.
   c. Use the Shared Folders utility to enable Offline Files
   d. Use the Shared Folders utility to configure your home folder to be available offline.

10. You have a shortcut to a shared folder located on a different Windows 2000 Professional computer. You are trying to configure the shortcut to be available offline, but the offline option is not available. Which of the following actions will enable the shortcut to be available offline?
   a. Recreate the shortcut and the offline feature will be available.
   b. Use Windows Explorer to configure the folder to be available offlinc.
   c. Use the Shared Folder utility to configure the folder to be available offline.
   d. This is not possible.

11. You are the administrator of a Windows 2000 network. You have five users who have laptops using the Windows 2000 Professional operating system. You have been asked to configure these computers to use network files while they are at home. Which of the following is the correct action to take?
   a. Make all files available offline, at the office.
   b. Copy all files to floppy disks.
   c. Connect to the network remotely and download all files needed.
   d. Don't take the laptop home. Use it only in the office.

12. You are the local administrator for a Windows 2000 Professional computer. The computer has a single hard drive divided into three partitions configured as follows: C: and D: are formatted with NTFS; and E: is formatted with FAT32. You have a shared folder named DOCS located on the D: drive and you want to move some of its files. Which of the following statements are true when moving files from drive D: to another location?
   a. Files moved to the C: drive will retain their original permissions, files moved to a different location on the D: drive will inherit the permissions of the folder that they are moved to and files moved to the E: drive will lose their permissions.
   b. Files moved to the C: drive will inherit the permissions of the folder that they are moved to, files moved to a different location of the D: drive will retain their original permissions, and files moved to the E: drive will lose their permissions.
   c. Files copied to the C: drive will retain their original permissions, files copied to a different location on the D: drive will inherit the permissions of the folder that they are moved to, and files moved to the E: drive will retain their original permissions.
   d. Files copied to the C: drive will inherit the permissions of the folder that they are moved to, files moved to a different location on the D: drive will retain their original permissions, and files moved to the E: drive will inherit the permissions of the folder that they are moved to.

13. You are the administrator for a Windows 2000 network. You have a user who has a laptop running Windows 2000 Professional. This user needs to work at home on some files that are actually stored on a network share. Before he leaves for the day, he enables Offline Files on his laptop. When he gets home he finds that copies of the files are not on his laptop computer. Which of the following actions should you perform to make the files available for offline use?

   a. Enable file and print sharing. The user will be able to access his files at home immediately.

   b. Synchronize all offline files. The user will be able to access his files at home immediately.

   c. At the office, make all files available offline. The user will be able to access his files the next time he logs off the network.

   d. At the office, create a shortcut to the Offline Files folder. The user will be able to access his files the next time he logs off the network.

Answers and Explanations

1. **a, c.** With NTFS you can apply permissions at the files and folders level. NTFS permissions are sometimes called local permissions. NTFS permissions cannot be applied to shares. That is done with the shared permissions, or network permissions. Printers also cannot have NTFS permissions applied.

2. **c.** Because the default permissions are applied to the subfolders, the parent folder's permissions will flow to the subfolders.

3. **b.** You have to prevent permission inheritance from the parent folder or the parent permissions will overwrite the permissions of each user folder. If you assign Full Control permission to each user for the Sales folder (parent folder), then all the users will have full control over each folder in the Sales folder. Denying access to everyone except the user it is intended for would be too much work.

4. **c.** We are only talking about NTFS permissions and not share permissions. You will combine the group permissions and the least restrictive permission will be the effective permission, which is Full Control.

5. **c.** Since Tom is a member of a variety of groups, the permissions are combined and the least restrictive is the effective permission for him. In this case his effective permission is Full Control.

6. **d.** The Shared Folder utility will allow you to identify the users connected to the shares and disconnect them if you need to. File Manager was used in Windows 3.1 and is not available in Windows 2000 Professional. You cannot use Windows Explorer to identify which users are connected to a share. Server Manager is a utility used in Windows NT 4.0 and is not available in Windows 2000 Professional.

7. **b.** Simply go to the Shared folder properties page, click the caching button, and deselect the "Allow caching" checkbox. Assigning special permissions will not prevent off-line caching. You do not want to use REGEDIT to remove the "Allow caching" setting, as this can be dangerous. You should never directly edit the Registry when there are specialized tools available to address the problem.

8. **a.** If you do not want the users of the Sales group to make changes, then you must give them the Read permission.

9. **a, b.** To make a file or folder use the Offline Files feature you must take two actions. First, Windows Explorer must be used to enable Offline Files. This is performed using the Tools option on the menu bar and selecting Folders Options, then clicking on the Offline Files tab. Then, you would again use Windows Explorer to make the particular folder available offline by right-clicking the folder and selecting "Make Available Offline".

10. **b.** You must use Windows Explorer to configure the local computer to use offline files and folders. The feature is enabled by default, but since the option is not available, someone must have turned it off. In Windows Explorer select the Tools option in the menu bar, then use the Offline Files tab to verify that the "Enable Offline Files" checkbox is checked.

11. **a.** You would enable OffLine Files at the office. This is done on the Offline Files tab in the folder's Options and making sure Offline Files is enabled. Then in Windows Explorer, right-click the file or folder and select "Make Available Offline".

12. **b.** You should select an answer that moves a file instead of copying a file, because copying a file produces different results. Files moved to the C: drive will inherit the permissions of the folder that they are moved to. Files moved to a different location on the D: drive will retain their original permissions, and of course files moved to the E: drive (non-NTFS) will lose their permissions. Copying files on the same or a different partition will change their original permissions to the folder that they are copied to.

13. **c.** Remember that the Offline Files process is a two-step process. First, Offline Files is enabled in Windows Explorer using the Tools option on the menu bar and selecting Offline Files on the pop-up menu, then using the Offline Files tab to make sure the "Enable Offline Files" checkbox is checked. Then you again use Windows Explorer and right-click the file or folder that you want to use offline and select "Make Available Offline" from the pop-up feature.

Challenge Solutions

1. The files must be made available offline. This is accomplished at the office. This is done in Windows Explorer by right-clicking the folder or file and selecting "Make Available Offline".

2. To make a file or folder use the Offline Files feature you must take two actions. First, Windows Explorer must be used to enable Offline Files. This is performed using the Tools option on the menu bar and selecting Folders Options, then clicking on the Offline Files tab. Then you would again use Windows Explorer to make the particular folder available offline by right-clicking the folder and selecting "Make Available Offline" on the pop-up menu.

3. You must use Windows Explorer to configure the local computer to use offline files and folders. The feature is enabled by default, but since the option is not available, someone must have turned it off. In Windows Explorer select the Tools option in the menu bar, then use the Offline Files tab to verify that the "Enable Offline Files" is checked.

4. Simply use Windows Explorer, right-click the folder, and select Properties. This will take you the shared folder Properties dialog box. Then use the caching button, and on the next screen deselect the "Allow caching" checkbox.

5. The correct answer to this problem is that the permissions that are applied to the parent folder will be inherited by the subfolder. This answer is true provided the "Allow inheritable permissions from parent to propagate to this object" checkbox is checked.

6. First, you have to deselect the "Allow inheritable permissions from parent to propagate to this object" checkbox, and then assign each user Full Control permission over their individual folder. If you don't deselect the checkbox, the parent folder's permissions will override the subfolder's permissions.

7. To determine his effective permission you add all the permissions: Read, Write, and Read & Execute. Then subtract the Write access that was denied by the Users group. This leaves Read and Read & Execute access.

8. Just add the permissions and subtract any denied permissions, and the least restrictive permission is the effective permission. In this case, Full Control is the effective permission.

9. First, you have to add all the permissions, which gives you Read & Execute, Write, and Full Control. Then you have to subtract the Write permission, and that leaves Read & Execute and Full Control. Because Full Control is the least restrictive, it is Jack's effective permission.

10. Since Tom is a member of a variety of groups, the permissions are combined and the least restrictive is the effective permission for him. In this case his effective permission is Full Control. Don't forget to subtract any permissions that are denied. The least restrictive permission means the highest permission.

11. Because you are dealing with share and NTFS permissions, the MOST restrictive permission applies, which is the Change permission. First, modify the NTFS permissions for the five files and change the permission to Read. This will make Read the effective permission for these five files. Then the users must be logged off the network. This is because when a person logs on to a network they receive a token, which includes permissions authorized through user and group accounts, and it remains active until the user logs off and back on to the network.

Networking

These are the areas that are generally testable on the MCSE Professional 2000 examination:

1. Install and configure network services for interoperability.

2. Install, configure, and troubleshoot network protocols.

3. Install, configure, and troubleshoot network adapters and drivers.

Introduction

In this chapter you will learn how to install and configure network adapters. You will learn how to install Plug-and-Play adapters, as well as older legacy adapters. After you have installed the adapter you must select the network protocol that will enable your computer to communicate on your network. We are sure that you will install TCP/IP. This is because the Internet uses this protocol and if it is needed to surf the Internet, you can also use it for all your networking needs.

If you are using a different protocol on your network, you must know how to configure it and how it works. Three protocols can be used with Windows 2000: TCP/IP, NetBEUI, and NWLink IPX/SPX/NetBIOS. We will discuss the attributes of each protocol and how to configure them. We will also provide you real-world Challenges to help you troubleshoot these network protocols.

Then, you will be shown how to use the IPCONFIG command-line utility. This utility basically enables you to troubleshoot the TCP/IP protocol located on your computer. You will learn how to use the PING command to test your network connectivity, if you are having problems connecting to a particular server.

You will then learn what network services can be provided on a Windows 2000 network. The most common services are DNS, DHCP, and WINS.

Finally, we will show you how to configure network clients to connect to a proxy server. This will enable them to utilize the Internet. We will also show you how to configure the users to bypass the proxy server for local access to servers.

NETWORK ADAPTERS

For a computer to communicate on the network, it must have a network adapter (network interface card) installed. A network adapter is a piece of hardware that provides the physical connection to the network. The adapter must have a protocol installed that will enable it to communicate with other computers. Three protocols are available with Windows 2000 Professional: TCP/IP, NWLink IPX/SPX/NetBIOS, and NetBEUI. When you install an adapter in your network, you will most likely install TCP/IP as the protocol of choice. This is because TCP/IP is the protocol used on the Internet.

Installing a Network Adapter

If your network adapter is compatible with Windows 2000 Professional and is Plug-and-Play, it will be auto-detected and automatically configured by the operating system. Plug-and-Play is great, just install the adapter, reboot the computer, and start using the network. Well, that is almost true. You must still make some entries for the TCP/IP protocol, if you are using a static IP address. Older (legacy) adapters require that you manually configure them to enable the cards to work properly. After you install a legacy adapter and start the computer, the Add Hardware Wizard should appear to guide you through the driver installation process. If the wizard does not appear, you can use the Add/Remove Hardware icon in the Control Panel to configure it.

Configuring a Network Adapter

You can configure your network adapter through its Properties dialog box, as shown in Figure 9-1. This dialog box can be accessed by double-clicking the Network and Dial-up Connection applet located in the Control Panel. Then double-click the Local Area Connection option and click the Configure button in the local area connection's Properties dialog box. This Properties dialog box has four tabs: General, Advanced, Driver, and Resources.

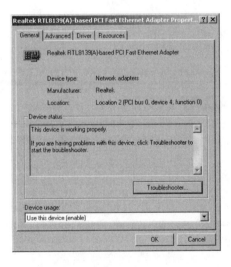

Figure 9-1: Network Adapter Properties Dialog Box

- *General* – This tab, illustrated in Figure 9-1, shows the name of the adapter, the device type, the manufacturer, and the location. In the middle of the tab is a Device status section that states whether the device is working properly or not. If the device is not working properly you can use the Troubleshooter button to run a wizard that will provide you with some assistance. *At the bottom of this tab is a Device usage section where you can enable or disable a device.* You normally disable a device when it conflicts with another device or just is not working properly.

- *Advanced* – We will not discuss the Advanced tab because you should not make any changes on this tab unless told to do so by the manufacturer.

- **Driver* – This tab, illustrated in Figure 9-2, shows the driver provider, driver date, driver version, and digital signer. The important items on this tab are located at the bottom of this tab. In particular, the "Update Driver" button will start an Upgrade Device Driver Wizard. Also notice the "Uninstall" button. This button is not normally used unless you are installing a new driver for the network adapter card. You should always check the vendor's Web site to obtain the latest drivers for your network adapter.

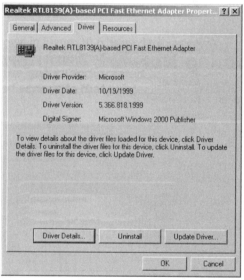

Figure 9-2: Network Adapter Properties Dialog Box, Driver Tab

- **Resources* - This tab, depicted in Figure 9-3, is used to view the adapter's resource settings. These settings include IRQ, Memory Range, and I/O. You can use the middle section to change the resource allocations. Simply click the "Change setting" button. You should use this tab immediately after you install a new network adapter to make sure it was installed properly. Finally, you have a Conflicting device list that will tell you whether there are any conflicting devices.

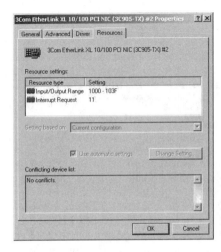

Figure 9-3: Network Adapter Properties Dialog Box, Resources Tab

NOTE: If you have used the Resources tab to configure the network adapter and it still does not work, you must troubleshoot the network adapter.

Troubleshooting Network Adapters

We have provided an easy-to-use visual guide in Table 9-1 to help you troubleshoot your network adapter.

Table 9-1: Troubleshooting Network Adapters

Problem	Solution
Improperly configured network protocols	Review the configuration of the network protocols and make sure they are configured properly. For example, if you are using TCP/IP, check the subnet mask to see if it is wrong. This could cause problems, as you will see later in this chapter.
Network adapter not on the HCL	There is no real solution to this problem. If you have this type of problem, the best thing to do is contact the vendor for assistance.
Outdated driver	*Obtain the latest driver from the vendor's Web site.*
Network adapter not recognized by Windows 2000	If your network adapter is not recognized, you will have to install it manually using the *Add/Remove Hardware* utility in the Control Panel. If the network adapter is not recognized by the operating system, this usually means you have a legacy device.

To make changes to the settings of the network adapter, you must use the tools that Windows 2000 provides for managing the device. Most of these tools are located under the Hardware tab of the System Properties dialog box, illustrated in Figure 9-4.

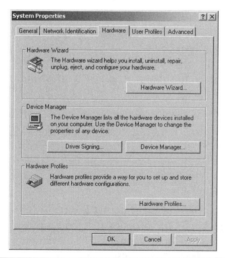

Figure 9-4: System Properties Dialog Box, Hardware Tab

NETWORK PROTOCOLS

Network protocols enable computers to communicate with each other. Table 9-2 lists the protocols that are supported by Windows 2000 Professional.

Table 9-2: Network Protocols Supported by Windows 2000 Professional

Protocol	Description
TCP/IP	Installed by default on clean installations. However, if you are upgrading from a different operating system the protocols that were installed in the other operating system will carry over into Windows 2000.
NWLink IPX/SPX/NetBIOS	Used to communicate with Novell NetWare computers.
NetBEUI	*Is not routable and is used for small Microsoft networks.*
AppleTalk	Used to support Apple Macintosh computers.
DLC (Data Link Control)	Used for printers and connecting to IBM systems.

TCP/IP

TCP/IP (Transmission Control Protocol/Internet Protocol) is installed by default on clean installations of Windows 2000 Professional. It is the protocol used on the Internet. It can be used in both large and small networks. The minimum requirements using TCP/IP are a unique IP address and a subnet mask in a nonrouted environment. "Nonrouted" means that your network does not communicate with the outside world. You won't see many of these networks in the corporate world today. When there is a router on your network, the default gateway must also be configured. This tells the computers on a particular network segment that the door to other network segments and to the outside world is through the default gateway. This default gateway (a router) is configured with a routing table that is used to direct the data packets to their final destination.

A unique IP address means an IP address that no other computer on the network has. A subnet mask is used to define which portion of the IP address makes up the network address and which portion is the host address. The **_default gateway_** is actually the IP address of the router that supports your particular segment. It is used to transmit data that is not addressed to the local network segment, (i.e., data that is transmitted outside your network). **_*The TCP/IP protocol can be used with any Windows client as well as when you want to communicate with UNIX hosts._**

On the exam you may be given a situation and then challenged to select the correct IP address for a new computer. You will be provided with a default gateway (router) address for your subnet and you must select the correct IP address and subnet mask for the new computer.

Lets say that you are installing a new computer named PRO1 on your Windows 2000 network. The router (default gateway) IP address is 10.1.2.1 with a subnet mask setting of 255.0.0.0. Select the correct IP address and subnet mask for the new computer to communicate properly.

Challenge #3

To send data to a segment of your network when the router does not have an entry in its routing table for it, you must establish a special entry in the router to handle the data. This is called the **_*default route_** and must be configured in the router that supports your network segment. This route is used to direct all traffic not specified in the routing table.

Jamie, your network engineer, is responsible for creating network routes in each of the network routers. He is concerned that the routes to some segments may not be defined in each of the router's routing tables. You believe that you are on one of the segments that does not have a routing entry and you need to send data to another segment of the network. How can you send the data to the remote segment?

Challenge #4

You can choose to manually configure your IP address. This is normally the case for a Windows 2000 Server. If you use a DHCP server (or another service) to automatically assign an IP address, the network users may have a hard time figuring out that address. A default installation of Windows 2000 Professional employs an automatic configuration of the IP address (using DHCP). However, if you choose to do so, you may manually configure an IP address for the computer using the Internet Protocol (TCP/IP) Properties dialog box. To access this location, you must right-click My Network Places and select the Properties option. Then, right-click the Local Area Connection option and select Properties. Then highlight the Internet Protocol (TCP/IP) entry and click the

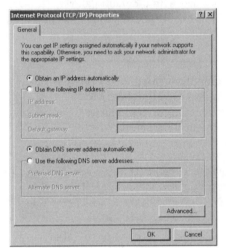

Properties button. This will bring up the Internet Protocol (TCP/IP) Properties dialog box, shown in Figure 9-5. Next, you should click the "Use the following IP address" radio button. This is where you enter the IP address, subnet mask, and default gateway address.

Notice the *Advanced* button at the bottom of the dialog box in Figure 9-5. It is important that you know what this button is used for. When clicked, it will bring up an Advanced TCP/IP Settings dialog box, illustrated in Figure 9-6. It can be used to configure additional DNS server IP addresses as well as WINS server addresses.

Figure 9-5: Internet Protocol (TCP/IP) Properties Dialog Box

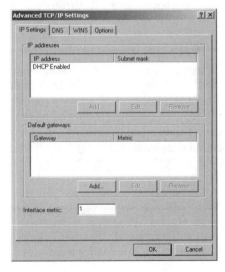

Figure 9-6: Advanced IP Dialog

The IPCONFIG and PING commands are used to test your IP configuration. You can enter the *IPCONFIG* command at the command prompt to test and display your local computer's IP configuration. There are some switches that can be used to perform different functions. These switches are listed in Table 9-3.

Table 9-3: IPCONFIG Command Switches

Switch	Description
/all	Shows the IP configuration settings on your computer, such as the computer's IP address, subnet mask, DNS servers, and more.
/release	*Use this switch to release an IP address that was assigned by a DHCP server.*
/renew	*Use this switch to renew an IP address that was assigned by a DHCP server.*
/flushdns	*Use this switch to flush (clear) and reset the contents of the DNS client resolver cache. This option is only available on computers running Windows 2000.*

The PING command is used to test network connectivity. Connectivity means that the computer can connect to network resources. The PING command should first be used with the local host address 127.0.0.1 (i.e., PING 127.0.0.1). This will check the local TCP/IP stack for errors. Next, you should ping the local computer's IP address. This double checks whether the TCP/IP address entries are working properly. Then you should ping an address of a computer that is on your local network segment. If this ping is successful, you should ping the default gateway's IP address. Finally, try to ping a remote computer's IP address. Any PING operation where you do not receive a successful return will help you identify where the connectivity problem is occurring.

Tammy is responsible for resolving host names on your Windows 2000 network. The network has a Windows 2000 Server with a DNS server installed to provide IP address-to-host name resolution. The rest of your network consists of 20 Windows 2000 Professional clients and one UNIX server. You are having problems resolving the host name of the UNIX server. You ping the UNIX server with its host name of UnixSvr and you do not receive a response. You review the DNS server configuration and notice that there is a record for the UNIX server. What should you do?

Challenge #5

The PING command can also be used to test your network connectivity. In Challenge 5 you should enter the PING command as follows: PING UnixSvr. If you do not receive a successful reply, it indicates that there is a problem in the DNS resolution process. Because you checked the DNS server and there is an entry there for the UNIX server, the next place to check is the DNS client. You should use the ipconfig /flushdns command and switch to clear the local computer's DNS cache and reset it. Just a word on this process. Before you perform a PING command with the DNS name, you should first check that the DNS can be contacted by the client by using the PING command and the IP address of the DNS server, (i.e., PING 14.10.11.1). If you receive a successful response, you know that you have network connectivity. The PING command is useful when you are having problems connecting to a particular server and want to verify that your computer can communicate with that server. Once you have ruled out connectivity problems such as NIC cards and cabling, you can move on to the DNS resolution.

The NWLink IPX/SPX/NetBIOS protocol enables your computer to communicate with Novell NetWare computers. This protocol enables you to route data to NetWare computers, but it does not provide you with access to NetWare File and Print Services. *If you need to use these services, you must install the NWLink protocol and Client Services for NetWare (CSNW) on the Windows 2000 clients. You can also provide these services through a Windows 2000 Server by installing Gateway Services for NetWare (GSNW).*

The NWLink protocol is easier to configure than TCP/IP. You only need to provide a network number and a frame type. When you install this protocol, the frame type is set to Auto Detect. You may have to change this setting if your network is using different frame types. Why would you want to change the frame type? *A common problem with NetWare networks is that if you are using different frame types on your network, your computer may not be able to communicate with a particular computer when both computers are not using the same frame type.* To change the frame type—right-click My Network Places and select Properties. Then, right-click the Local Area Connection option and select Properties. Finally, highlight the NWLink protocol and click the Properties button. This will bring up the screen depicted in Figure 9-7. You need to select the "Manual frame type detection" option and enter the frame types being used on your network.

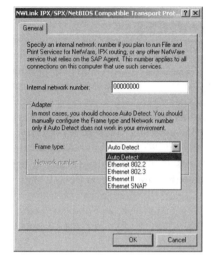

Figure 9-7: NWLink Protocol Dialog Box

Jerald is your current Windows 2000 Administrator and is having problems with one of his Windows 2000 Professional computers. The computer needs to access file and print resources on a NetWare 4 server, but cannot. He believes that the TCP/IP protocol is the only protocol installed on the Windows 2000 server. In order to provide this access, what must be installed on the Windows 2000 Server?

Challenge #6

You have been contracted to administer a mixed network operating System network. The network consists of five Windows 2000 Servers, 30 Windows 2000 clients, and three NetWare servers. You need to ensure that all the Windows 2000 computers on the network are able to communicate with the NetWare servers. On each of the Windows 2000 computers you install the NWLink IPX/SPX/NetBIOS compatible Transport Protocol. After installing the protocol, you discover that the Windows 2000 machines can communicate with only one of the NetWare servers. You must correct this problem immediately, but you're not sure of what the problem is. What is the most likely reason for this problem and how would you solve it?

Challenge #7

NETWORK SERVICES

The topic of Network Services is usually covered in the Windows 2000 Server subject area. However, because you need to troubleshoot the total network environment, you must be familiar with the basics of network services to answer many Windows 2000 Professional exam questions. Windows 2000 Server provides support for DHCP, WINS, and DNS servers. These services must be installed on a Windows 2000 Server. You can install them with the Add/Remove Programs utility in the Control Panel. After you have installed the services, their icons will be available in the Administrative Tools utility. If you wish you may also add each service as a snap-in to the MMC.

DHCP

The Dynamic Host Configuration Protocol (DHCP) is used to automatically assign an IP address to the clients on your network. DHCP clients can run most Microsoft operating systems, as well as UNIX or Macintosh. This eliminates the need to manage which IP address is configured on each computer in your network. *As stated before, this service can only be installed on a Windows 2000 Server or a Windows NT 4.0 Server.* The server must also have a static (manual) IP address and a valid range of IP addresses that can be assigned to the DHCP clients.

DHCP Server Configuration

After the DHCP service has been installed, you must configure a scope. This is done by accessing the Administrative Tools applet and clicking the DHCP icon. This brings up the DHCP window. Next, right-click your server in the left pane and select the New Scope option. Simply follow the instructions on the screens that follow. It is wise also to configure the DHCP server to assign the default gateway, DNS servers, and WINS server options. One additional note: When the DHCP server is part of the Active Directory, it must be authorized to perform its services.

NOTE: If your network is configured to use DHCP services, and a DHCP server cannot be contacted, the computer will issue its own IP address of *169.254.x.x* and will not be able to communicate with any other computers.

WINS

WINS servers are used to resolve NetBIOS computer names to IP addresses. This service is normally used to provide IP address resolution for operating systems prior to Windows 2000, such as Windows 9x and Windows NT 4.0 clients. A WINS server must have a static IP address in order to operate properly. *If you choose not to use a WINS server, you can use the LMHOSTS file to provide this service.*

DNS

DNS servers are used to resolve host names to IP addresses. The DNS server must be configured with a static IP address. *If you choose not to use a DNS server, you can use the HOSTS file to provide this service.*

DNS is dynamic in Windows 2000. This means that it automatically creates records that point to computers and services. However, sometimes you need to recreate a record from the Windows 2000 client. Remember the IPCONFIG utility? Use this command with the **/registerdns switch from the client and it will re-create the DNS records on the Windows 2000 Server.** Furthermore, if you want to integrate the DNS server with Active Directory, the partition holding the zone file must be formatted with NTFS.

There is another command-line tool you can use to resolve a domain name. ***The tool is called the NSLOOKUP command.*** Let's say that you know the TCP/IP address of the Windows 2000 Server but you are unsure of its domain name. At the command line, type NSLOOKUP along with the IP address of the server and the domain name will be returned to you.

NETWORKS USING MULTIPLE PROTOCOLS

Some networks employ different network protocols for communication between different computers. The most common network protocols you will encounter together on the same network are TCP/IP and IPX/SPX. On the exam you may be challenged to identify how you can increase your network's performance when you are using multiple network protocols. In Figure 9-8, is the Advanced Settings dialog box, with the Adapters and Bindings tab selected. ***At the bottom of the figure you can see a section called "Bindings for Local Area Connection".*** In this section, you will use the Client for Microsoft Networks item and move the most used network protocol to the top of the list. As an example—say that you use both TCP/IP and IPX/SPX on your network. However, the TCP/IP protocol is used 80 percent of the time. In this case, you would place the TCP/IP protocol at the top of the binding order on the client computer. If you leave IPX/SPX at the top, each time a packet arrives, the computer will try to use the IPX/SPX protocol first, and then apply the TCP/IP protocol.

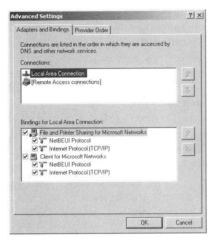

Figure 9-8:
Advanced Settings
Dialog Box,
Adapters and
Bindings Tab

EXAM TIP: Know that when your network uses more than one network protocol, you can increase network performance on the client by moving the most used protocol to the top of the protocol binding order.

INTERNET EXPLORER

Nearly all companies use Internet Explorer to access the Internet. However, before your users can connect to the Internet, they probably will pass through some type of proxy server. You must manually configure each client to use the proxy services. To access these settings in Internet Explorer, right-click the Internet Explorer icon located on the desktop and select Properties. This will bring up the Internet Properties dialog box. Then, click the Connections tab and, at the bottom of the page, click the LAN Settings button. This will bring up the Local Area Network Settings dialog box, as seen in Figure 9-9.

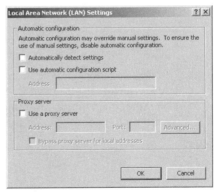

Figure 9-9: Local Area Network
Settings Dialog Box

In the figure, direct your attention to the "Use a proxy server" checkbox. You must select this checkbox and then enter the IP address of the proxy server along with a port number (usually port 80). An important item to discuss is the *"*Bypass proxy server for local addresses"** option located at the bottom of the screen. This will enable users to bypass the proxy server for access to servers located on your local network.

Review Questions

1. James is responsible for network connectivity for all the Windows 2000 Professional computers on the network. He is having problems connecting one Windows 2000 Professional computer to the network. This computer has an integrated 10 MB Ethernet network interface card and he wants to replace it with a new 100 MB Ethernet network card. "Integrated" means that it is built in to the motherboard. The new adapter is a newer PCI adapter card. After the card has been installed and the computer is restarted, he receives error messages in the System log stating that the new adapter is missing or is not working. Which of the following procedures will enable him to use the new network adapter card?
    a. Create a new hardware profile.
    b. Use Device Manager to remove the integrated 10 MB Ethernet adapter.
    c. Use Device Manager to disable the integrated 10 MB Ethernet adapter.
    d. Delete the device driver for the integrated 10 MB Ethernet adapter from the Systemroot\system32\Driver Cache folder.

2. Tammy is responsible for resolving host names on your Windows 2000 network. You have a Windows 2000 Server that has a DNS server installed to provide resolution of IP addresses to host names. The rest of your network consists of 20 Windows 2000 Professional clients and one UNIX server. She is having problems resolving the host name of the UNIX server. She pings the UNIX server with its host name of UnixSvr and does not receive a response. Tammy reviews the DNS Server configuration and notices that there is a record for the UNIX server. Which of the following actions must she perform next to solve this problem? (Select two answers.)

   a. Restart DNS on the Windows 2000 server.
   b. Windows 2000 server does not support Unix server entries.
   c. Run ipconfig /registerdns on the unix server.
   d. Stop the DNS client service and restart it.
   e. Run the ipconfig /flushdns command.

3. You have just taken a position with a south Florida company managing their Windows 2000 network. The network consists of 5 Windows 2000 Servers, 20 Windows 2000 Professional clients, 10 Windows 98 clients, and 3 UNIX hosts. You want to make sure that the UNIX hosts can communicate with the other Windows clients. Which of the following protocols can be used to enable the Windows clients and the UNIX hosts to communicate with each other?

   a. NetBUIE
   b. IPX/SPX
   c. TCP/IP
   d. SNMP

4. Jeraldine is your current Windows 2000 Administrator and is having a problem with one of her Windows 2000 Professional computers. The computer must access file and print resources on a NetWare 4 server, but cannot. She wants to access the resources using a Windows 2000 Server and she believes that the TCP/IP protocol is the only protocol installed on the Windows server. Which of the following items must be installed to enable the Windows 2000 Server to utilize the file and print resources on the NetWare server? (Select two answers.)

   a. NWLink IPX/SPX/NetBIOS
   b. GSNW
   c. File and Print Services for NetWare
   d. CSNW

5. Jamie, your network engineer, is responsible for establishing network routes in each of your network routers. He is concerned that routes to some segments may not be defined in each of the routers' routing tables. You believe that you are on one of the segments that may not have a routing entry and need to send data to another segment of the network. Which of the following should be used to send data from your segment, based on the current configuration of your network?

   a. Default route
   b. Default router
   c. Default subnet mask
   d. Primary route

6. You have been contracted to administer a mixed network operating system network. The network consists of five Windows 2000 Servers, 30 Windows 2000 clients, and three NetWare servers. You need to ensure that all the Windows 2000 computers on the network are able to communicate with the NetWare servers. On each of the Windows 2000 computers, you have installed the NWLink IPX/SPX/NetBIOS Compatible Transport Protocol. After installing the protocol, you discover that the Windows 2000 machines can communicate with only one of the NetWare servers. You must correct this problem immediately, but you don't know what the problem is. Which of the following correctly identifies the problem and the best way to solve it?

   a. The default gateway or subnet mask is not configured correctly on the Windows 2000 computer. Use the IPCONFIG utility to check your configuration and make any necessary changes.
   b. You must change the Internal Network Number on the Windows 2000 computers to allow communication with Netware servers. The default value of 00000000 must be changed to a number that is unique on the local network.
   c. The NetBIOS scope ID is not set correctly. In order to support communication with servers that might have multiple scope IDs, you must specify each of the scope IDs individually in the TCP/IP properties of the Windows 2000 computers.
   d. The frame type is not set correctly. You must reconfigure the Windows 2000 computers for manual frame detection.

7. Jodie is your current TCP/IP manager and wishes to configure your Windows network so that it automatically issues the clients' IP addresses. Your network contains two Windows 2000 domain controllers, four Windows 2000 member servers, two Windows NT 4.0 servers, and 50 Windows 2000 Professional clients. In order to set up the automatic IP addressing configuration, Jodie knows that he needs to install a DHCP server on the network. He is not sure of which computer to install the DHCP server on. Based on your network configuration, which of the following can be used for this purpose?

a. Windows 2000 domain controller
b. Windows 2000 member server
c. Windows 4.0 server
d. Windows 2000 Professional

8. You are new to the network and need to solve an IP configuration problem. The problem is that of your two routed subnets—Subnet1 and Subnet2—only Subnet2 is receiving DHCP messages from the DHCP server. Subnet2 has a DHCP server installed on a Windows 2000 Server. This server has scopes created for both network segments. However, Subnet1 does not have a DHCP server and you believe that this may be the problem. Which of the following is the best solution to enable clients on Subnet1 to receive dynamically assigned IP addresses?

a. Install a DHCP relay agent on Subnet1.
b. Install and configure another DHCP server on Subnet2.
c. Create a superscope on the DHCP server in Subnet2, which contains both the scope for Subnet1 and the scope for Subnet2.
d. Configure a WINS Server on Subnet1.

9. Denny is the administrator for a small Windows 2000 network. You have a Windows 2000 Server running Microsoft Proxy Server. The members of the Sales group constantly access the Internet through the proxy server and must provide their user name and password each time. This group must also provide the same credentials each time they want to use the local Intranet server. The Accounting group is not authorized to use the proxy server and cannot even access the local intranet server. Denny would like both of these groups to have access to the local intranet server without needing a user name or password. Which of the following actions will allow him to meet his goals?

a. Move the intranet server to the client segment of the network.
b. Move the proxy server to the server segment of the network.
c. Configure each client computer to bypass the proxy server for local addresses.
d. Configure each client computer to use port 81 for the proxy server.

10. You are the DNS server administrator for your Windows 2000 network. You need to quickly resolve a Windows 2000 Server's domain name. You know the IP address of the server. Which of the following tools can be used to learn the server domain name with a known IP address?
   a. Type "ping" and the IP address of the server.
   b. Type "NSLOOKUP" and the IP address of the server.
   c. Type "DOMAINAME" and the IP address of the server.
   d. Type "tracert" and the IP address of the server.

11. You have just installed Windows 2000 Professional on a new computer in your Windows 2000 network. It was manually configured with a valid IP address and you are able to join the domain. You are not able to access the DNS names of computers on and outside your subnet. Which of the following should be checked first?
   a. Check to see if the network card is plugged in to the network.
   b. Check that the client computer has valid DNS servers entered in TCP/IP properties.
   c. Check that the server has valid DNS servers entered in TCP/IP properties.
   d. Verify that an object has been created for the computer in Active Directory.
   e. Verify that the entries are in your local LMHost file.

12. You are the administrator of a routed network. You have 10 Windows Professional computers on one side of a network router. Nine of these computers use dynamic TCP/IP and NWLink 802.2. The tenth computer is only using NWLink 802.3. You have noticed that none of the nine TCP/IP computers can communicate with different network segments. After investigating, you find that these computers are configured with the wrong gateway address. You also notice that the nine TCP/IP computers cannot communicate with the tenth computer, which is configured with only NWLink 802.3 and is located on the same network segment. Which of the following will enable all the computers on this segment to communicate with each other and the nine computers to communicate with other network segments? (Select two answers.)
   a. The DHCP server was handing out bad gateway addresses.
   b. Configure the Nwlink PC to use DHCP.
   c. Configure the Nwlink PC to use 802.2.
   d. Configure everyone to use NETBEUI.

13. You are the administrator of a Windows 2000 network. This network has two network segments—Seg1 and Seg2. You are installing a new computer with Windows 2000 Professional on Seg1 and you have to assign this computer a static IP address because this segment does not have a DHCP server. The DNS server is located on Seg2 and is configured to support both segments. Which of the following must also be configured on the client to ensure that it communicates on the network properly? (Select all that apply.)
    a. Default gateway
    b. IP Address of the certificate server
    c. IP Address of the DNS server
    d. IP Address of the global catalog server
    e. IP Address of the terminal server
    f. Subnet mask

14. You are the network administrator for a small Windows 2000 network. You are required to install a new computer with Windows 2000 Professional configured to use DHCP services. The IP address range that will be used is 10.2.3.1 – 10.2.3.100. When you review the IP address with the IPCONFIG utility, you notice that the computer is configured with an IP address of 169.254.134.194 and that the computer cannot use any network resources. Which of the following is the most likely cause of the problem?
    a. The DHCP server is unavailable. Your computer has assigned itself an IP address from the 169.254.0.0 range.
    b. The DHCP server is available, but it is set up with the wrong IP address range.
    c. The DNS server is not available and cannot be contacted to issue IP addresses.
    d. The WINS server is not available and cannot be contacted to issue IP addresses.

Answers and Explanations

1. **c.** Integrated devices have the tendency to interfere with other devices of the same type that you are trying to install. Disabling the device will allow you to install the new device. Just as a side note, you may have to uninstall the device if the disable does not work.

2. **d, e.** The ipconfig/flushdns command provides you with a means to flush and reset the contents of the DNS client resolver cache. Although the ipconfig command is provided for earlier versions of Windows, the /flushdns option is only available for use on computers running Windows 2000. Then the DNS client service must also be started.

3. **c.** TCP/IP is becoming a universal protocol. The UNIX hosts can communicate with the Windows hosts using this protocol. UNIX hosts cannot by default communicate using the IPX/SPX protocol. SNMP is used in TCP/IP networks to monitor services.

4. **a, b.** To allow the Windows 2000 Server file and print access to the Netware 4 resources, you need to install Gateway Services for NetWare and NWLink IPX/SPX/NetBIOS.

5. **a.** The default route is an entry in the routing table that states where to send data that cannot normally be routed. The default router is the default gateway and will not send the data to another router unless there is an entry in the routing table. The default subnet mask is used to identify on which segment a particular host resides. Answer d. is not correct because the primary route is not used to direct host traffic that has not been specified in the routing table.

6. **d.** This is a very common problem with Netware networks. NetWare can use many different frame types, but if all the computers on the network do not use the same frame type, they will not be able to communicate with each other. If the default gateway or subnet mask is configured incorrectly, the Windows 2000 computer will not be able to communicate with other segments or their local segment. if the Internal Network Number is configured incorrectly, the Windows 2000 computers will not be able to communicate with any Netware servers. If the NetBIOS scope ID is not set correctly, it will not create a problem with the Windows 2000 computers communicating with the NetWare computers.

7. **a, b, c.** A Windows 2000 Server domain controller, a Windows 2000 member server, and a Windows NT 4.0 server can provide services as a Dynamic Host Configuration Protocol server. However, a Windows 2000 Professional cannot.

8. **a.** A DHCP relay agent located on Subnet1 will forward DCHP information to the clients on Subnet1. You would not want to install another DHCP server on Subnet2, because the IP information would still not be forwarded to Subnet2. A superscope is used on a DNS server, and not a DHCP server. You need to install a DHCP relay agent on Subnet1. A WINS server is used to resolve NetBIOS names to IP addresses and is not used to dynamically issue IP addresses to clients.

9. **c.** Configuring each client to bypass the proxy server for the local addresses will allow users to use the intranet and no password will be required. The configurations are actually made in Internet Explorer, Tools, Options. Changing the port that clients use will not stop the need for the proxy server to require authentication. Moving the proxy server to the server segment of the network will not change the number of passwords that are required for the different servers. Moving the intranet server to the client segment of the network will not solve your problem.

10. **b.** Using the NSLOOKUP command and the IP address of the server will return the name of the server. Tracert with the IP address of the server will not provide you the name of the server. PING will return a reply, but not the name of the server.

11. **b.** If you are using static entries on your network, check the client computer's TCP/IP entries to ensure that valid DNS servers are listed. An object being created for the computer in Active Directory has nothing do to with the DNS settings. The LMHost file is used for resolution of Netbios names to IP addresses. If this answer was the Host file then you would be right.

12. **a, c.** If the nine TCP/IP clients are using a DHCP server, the DHCP server provides gateway addresses to its clients. If the gateway address is wrong, the DHCP server is configured wrong. To allow the nine TCP/IP computers to communicate with the tenth computer, you must configure the NWLink PC with the 802.3 to 802.2. NWLink PCs cannot use DHCP.

13. **a, c, f.** Since your network has two subnets they must be connected together with routers and therefore the default gateway IP address must be configured on the clients. The DNS server IP address is required to provide host name to IP address support. In order for the computers to communicate properly, the clients must be configured with a subnet mask. The IP address of the certificate server is not necessary. The IP address of the global catalog server is not required. The IP address of the terminal server is not required.

14. **a.** This type of problem commonly occurs when a DHCP server is not available to issue IP addresses to its clients. If the DHCP server is either down or on a different network segment, and no relay agent is available, the local computer will issue its own IP address of 169.254.0.0 range.

Challenge Solutions

1. A common problem with integrated devices is that if you try to install another device the integrated device does not allow the additional device to operate properly. The best way to correct this problem is to disable the integrated device using Device Manager. However, you may have to uninstall the integrated device if disabling the device is not successful.

2. Simply use the Hardware tab of the System Properties dialog box, as illustrated in Figure 9-4.

3. You should choose the following IP address and subnet mask for this computer: 10.1.2.100 and 255.0.0.0. You may also see it listed as 10.0.2.100/8. The 8 means that you are using 8 bits for the network address and means the same thing as 255.0.0.0.

4. If you are trying to send data to a segment of your network and the router doesn't have an entry in its routing table, you must have a special entry in the router to handle the data. This is called the default route and it must be configured on the router that supports your network segment. This entry in the routing table is used to direct all traffic that is not specified elsewhere in the routing table.

5. The ipconfig/flushdns command, performed at the Windows 2000 Professional client, provides you with a means to flush and reset the contents of the DNS client resolver cache. Then, you must stop the DNS client service and restart it.

6. Because you want to use a Windows 2000 Server to access file and print resources on a NetWare 4 server, you need to install NWLink IPX/SPX/NetBIOS and Gateway Services for NetWare on the Windows 2000 Server.

7. The frame type is not set correctly. You must reconfigure the Windows 2000 computers for manual frame detection of all the frame types used on the network. Then you must manually enter the frame types you wish to use. This is a very common problem with NetWare networks. NetWare can use many different frame types, but if all the computers on the network do not use the same frame type, they will not be able to communicate with each other.

8. A DHCP relay agent located on Subnet1 will forward DCHP information to the clients on Subnet1. You could install a DHCP server on Subnet1, but a DHCP relay agent is much easier to manage and configure.

9. Since you have just installed this computer, check the TCP/IP Properties dialog box at the client and make sure the IP address of the DNS server is entered and is correct.

10. A proxy server can be configured to force users to enter a user name and password prior to connecting to the Internet and, by default, the access to the local intranet server. Simply select the "Bypass proxy server for local address" checkbox. This will stop users from using the proxy server for local servers.

Chapter 10

Printing

These are the areas that are generally testable on the MCSE Server 2000 examination:

1. Monitor, configure, troubleshoot, and control access to printers.

2. Manage printers and print jobs.

3. Control access to printers by using permissions.

4. Connect to a local print device.

Introduction

Read this section very carefully because there is so testable much information located here. Setting up a printer is very important in today's networks. If users cannot print, they may become very upset and nonproductive. You will first learn how to correctly install a printer using the Add Printer Wizard. Then you will be shown how to perform maintenance of a printer using the printer Properties dialog box. You will discover that you must be logged on as a member of the Administrators or Power Users group to add a printer.

When you initially create a printer, by default the only print driver loaded is the Windows 2000 driver. You will learn how to add more drivers to support the users on your network, using the "Additional Drivers" button located on the Sharing tab of the printer's Properties dialog box. We also provide information about the rest of the tabs located in the printer Properties dialog box.

Finally, you will receive some valuable information on how to manage print servers. One important note on print servers: a Print Server can be a local Windows 2000 Professional computer that has a printer attached directly to it.

CREATING A PRINTER

In Windows 2000, the physical printer is called the print device. The logical printer (software), which is called the printer, is used to connect to the print device. You create a printer with the Add Printer icon located in the Printers folder, as shown in Figure 10-1. The path to this folder is—Start, Settings, Printers, Add Printer. Simply double-click the Add Printer icon and a wizard will guide you through the installation process. *To use this wizard, you must be logged on as a member of the Administrators or Power Users group.* We won't go through the individual steps needed to create a printer because you don't need to know that information for the exam. What you do need to know is what you do with the printer after it has been created.

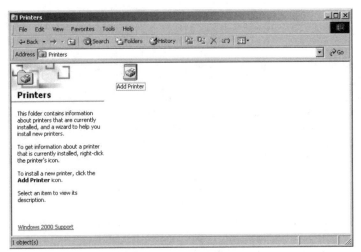

Figure 10-1: Add Printer Icon

Printer Properties

After you create the printer using the Add Printer Wizard, you can make changes to that printer through the printer's Properties dialog box. You can access this dialog box by opening the Printers folder, right-clicking the printer you want to manage, and choosing the Properties opti0n from the pop-up menu. The tabs located on the printer Properties dialog box can vary depending on the type of printer installed. In the following sections, we will cover the most common tabs. Once again, we cover only what you need to know for the exam.

General Tab

The General tab of the printer Properties dialog box, illustrated in Figure 10-2, lists information about the printer, such as printer name, location of the printer, and comments. Below this is printer model information and features. The most important part of this tab is the *"Print Test Page"* button. You can use this button to print a test page, which will, after printing, be a good indicator of whether the printer is operating correctly. You will use this button immediately after you create the printer, so that if the test page does not print, you can start troubleshooting immediately.

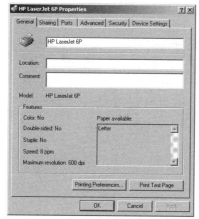

Figure 10-2: Printer Properties Dialog Box, General Tab

EXAM TIP: You must know that the Print Test Page button is located on the General tab of the printer Properties dialog box. We can't emphasize how important the CHALLENGES are. Read them and reread them until you know the subject matter.

Sharing Tab

The Sharing tab, depicted in Figure 10-3, enables you to share a printer for other users to print to. The only required entry is the "Shared as" name that will be seen by users printing to your printer. Notice the *"Additional Drivers"* button. This enables you to identify the print drivers that will be automatically downloaded when users print to the device. *By default, the only driver loaded when you create a printer is the Windows 2000 driver.*

Printing   **243**

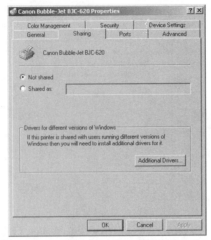

Figure 10-3: Printer Properties Dialog Box, Sharing Tab

George is the printer manager for your Windows 2000 network. The network contains five Windows 2000 Servers, 50 Windows 2000 Professional clients, and 50 Windows NT 4.0 Workstation clients. He installs a printer on one of the Windows 2000 Professional computers. He creates a printer on this computer called Printer1. He shares Printer1 and creates print permissions that allow everyone on the network to print to this device. Later that day, he starts to receive complaints from the Windows NT 4.0 Workstation clients. They claim that when they try to use the printer, they receive an error dialog box. He has verified that the problem has to do with print drivers. He must configure the Windows 2000 Professional computer to automatically install the print drivers for the 50 Windows NT 4.0 Workstation clients when they connect to Printer1. How can you help George?

EXAM TIP: When you initially create a printer, by default, the only print driver loaded is the Windows 2000 driver. If you want to add more drivers to support the users on your network, use the "Additional Drivers" button located on the Sharing tab of the printer's Properties dialog box.

Ports Tab

The *Ports tab* is an important item on the exam, so we have marked it in bold. This tab is used to configure local ports (physical ports) and standard TCP/IP ports (logical ports). Local ports are used for printers attached directly to the computer. Standard TCP/IP ports are used when a printer has a network card installed in it and becomes a networked printer. *To establish a TCP/IP port, you must provide the IP address of the network printer.* The Ports tab enables you to add, delete, and configure a port with the appropriately labeled buttons. *Finally, take note of the "Enable printer pooling" checkbox.* You can see this tab in Figure 10-4.

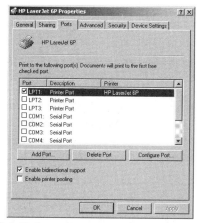

Figure 10-4: Printer Properties Dialog Box, Ports Tab

Printer pools are used when you have multiple physical print devices printing from a single logical printer (software). *Printer pools must be in the same location, be of the same type, and use a single print driver.* The biggest advantage of using a printer pool is that the first available print device will print the job. *After you enable printer pooling by selecting the "Enable printer pooling" checkbox, you must check all the ports that the print devices in the pool will use*, as illustrated in Figure 10-4.

You have three identical print devices that are located in the same office and you want to establish a printer pool. You have learned that a printer pool will send a print job to a different print device when a print device fails. You are not sure of how to set up a printer pool and need help. What is the correct procedure to create a printer pool?

Redirecting Print Jobs

You redirect print jobs if a print device fails and you want another print device to handle them. In order for this process to work, the new print device must use the same print driver as the original device. *To redirect print jobs, access the printer Properties dialog box, select the Ports tab, as shown in Figure 10-4, click the "Add Port" button, then highlight New Port and choose New Port Type. In the Port Name dialog box you must enter the UNC name of the printer to which the print jobs will be redirected (i.e., \\computername\printer).*

Mr. Jones is the assistant printer manager for a medium-sized Windows 2000 network. He wants to install an expensive color printer on a Windows 2000 Professional computer called PRO1. During the installation he calls the printer Color1. He receives another print device exactly like the first printer and installs it on another Windows 2000 Professional computer called PRO2. This printer he calls Color2. The printer on PRO1 stops working and Mr. Jones needs to redirect the print jobs already in the print queue on Color1 to Color2. There are many print jobs currently in the print queue of Color1, and he does not want to be embarrassed by asking the users to resubmit them. How can he best accomplish this?

EXAM TIP: The Ports tab is hit hard on the exam. You must be aware that you must know the IP address of the network printer to create a TCP/IP port. You must also know how to enable a printer pool with this tab. Finally, you may be required to know how to redirect print jobs to another print device.

Advanced Tab

The Advanced tab, illustrated in Figure 10-5, has a lot of testable information. This tab is used to configure the following options. We need to discuss each separately.

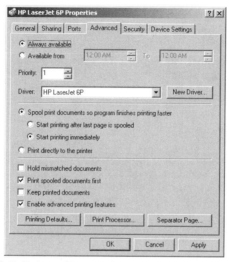

Figure 10-5: Printer Properties Dialog Box, Advanced Tab

- ***Availability*** – There are two options for when the printer will be available for printing jobs: Always available, and Available from. The *"Available from"* option is used when you have multiple printers using a single print device. You normally use this option when you want to control some printing situation such as when large monthly reports slow down the availability of the printer during daytime hours. For this example, we would recommend that you configure two printers. One will be called USERS, which will always be available. This printer can be used for normal daytime use. You should then create another printer called REPORTS, which can be configured to be available only during after-duty hours. You would inform the individuals that create the reports to print their jobs to this printer and that they should only print during the time frame selected.

David is the administrator for your large Windows 2000 network. He has a network printer that is used by three different offices. At the end of each month, he receives complaints from users stating that it takes too long to print even the smallest jobs. This does not occur during the beginning of the month and he must investigate the situation. Finally, he pinpoints the source of the problem. It appears that at the end of each month, the Accounting Department prepares and prints many large reports that delay the print jobs of normal users. David needs to correct this problem and enable the normal users to print efficiently during duty hours. What action will correct this problem?

- ***Priority*** – The Priority option can be configured when you have one or more groups using the same print device. Priority 1 is the lowest while Priority 99 is the highest value. Let's say that you have an Accounting group and a Supervisors group that send documents to the same printer. The Supervisors want their jobs to print before the Accounting group's jobs. To make this happen, you would create a printer called Accounting and specify a priority of 1 in the "Priority" section. Then, create another printer called Supervisors with a priority of 99. Afterward, any time members of the Supervisors group send a print job to the print device, they will have priority and therefore be printed first. After the separate printers are created, you must use the Security tab to restrict which groups use each printer.

- *Driver* – The Driver section allows you to select the driver that is used with this printer, if you have more than one driver installed. The New Driver button starts the Add Printer Driver Wizard. Don't confuse this button with the ***"Additional Drivers"*** button located on the Sharing tab. The New Driver button will enable you to add or update the driver used for the local print device.

- ***Spooling*** – Spooling is used to save print jobs to disk before sending them to the printer. This arrangement prevents print jobs from trying to print at the same time. You can set the printer to print directly to the printer. The default setting is set to enable spooling and start printing immediately. You can also set the spooling option to print after the last page has been spooled. This option enables smaller jobs to be printed before larger jobs. The Print directly to the printer option does not use spooling and is commonly used to troubleshoot printer problems. If a job will print only with this option selected, then there may be a problem with your hard drive. This option is used when printing from DOS. You can also use the NET USE command at the command prompt to map a physical port. This command will point DOS to the network printer and allow it to print.

- *Keep printed documents* – When this option is selected, it will save the print job after it has been spooled. This can be helpful if you suspect that someone is misusing the print device and you want to identify that individual.

EXAM TIP: The Advanced tab has so much testable material that you really need to read this section a couple of times. First, you need to know how to use the availability options to select when the printer will be available for use. The Priority section enables you to select the priority of the selected printer. Note that 1 is the lowest priority and 99 is the highest priority. Finally, know how enabling spooling will affect the performance of printing jobs on your printer.

Security Tab

The Security tab, shown in Figure 10-6, is used to control who uses the printer. *One important item to consider is that if a user or group is denied access to a printer through one group and granted access through another group, they will be denied access to that printer.*

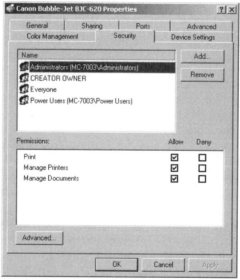

Figure 10-6: Printer Properties Dialog Box, Security Tab

Table 10-1 lists the printer permissions that can be given to particular users and groups.

Table 10-1: Printer Permissions

Permission	Description
*Print	Used to permit users or groups to submit print jobs to the printer.
*Manage Printers	Used to give users or groups complete control over the printer.
*Manage Documents	Used to enable users or groups to manage documents, but not to change any printer settings.

NOTE: By default the Administrators and Powers Users groups are given all three printer permissions. The Everyone group has the Print permission and the Creator Owner has the Manage Documents permission.

Challenge #6

Denise is the administrator of all the printers for your Windows 2000 network. She has created a printer that is centrally located to provide all the company users with convenient access. Lately, it appears that too many people are using the printer and the company managers want her to correct the problem. She responds quickly by creating a new printer with a higher priority. She instructs the managers to use this printer when they want to print documents. She sets up the permissions for the groups as follows: Administrators, Everyone, Managers, Accounting, and IT. Denise is troubled because the print queue is still backed up and the managers are still complaining. She verifies that the Managers have Print permissions by making sure the checkbox to allow Print permissions is selected. She selects the checkbox to allow Print permissions for the Executives group. She only wants the Administrator, Managers, Accounting, and IT groups to be authorized to print. Based on the groups above, what can she do to reduce the printing backlog?

EXAM TIP: Don't overlook this section. Be familiar with all the permissions in the printer permissions table and know what each permission enables a user or group to do with the printer. Know that when a user or group is denied access to a printer through one group and granted access through another group, they will be denied access to that printer.

PRINT SERVERS

A print server is a computer that has a physical printer directly attached to it. You can configure a print server's properties through the Print Server Properties dialog box. This is accomplished by opening the Printers folder and selecting File and then Server Properties. There are two important tabs located in the Print Server Properties dialog box. These are— Forms, Ports, Drivers, and Advanced tabs. We will discuss only the important tabs.

Ports Tab

The Ports tab, illustrated in Figure 10-7, is used to configure ports for the print server. It is similar to the Ports tab of the Printer Properties dialog box. *This tab can be used to manage all the ports for the print server instead of individually managing each port for a print device.*

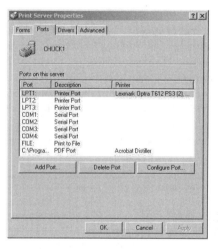

Figure 10-7: Print Server Properties Dialog Box, Ports Tab

Advanced Tab

The Advanced tab, depicted in Figure 10-8, is used to identify the location of the spool file. There is a checkbox on this tab that can be used to send a notification to users after their print job has finished printing. This checkbox is called *"Notify when remote documents are printed".* If users complain about getting this notification, simply remove the checkmark to shut off this feature.

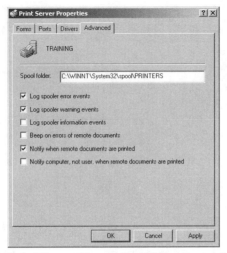

Figure 10-8: Print Server Properties Dialog Box, Advanced Tab

Jimmy is the printer manager for a very small Windows 2000 network. His network contains one Windows 2000 Server and 10 Windows 2000 Professional clients. He creates a new printer on one of the Windows 2000 Professional computers, which has limited disk space on the system drive. He receives numerous calls from the 10 Windows 2000 Professional clients stating that each time they try to print to the printer, they receive an error message. He has determined that the message occurs because the spool file has run out of disk space. What process will enable Jimmy to change the location for the spool file?

EXAM TIP: Know that you can change the location of the spool file through the Advanced tab located on the Print Server Properties dialog box.

1. Denise is the administrator of all the printers for your Windows 2000 network. She creates a printer that is centrally located to allow all the company users convenient access. Lately, it appears that too many people are using the printer and the company managers want her to speed up their printing. She responds quickly by creating a new printer with a higher priority. She instructs the managers to use this printer when they want to print documents. She sets up the permissions for the groups identified as:

   Administrators
   Everyone
   Managers
   Accounting
   IT

   Denise is troubled because the print queue is still backed up and the managers are complaining again. She verifies that the Managers have the Print permission by making sure the checkbox to enable Print permissions is selected. She selects the checkbox to enable Print permissions for members of Executives group. She only wants the members of Administrator, Managers, Accounting, and IT groups to be authorized to print. Based on the groups above, what can she do to reduce the printing backlog? (Select all answers that apply.)
   a. remove the Everyone group.
   b. Select the checkbox to Deny Print permission to Everyone.
   c. Select the checkbox to Deny manage documents.
   d. Select all Deny checkboxes for the Everyone group.
   e. Clear all allow checkboxes for the Everyone group.

2. You have a Windows Professional computer that you are trying to add a fax printer to. You confirm that you should be using the Fax icon, but the icon is missing from the Control Panel. Which of the following will correct this problem?
   a. Restart the Fax service.
   b. Reinstall the Fax service.
   c. Remove the local computer policy.
   d. You must be a member of to the local Administrators group.

3. David is the administrator for your large Windows 2000 network. He has a network printer that is used by three different offices. At the end of each month, he receives complaints from users stating that it takes too long to print even the smallest jobs. This problem does not occur during the beginning of the month, and he must investigate the situation. When he pinpoints the problem, it appears that at the end of each month the Accounting Department prepares many large reports that delay the print jobs of normal users. David needs to correct this problem and enable the normal users to print efficiently during duty hours. Which of the following procedures will correct this problem?

    a. Create two printers that will use the same print device. Call these printers Users and Reports. Give the Users printer a priority of 1 and Reports a priority of 99. Tell the users that when they need to print a report they should use the Reports printers.

    b. Create two printers that will use the same print device. Call these printers Users and Reports. Configure the Users printer to be available 24 hours a day and the Reports printer to be available only during off-duty hours. Inform the Accounting Department to send the long reports to the Reports printer.

    c. Tell all the users that they must stay after work to print reports.

    d. Create one printer that will point to two print devices.

4. Mr. Jones is the assistant printer manager for a medium-sized Windows 2000 network. He wants to install an expensive color printer on a Windows 2000 Professional computer called PRO1. During the installation he calls this printer Color1. He installs another print device that is exactly the same as the first printer on another Windows 2000 Professional computer called PRO2. This printer is called Color2. The printer on PRO1 stops working and Mr. Jones needs to redirect the print jobs already in the print queue of Color1 to the Color2 printer. There are many print jobs currently in the print queue of Color1 and he does not want to be embarrassed by asking the users to resubmit those print jobs. Which of the following will enable him to complete the task?

    a. Select a second printer port on PRO1 and redirect the port to \\PRO2\Color2.

    b. Replace the print device on PRO1.

    c. Stop and restart the print service.

    d. Go to the printers folder and use the Add Printer icon to replace printer Color1.

5. Tony is the print manager for your Windows 2000 network that uses TCP/IP as its only protocol. He has heard that network printers are faster than printers that are directly attached to a computer. He finally gets his wish and receives a new network printer. He successfully installs the network printer and now must connect the Windows 2000 Professional clients, but does not know how to do this. You advise him that the installation requires only two pieces of information. Which of the following pieces of information will allow Tony to connect the clients to a TCP/IP based network print device? (Select two answers.)
   a. Name or IP address of the TCP/IP-based network printer
   b. Port number
   c. The type of NIC used in the printer
   d. Community name

6. You have three identical print devices that are located in the same office and you want to establish a printer pool. You have learned that a printer pool will send print jobs to a different print device when a print device fails. You are not sure of how to set up a printer pool, so you do some research. Which of the following actions will enable you to correctly set up a printer pool?
   a. Using the Ports tab of the printer Properties dialog box, select the Enable printer pooling checkbox, then check all of the ports that the print devices are attached to.
   b. Use the Add Printer Wizard and you will be prompted to configure multiple ports.
   c. In the Advanced tab of the printer Properties dialog box, select the Enable Printer Pooling checkbox, then check all the ports that the print devices are attached to.
   d. In the Ports tab of the printer Properties dialog box, select the ports the print devices are attached to.

7. George is the printer manager for your Windows 2000 network. His network contains five Windows 2000 Servers, 50 Windows 2000 Professional clients, and 50 Windows NT 4.0 Workstation clients. He installs a printer called Printer1 on one of the Windows 2000 Professional computers. He shares Printer1 and creates Print permissions to enable everyone on the network to print to this device. Later that day, he starts to receive complaints from the Windows NT 4.0 Workstation clients. They claim that when they try to use the printer, they receive an error dialog box. He has determined that the problem has to do with print drivers. He needs to configure the Windows 2000 Professional computer to automatically install the print drivers for the 50 Windows NT 4.0 Workstation clients when they connect to Printer1. Which of the following options will enable him to accomplish this task? (Select two.)

   a. Copy the Windows NT 4.0 printer drivers to the Netlogon shared folders on all Windows NT Server 4.0 computers still configured as BDCs.

   b. Copy the Windows NT 4.0 printer drivers to the Netlogon shared folder on the PDC emulator.

   c. Change the sharing options on the printer to install additional drivers for Windows NT 4.0 Workstation computers.

   d. Copy the Windows NT 4.0 printer drivers to the Winnt\System32\printers\ drivers folder on the Windows 2000 print server.

8. Jimmy is the printer manager for a very small Windows 2000 network. His network contains one Windows 2000 Server and 10 Windows 2000 Professional clients. He creates a new printer on one of the Windows 2000 Professional computers that has limited disk space on its system drive. He receives numerous calls from the 10 Windows 2000 Professional clients stating that every time they try to print to the printer they receive an error message. He has determined that the messages occur because the spool file has run out of disk space. Which of the following will enable Jimmy to select a different location for the spool file?

   a. The Advanced tab of the printer Properties dialog box
   b. The Advanced tab of the server Properties dialog box
   c. The Spool tab of the server Properties dialog box
   d. You can't change the location of the spool file

9. You are the local administrator for a Windows 2000 Professional computer. This computer has a local printer and is shared for 20 users. The users are recruiters and are constantly printing many small documents to this printer. The printer is configured to notify the user when the document has printed. The users are tired of this message and ask you to turn it off. Which of the following will accomplish this?

    a. In the Printer Properties dialog box, disable "Notify when remote documents are printed".
    b. In the Print Server Properties dialog box, disable "Notify computer, not user, when remote documents are printed".
    c. In the Printer Properties dialog box, disable bi-directional support
    d. In the Print Server Properties dialog box, disable " Notify when remote documents are printed".

10. You are the printer manager for a small Windows 2000 network. You have a Windows 2000 Professional computer with a color laser printer attached locally. The printer is shared between two groups: IT and Accounting. The Accounting group prints a large amount of multiple-page documents that slow down the printer. The users in the IT group usually print smaller print jobs and have to wait hours before they receive their documents. Which of the following actions can you take to ensure that the IT department can print their jobs before the Accounting department?

    a. Configure the priority of the current printer to 50, and instruct the Accounting group to use this printer. Add a new printer, and set the priority to 1. Instruct the IT group to print to this new printer and deny print permissions to the Accounting group.
    b. Configure the priority of the current printer to 50, and instruct the Accounting group to use this printer. Add a new printer, and set the priority to 95. Instruct the IT group to print to this new printer and deny print permissions to the Accounting group.
    c. Monitor the print queue, and raise the priority of all the print jobs that are sent by users who are not members of the Accounting group.
    d. Delete the old printer. Add a new printer, and set the priority to a higher value. Pause the print queue only when Accounting group jobs are printing.

11. You have a Window 2000 Professional computer that is configured with a local laser printer. Which of the following is the correct term for the laser printer?
    a. Printer
    b. Printer device
    c. Print server
    d. Physical printer

Answers and Explanations

1. **a, e.** You could remove the Everyone group from the Security tab of the printer Properties dialog box, or you could just clear all allow checkboxes for the Everyone group. Answer b. is wrong because if you deny print permissions for the Everyone group nobody, including the Administrator, would be able to print. Print permissions are cumulative except for the deny permission, which cancels all other permissions.

2. **d.** You must be logged on with Administrative privileges to be able to use the fax services.

3. **b.** Create two printers and have the users print to the Users printer 24 hours a day (normally used in the day time), and require the reports to be printed only during off-duty hours. This will stop the problem of the end-of-month reports back-logging the printer queue. Answer a. will give the Reports printer priority over the Users printer and therefore the normal users will not be able to print when they want to.

4. **a.** Use this method to redirect the printer port on the Color1 printer to PRO2. Physically replacing Color1 printer could take some time and the users would have to resubmit their print jobs. Stopping and restarting the print service will not accomplish anything. Replacing the printer software for PRO1 will not help if the physical printer device fails.

5. **a, b.** In order to set up a TCP/IP-based network printer you are required to enter the name or IP address. You also have to know the port number.

6. **a.** Enabling the printer pooling by selecting the checkbox is the only way that you can select multiple ports. You will not be prompted to configure multiple ports in the Add Printer Wizard.

7. **c, d.** You can also copy the Windows NT 4.0 printer drivers to the
    Winnt\System32\printers\drivers folder on the Windows 2000 print server.
    Copying the print drivers to the Netlogon shared folder (located on a PDC or a
    BDC) will not allow the Windows NT 4.0 computer to print. Making any changes
    on the print device itself will not allow the driver to be automatically downloaded
    when the Windows NT 4.0 computers try to print.

8. **b.** The Advanced tab of the server Properties dialog box allows you to specify a
    different location for the spool file.

9. **d.** The Print Server Properties dialog box must be used to remove the checkmark
    of the "Notify when remote documents are printed" on the Advanced tab.

10. **b.** Remember that 95 is a higher priority, and each time someone from the IT group
    prints a job, it will be printed before the Account group's print jobs.

11. **b.** The printer device is the actual piece of hardware that prints the document. The
    printer is the software that creates a connection to the printer device and enables
    you to print to the actual printer device.

Challenge Solutions

1. The answer is to use the General tab on the printer Properties dialog box. Look at
    Figure 10-2 and identify the location of the "Print Test Page" button.

2. Change the sharing options on the printer to install additional drivers for Windows
    NT 4.0 Workstation computers. Remember that this is accomplished on the
    Advanced tab of the printer Properties dialog box by using the "New Driver"
    button, then installing the additional driver.

3. In the Ports tab of the printer Properties dialog box, select the "Enable printer
    pooling" checkbox, then check all of the ports that the print devices will be
    printing to. Enabling the printer pooling by selecting the checkbox is the only
    way that you can select multiple ports.

4. Select a second printer port on the printer on PRO1 and redirect the port to
    \\PRO2\Color2. On the exam you may be tempted to use the second computer
    (PRO2) to redirect the print jobs. Don't fall for this, because you must use the
    computer whose printer has failed to redirect the print jobs.

5. Create two printers that point to the same print device. Call these printers Users and Reports. Configure the Users printer to be available 24 hours a day and the Reports printer to be available only during off-duty hours. Tell the Accounting users to send the long reports to the Reports printer, and of course tell the normal users to print to the Users printer.

6. Remove the Everyone group, or you could just clear all the checkboxes for the Everyone group. This is because the Everyone group, by default, has Print permissions.

7. You can change the location of the spool file by using the Advanced tab of the Print Server Properties dialog box, shown in Figure 10-8.

Chapter 11

Dial-up Networking

These are the areas that are generally testable on the MCSE Server 2000 examination:

1. Install, configure, and manage modems.

2. Connect to computers by using dial-up networking.

    • Create a dial-up connection to connect to a remove access server.

    • Connect to the Internet by using dial-up networking.

    • Configure and troubleshoot Internet Connection Sharing.

3. Enable viewing of web pages offline.

4. Use Peer Web Services.

5. Create an Internet printer.

Introduction

This chapter has 12 Challenges, so pay particular attention to all the problems presented. We will first provide you with information about how to properly install a modem that will be used to connect to a remote server.

After the modem has been installed, you will learn how to configure it using the Device Manager. You will also learn how to use the "Troubleshooter" utility located on the General tab of the modem Properties dialog box. The General tab will also enable you to test the modem by querying it.

Then, we will cover how to configure a dial-up connection that could be used to connect to a RAS server or a VPN server. When the dial-up connection is created, you must make sure that you select the correct type of authentication to be used. If you choose the wrong type at this point, you could have a security problem.

Next, you will be shown how to enable network computers to connect to a computer set up to share a dial-up connection that can be used to connect to the Internet. First, you will learn that a host ICS computer must have a modem installed and must be configured to share the connection. Then you will use the Internet Explorer to permit the ICS clients to connect to the host ICS computer and access the Internet.

Then, you will learn how to authorize a user to dial into the RAS server and how to enable the callback option. RAS enables users to connect to the network remotely and access resources as if they were connected locally to the network. A Windows 2000 server can be configured as a RAS server to provide this service using the Routing and Remote Access service.

You will learn how to enable the RAS server to use multiple modems (referred to as a multilink connection). You will also discover how to enable your computer to view web pages when a connection to the Internet is not available. Peer Web Services will then be discussed, and specific procedures will be provided to enable your Windows 2000 Professional to act as a small-scale web server.

Finally, you will learn how to create an Internet printer and how to manage this printer from anywhere in the world using your Internet browser.

INSTALLING A MODEM

First, let's define what dial-up networking really is. About 75 percent of the people that connect to the Internet from their homes use dial-up networking. Some even use dial-up networking to connect to their company's RAS server so that they can do work from home. To use dial-up networking, you must first have a modem installed in your computer. Newer computers come with a built-in modem. However, because there are many older computers still without modems, you must be able to install a modem and be able to use dial-up networking to connect either to the Internet or to a company's remote server. First, we will go through the process of installing a modem.

If you purchase a new modem, you will more than likely receive a Plug-and-Play modem. As stated in Chapter 3, a Plug-and-Play device can be installed and it should automatically be detected and configured with the correct driver. This is a great improvement over installing a non-Plug-and-Play (legacy) device, which has to be manually installed.

After the modem has been installed (either automatically or manually), you can manage and configure it using the Device Manager. Remember how to get to Device Manager? There are several ways, but we'll give you the path that Microsoft prefers. First, right-click My Computer on the desktop and select the Manage entry from the menu. This brings up the Management Console.

Next, select System Tools, and finally Device Manager. Once in Device Manager, double-click the modem to be configured and the modem Properties dialog box will appear, as shown in Figure 11-1. Notice that depending in the type of modem installed, you may have five or six tabs. This example shows five tabs—General, Modem, Diagnostics, Advanced, and Driver. Other modems may display a Resources tab. We will not discuss each tab, only the important ones.

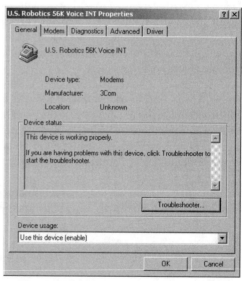

Figure 11-1: Modem Properties Dialog Box, General Tab

- *General tab.* This tab, shown in Figure 11-1, shows the Device type, Manufacturer, and Location. Right below this information is a Device status window that will tell you whether your modem is working properly or not. Notice the *"Troubleshooter"* button near the bottom. Click this button to start the Troubleshooter utility that can help you identify what is wrong with your modem. Be aware that the Troubleshooter does not actually fix the device. You must perform that job manually. Then at the bottom of the screen you will see the Device usage area. *This is where you would enable or disable a modem.* We normally use this when we have a built-in modem and then want to add a newer modem adapter to the system. Normally, you must disable the built-in modem to properly install the new modem. We will skip the Modem tab because it is not on the test.

- *Diagnostics tab.* This tab is shown in Figure 11-2. The only important item here is the *"Query Modem"* button near the bottom of the screen. If you are having problems with your modem, you would use this button to assist in the troubleshooting process. After clicking it, the modem is sent some modem commands and should respond with replies. We will skip the Advanced tab and move on to the Driver tab.

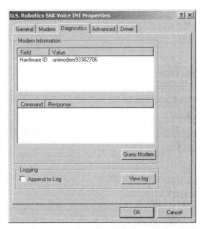

Figure 11-2: Modem Properties Dialog Box, Diagnostics Tab

- *Driver tab.* This tab is illustrated in Figure 11-3. You have already been shown how to install drivers for devices in Chapter 3. However, we really believe this is an important topic as it relates to modems. This tab contains the modem's device driver information. Some of the most important features are two of the buttons located at the bottom of the screen. These are *"Uninstall" and "Update Driver".* You should uninstall a driver when you are installing a completely new driver. You should update a driver when you are installing the same type of driver, but in a newer version.

You have a user that employs a laptop to access the network from his home. The computer is running Windows 2000 Professional and has a modem installed. You configure the modem to connect to the RAS Server. The next day, the user claims that he was not able to connect to the network. You believe that the modem is not working properly. How could you test whether the modem is working properly?

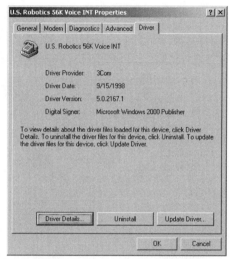

Figure 11-3: Modem Properties Dialog Box, Driver Tab

EXAM TIP: Know how to install a modem and how to configure it with Device Manager after it has been installed. Know that the "Troubleshooter" can be used to roubleshoot a modem, and that it is located on the General tab of the modem Properties dialog box. Also, be aware that this tab is used to enable and disable the modem. Finally, know that the Query Modem button is on the same Properties dialog box on the Diagnostics tab and can be used to test the installed modem.

CONFIGURING A DIAL-UP CONNECTION

Once you have a modem installed and working properly, you can configure the dial-up connection to connect to the Internet, or to a Remote Access Service (RAS) server. You can also make a connection using Virtual Private Network (VPN) or Internet Connection Sharing (ICS). In this section we will only discuss configuring a dial-up connection to a RAS server. Then we will really hit the Internet Connection Sharing section hard. This subject area alone could have at least three exam questions.

Remote Access Service Server Connection

Remote Access Service (RAS) enables users to connect to the network remotely and access resources as if they were connected locally to the network. A Windows 2000 Server can be configured as a RAS server using the Routing and Remote Access service. To configure a dial-up connection to a RAS server you would use the Network and Dial-up Connections utility shown in Figure 11-4. This utility can be accessed by double-clicking the *Network and Dial-up Connections icon located in the Control Panel.*

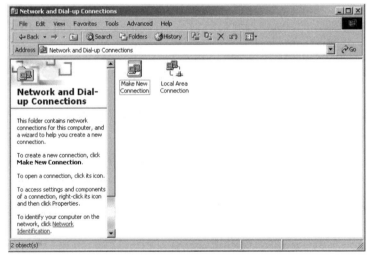

Figure 11-4: Network and Dial-up Connections Window

Notice the Make New Connection icon. If you click it, the Network Connection Wizard will start. Click the Next button to display the screen depicted in Figure 11-5. This screen is important, because it is here that the type of connection is configured. Notice that there is an entry for a dial-up connection "using my phone line (modem or ISDN)". This option is used for the RAS connection. Then, briefly examine the others—Dial-up to Internet (ISP), VPN connection, and others.

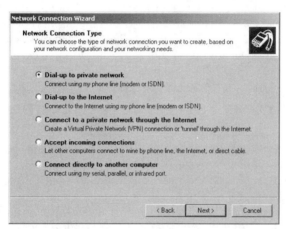

Figure 11-5: Network Connection Type

Before you can use dial-up connection, you must configure the connection's properties. These can be accessed by right-clicking the connection you just created and selecting Properties. This will bring up the Dial-up Connection Properties dialog box, shown in Figure 11-6. This figure has the Options tab selected.

Figure 11-6: Dial-up Connection Properties Dialog Box, Options Tab

- *Options tab.* Two items on this tab are important. The first one is the ***"Prompt for name and password, certificate, etc."*** checkbox. When this checkbox is enabled, you will be prompted for a user name and password before the connection is started. It is used in combination with the ***"Include Windows logon domain"*** checkbox to enable you to log on to the correct domain with the correct user name and password.

- *Security tab.* This is a very important tab because this is where the connection security is configured, as shown in Figure 11-7. You should normally use the "Typical" security option to dial into a normal Windows 2000 network. With the Typical setting you are given three ways to validate your identity. They are—Allow unsecured password, Require secured password, and Use smart card option.

Figure 11-7: Dial-up Connection Properties Dialog Box, Security Tab

You are a user that normally accesses your company's remote Windows 2000 network from your home. You use a laptop computer running Windows 2000 Professional to connect to the RAS server. You decide to create a new dial-up connection to the company's remote access server and you want to configure the connection to require secured passwords and to use the Windows logon name and password. What should you do?

Challenge #2

If you are really concerned with security and want to select a specific security option, you would select the "Advanced (custom settings)" radio button, shown in Figure 11-7. Then you would select the "Settings" button to bring up the Advanced Security Settings dialog box, illustrated in Figure 11-8.

Table 11-1 lists the definitions of the security protocols shown in Figure 11-8. The acronym CHAP stands for "Challenge Handshake Authentication Protocol." MS-CHAP is the Microsoft version of this encrypted authentication protocol.

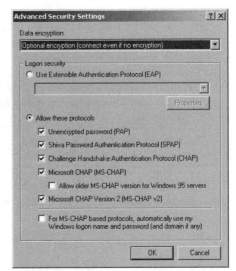

**Figure 11-8: Advanced Security
Settings Dialog Box**

Table 11-1: Security Protocol Definitions

Method	Description
Extensible Authentication Protocol (EAP)	Enables your connection to use smart cards, which is the highest type of encryption.
Microsoft Encrypted Authentication Version 2 (MS-CHAP v2)	Uses a higher level of security than MS-CHAP. It provides mutual authentication between the RAS server and RAS clients. It also uses an encrypted password process.
Microsoft Encrypted Authentication (MS-CHAP)	Uses an encrypted password process that is a nonreversible authentication.
Encrypted Authentication (CHAP)	Used by non-Microsoft clients for challenge-response authentication. This type of authentication uses a hashing scheme to encrypt the response sent from the RAS client to the RAS server.
Unencrypted Password (PAP)	Uses plain text passwords. It is the least secure authentication method.

Kale is an assistant administrator for a large Windows 2000 network. He uses a Windows 2000 Professional computer to dial into the network from home, where he connects to a RAS Server. He wants to use plain text passwords with this dial-up connection, but is not sure of which protocol he will use. Which authentication protocol will support plain text passwords?

Sharon must configure a Windows 2000 Server to enable users to dial in to the network from their homes. She has determined that she must install a RAS server, but she is not sure of how to accomplish this. You show her how to enable the Routing and Remote Access Service (RRAS) on one of Windows 2000 Servers and configure it as a RAS server. Sharon wants to use mutual authentication between the RAS server and RAS clients and at the same time ensure that data passing between the RAS server and RAS clients is encrypted. Which authentication protocol should you instruct Sharon to use for incoming connections?

Tamrica is your network administrator. She has just installed a new RAS Server to enable remote users to connect to the network. You have a laptop computer with Windows 2000 Professional installed at home and you want to use it connect to the RAS server. Your home computer has a smart card installed to provide you with the highest level of security. You are not sure of which authentication protocol should be used with a smart card. Which protocol offers the best choice?

Sally is your resident expert on dial-up connections. She has been asked to set up a RAS server on one of the network's Windows 2000 Servers. First, she needs to configure a dial-up connection for users to connect to the network. Sally is concerned about network security and decides to establish a dial-up connection that will require encrypted authentication. She is not sure of which authentication protocol to use. Which protocol should Sally use?

EXAM TIP: Review Challenges 3 through 6 carefully. They will reinforce the types of authentication that you should use in specific circumstances.

- *Networking tab.* When you are dialing in to a RAS Server, you must be aware of this tab. If the network you are dialing in to has multiple network segments, you must access this tab and click the Internet Protocol (TCP/IP) checkbox, followed by the Properties button. This will bring up the Advanced TCP/IP Settings (TCP/IP Properties) dialog box that can be used to access different network segments after you have established a dial-up connection with the RAS Server. Pay special attention to the Dial-up Connection Properties' Networking tab, shown in Fig 11-9. In Figure 11-10 you can see the TCP/IP Properties dialog box with the *"Use default gateway on remote network" checkbox*. This checkbox must be checked to enable you to access the other network segments.

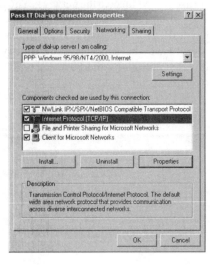

Figure 11-9: Dial-up Connection Properties Dialog Box, Networking

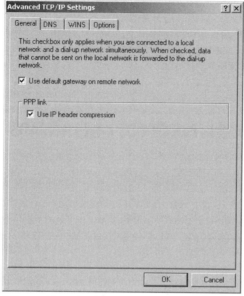

Figure 11-10: TCP/IP Protocol Dialog Box

You are a typical user of a Windows 2000 network. You have just been authorized to dial in to the company network from your home. You configure the dial-up connection properly and are successful in connecting to the RAS server. You can access the resources on the network segments where the RAS server is located, but not on any of the other company's network segments. What can be done to provide you with access to the other network segments?

You have installed a RAS server on one of your network's Windows 2000 Servers. The RAS server and the local network are configured to only use the TCP/IP protocol. The next day, all the remote access users complain that when they connect to the RAS server they receive an error message stating that the IPX/SPX compatible protocol is not available. You also discover that if the users wait long enough, they can finally connect to the network using TCP/IP. You know that this problem is not critical, but you want to keep the message from being displayed on the client computers. What is the best solution for this situation?

INTERNET CONNECTION SHARING

What is Internet Connection Sharing (ICS)? Well, if you don't have a dedicated connection to the Internet and only have a modem, you would be a good candidate for ICS. In a nutshell, ICS allows you to configure one computer at the office (or home) to connect to the Internet and the other computers use that computer as a gateway to access the Internet. ICS is a watered-down version of Network Address Translation (NAT), not discussed on this book.

Pay close attention to this section. The Internet Connection Sharing (ICS) feature is normally used for small companies that do not have a dedicated Internet connection, like a T-1 or ISDN connection, and do not have a large budget. One computer in the company dials up to the ISP and establish the Internet connection for the other company computers. This computer is responsible for network address translation, IP addresses, and name resolution for all the computers that connect through this computer. The computers behind the hosting computer can use the Internet just as if they were directly connected themselves. Depending on how many computers will be using the ICS connection, you may notice that access to the Internet may be considerably slower on a modem dial-up connection.

Before you can implement ICS on your network, the following requirements must taken into consideration:

- *Network client as well as the host computer must use DHCP services. This means that they will receive their IP addresses dynamically.* When ICS is installed a DHCP address allocator is installed that is pre-configured with an address range of 192.168.0.1-192.168.0.254 with a subnet mask of 255.255.255.0. This mini-DHCP Server can not be configured. .

- *The network clients must be set up to use the ICS services.*

- *One computer (called the host) must be enabled to host the ICS services.*

Setting up the host computer for ICS:

- *The host must be correctly configured before the clients are able to use the Internet through the Host computer.* Before you can set up a computer to be an ICS Host, you create a dial-up connection to the Internet, which is accomplished using the Network and Dial-up Connection window. After the dial-up connection is created, you would right-click it and select Properties. This brings up that connection's Properties dialog box, which you will select the Sharing tab. Figure 11-11 shows this dialog box. Before you set up the Host, you have to make sure that you have a modem (or NIC) that is used to connect to the Internet and an additional NIC that will be connected to the LAN. You can also implement ICS on a normal dial-up VPN connection. To enable ICS you have to be logged in to the computer with Administrative privileges or you will not see the Sharing tab.

Figure 11-11 is so important. Notice the *"Enable Internet Connection Sharing for this connection"* checkbox. This box must be selected to enable the computer to operate as a ICS host. If you want to stop ICS, you would remove the checkmark. On the same tab, notice the *"Enable on-demand dialing"* checkbox. This box must be checked to enable other computers to automatically dial up the Internet connection when the ICS host is not currently connected. If this box is not checked and the ICS host is not currently connected to the Internet, the ICS client will be denied service.

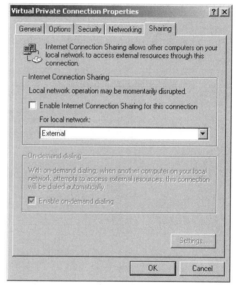

Figure 11-11: Virtual Private
Connection Properties, Sharing Tab

EXAM TIP: You must know that you must already have a dial-up connection created in order to establish a host ICS computer. The host computer must be configured to provide DHCP services to the ICS clients. Finally, know that the Sharing tab of the Dial-up Connection Properties dialog box is used to enable ICS and on-demand dialing.

You have a network computer installed with Windows 2000 Professional and you want to use this computer to connect to the Internet on a 56k connection. You also want other network users to access the Internet using the Internet Connection Sharing (ICS) feature. What can you do to enable ICS on this Windows 2000 Professional computer?

Setting up the client computers for ICS:

- The other side of the ICS configuration is the ICS client setup. This process enables a computer to access the Internet through the ICS host computer. This is a fairly simple process and does not require any additional software. The process goes like this. On the client computer, right-click the Internet Explorer icon on the desktop and select Properties. This will bring up the Internet Properties dialog box. Make sure you use the Connections tab, as shown in Figure 11-12.

Figure 11-12: Internet Properties Dialog Box, Connections Tab

Now, click on the "Setup..." button to start the Internet Connection Wizard, as shown in Figure 11-13. On the first screen of this wizard, you will select the "I want to connect through a Local Area Network (LAN)" option. What this really means is that you want to connect to the Internet through the ICS host computer, that happens to be located on your LAN. You will be taken through three more screens and the process is complete. Simple, isn't it.

Figure 11-13: Internet Connection Wizard, Setting Up Your Internet Connection

You are the local administrator of a small Windows 2000 network. The network has five Windows 2000 Professional computers. On one of the computers you create a dial-up connection to the Internet. This computer is then configured as a Internet Connection Sharing (ICS) host computer. The next day you decide to access a shared folder on a different computer, but you can't find the folder or the computer in Windows Explorer. In fact, you can't see any of the other computers. What should you do to correct this problem?

Challenge #10

EXAM TIP: Know that you use Internet Explorer to enable the ICS clients to use the ICS host computer's connection to the Internet.

DIAL-IN PERMISSIONS FOR USERS

Even though this topic is covered in Windows 2000 Server, we feel it necessary that you know how to configure the client to use dial-in connections. You will have some questions on the exam where the additional information will help. After you set up your RAS server, users are not automatically authorized to use the service. *You must authorize the users to dial in to your RAS server.* You grant dial-in permissions using the Local Users and Groups utility (member server), or with the Active Directory Users and Computers utility (domain controller), depending on how your network is set up. Using one of these utilities, open the user Properties dialog box by expanding the Users folder and double-clicking the user account to which you wish to grant dial-in access. *After the user Properties dialog box appears, click the Dial-in tab, as illustrated in Figure 11-14.* The Dial-in tab enables you to Allow access, Deny access, or Control access through Remote Access Policy, as well as to set the following callback options—No callback, Set by Caller, and Always Callback to a particular telephone number. *Setting the Callback Option to Always Callback to a particular telephone number provides additional security by calling a user back at a predetermined telephone number.*

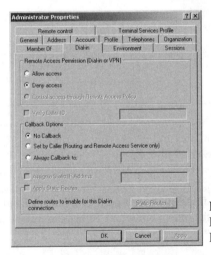

Figure 11-14: User Properties Dialog Box, Dial-in Tab

EXAM TIP: Know that you must authorize users to dial in to the RAS server. This is done in the user Properties dialog box on the Dial-in tab. Also, know what it means to enable the Callback Options.

Enabling a Multilink Connection

If you want your remote users to connect to your network, you must use the PPP tab on the RAS Server Properties dialog box. This tab, illustrated in Figure 11-15, provides you with the options required to configure the Point-to-Point Protocol (PPP). Notice the "Multilink" connections checkbox. We will discuss only the Multilink connections checkbox because that is all you need to know from this screen. *This checkbox is marked to enable two or more physical connections to be combined into a single logical connection.* If you use Multilink, you also have the option to set the amount of bandwidth utilized by employing the Bandwidth Allocation Protocol (BAP) or the Bandwidth Allocation Control Protocol (BACP).

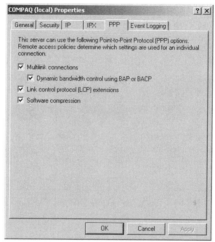

Figure 11-15: RAS Server Properties Dialog Box, PPP Tab

Winters is a new member of your Windows 2000 staff. He has limited knowledge about RAS servers. He receives a call from a user who wants to use her Windows 2000 Professional computer to connect to the RAS server from home. Winters creates a new dial-up connection for this user and configures it to use a multilink that will provide more bandwidth by using both of the server's modems. The next day the same user calls Winters and complains that she was able to use only one of the modems. What can Winters do to enable the user to dial in and use both modems?

Challenge #11

Web Page Offline Viewing

You can set up Windows 2000 Professional to provide offline viewing of web pages. This means that you can configure your computer to allow viewing of web pages on your local machine if a network connection to the Internet is not available. When configuring the computer for this feature, you are guided through a process that will actually download (cache) a copy of the web page to your local computer. This is handy when you lose access to the Internet and must still use a particular web page to perform your duties. The process is quite simple. Open Internet Explorer and click the Favorites entry on the menu bar. Then, select the Add to Favorites option. This is shown in Figure 11-16.

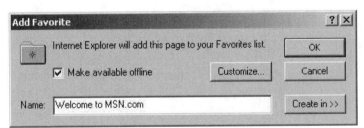

Figure 11-16: Enabling Web Page Offline Viewing

In Figure 11-16, notice the checkbox labeled "Make available offline". *To enable offline viewing of web pages, this box must be checked. Then you should click the "Customize" button located just to the right of the checkbox.* An Offline Favorite Wizard will start and guide you through the enabling process. Click the Next button and another screen will appear to provide you with options to determine whether you want links to other web pages to also be available offline. This is shown in Figure 11-17. You should keep this selection to a minimum if you have limited hard drive space because you may fill it up quickly.

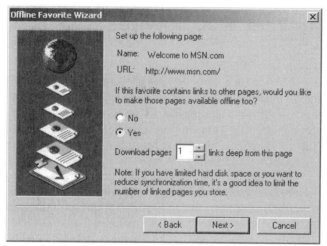

Figure 11-17: Making Links to Other Web Pages Available Offline

The screens following this one enable you to specify how often you want to synchronize the web page (update locally). Of the two previous figures, the most important is Figure 11-16. Know how to enable offline viewing of web pages.

You are the local administrator of a Windows 2000 Professional Computer. You work continuously with a particular web page and need to make sure it can be viewed when the network connection to the Internet is not available. What process can you use to make a web page available for offline viewing?

Challenge #12

EXAM TIP: Know exactly how to enable your computer to view web pages when the connection to the Internet is lost.

Installing Peer Web Services

Peer Web Services (PWS) is used to configure your Windows 2000 Professional computer as a web server for a small network. Note that the functionality of PWS is limited and should not be confused with the full-scale version seen in the Internet Information Services (IIS)—which must be installed on a Windows 2000 Server. You install PWS through the Add/Remove Programs icon located in the Control Panel. After you double-click this icon, you will be given an Add/Remove Programs window. You should then select the Add/Remove Windows Components option. This will start the Windows Components Wizard. *Notice that you will select the "Internet Information Services (IIS)" checkbox and simply follow the directions given by the wizard, as illustrated in Figure 11-18.* One important thing to note is that even though you have selected to install IIS, when you install these services on a Windows 2000 Professional computer, you are actually installing Peer Web Services. Also, be aware that before you can install PWS, the computer must already have TCP/IP installed.

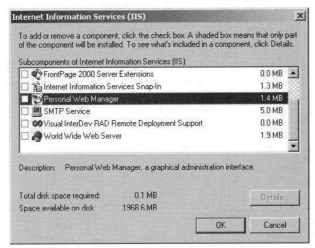

Figure 11-18: Windows Components Wizard, Installing Peer Web Services

After PWS has been installed, you will be able to use the following installed protocols:

- *Simple Mail Transfer Protocol (SMTP).* As the name implies, this is a simple method of transferring mail from one SMTP mail system to another.

- *Hypertext Transfer Protocol (HTTP).* This particular protocol is already installed with the Windows 2000 Professional operating system to enable you to navigate web sites. However, when you install PWS, you can use this protocol to publish your own web site to the outside world.

- *File Transfer Protocol.* This protocol enables you to transfer files from one computer to another.

Also notice that there are two new icons in the Administrative Tools folder called Personal—Web Manager and Internet Services Manager. We will not explain each of these options. Simply be aware that they are created when you install PWS.

Installing Internet Printers

Windows 2000 Professional comes with a new protocol called the *Internet Printer Protocol (IPP)*, which enables you to send print jobs across the Internet to another printer. This functionality greatly enhances your ability to print worldwide. The IPP protocol converts the print job into HTML format and transfers it to a selected printer over the Internet. One important item to note is that the Windows 2000 Professional computer receiving the print job must be running PWS. Installing an Internet printer is similar to installing a normal network printer except that you must enter the URL of the printer, as illustrated in Figure 11-19. *The format for the URL to be entered in is:*

http://computername/printer/share_name/.printer

Click the Next button to finish the process.

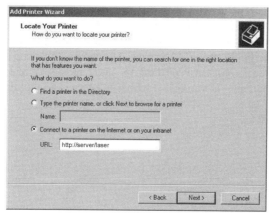

Figure 11-19: Adding an Internet Printer

Let's say that an Internet printer has been created and you want to manage the printer. You can manage the printer as if you were sitting right there. Before you can attempt to manage printers, you must have Internet Explorer 4 or later installed. Simply open your web browser and **_type http://print_server/printer_** in the URL address element and press ENTER. You may be prompted for your user name, password, and domain name. Click the link for the printer to be managed and under Printer Actions, click the Connect option.

EXAM TIP: Know how to install a printer over the Internet and how to use your web browser to manage printers over the Internet.

Review Questions

1. Kale is an assistant administrator for a large Windows 2000 network. He uses a Windows 2000 Professional computer from home to dial in to the network where he connects to a RAS server. He wants use plain text passwords with this dial-up connection, but is not sure of which protocol he will use. Which protocol supports plain text passwords?

   a. CHAP
   b. MS-CHAP v2
   c. PAP
   d. EAP

2. Sharon needs to configure a Windows 2000 Server to allow users to dial in to the network from their homes. She has determined that she must install a RAS server, but she is not sure of how to accomplish this. You tell her to enable the Routing and Remote Access Service (RRAS) on one of her Windows 2000 Servers and configure the computer as a RAS server. Sharon wants to use mutual authentication between the RAS server and RAS clients and at the same time ensure that data passing between the RAS server and RAS clients is encrypted. Which protocol should you instruct Sharon to use for incoming connections?

   a. CHAP
   b. MS-CHAP v2
   c. PAP
   d. SPAP

3. Tamrica is your network administrator. She has just installed a new RAS server to be used by remote users to connect to the network. You have a laptop computer with Windows 2000 Professional at home that you will be using to connect to the RAS server. Your home computer has a smart card installed to provide you with the highest level of security. You are not sure which protocol should be used with a smart card. Which of the following is the best option?
   a. EAP
   b. PPTP
   c. IPSec
   d. NetBEUI

4. Sally is your resident expert on dial-up connections. She is asked to set up a RAS server on one of the network's Windows 2000 Servers. Next she needs to configure a dial-up connection for users to connect to the network. Sally is concerned about network security and has decided to establish the dial-up connection to require encrypted authentication. She is not sure which protocol to use. Which protocols should she use? (Select all that apply.)
   a. MS-CHAP
   b. MS-CHAP v2
   c. PAP
   d. EAP

5. You have installed a RAS server on one of your network's Windows 2000 Servers. The RAS server and the local network are configured to use only the TCP/IP protocol. The next day, all of the remote access users complain that when they connect to the RAS server they receive an error message stating that the IPX/SPX compatible protocol is not available. You also discover that if the users wait long enough, they can finally connect to the network using TCP/IP. Which of the following is the best way to keep the error messages from being displayed?
   a. Configure the client computers to use only TCP/IP for the connection to the RAS server.
   b. Configure the client computers to use a defined IPX network address for the connection to the RAS server.
   c. Configure the RAS server to allow IPX-based remote access and demand dial connection.
   d. Configure the RAS server to disable multilink connection.

6. You are a typical user on a Windows 2000 network. You have just been authorized to dial in to the company network from your home. You configure the dial-up connection properly and are successful in connecting to the RAS server. You can access the resources on the network segment where the RAS server is located, but not on any of the company's other network segments. What can be done to provide you with access to the other network segments?
    a. Configure the company's remote access server to accept Multi-link connections.
    b. Configure the TCP/IP properties for the dial-up connection to disable IP header compression.
    c. Configure the TCP/IP properties for the dial-up connection to use the default gateway on the remote network.
    d. Grant your user account dial-in permission on the company's remote access server.

7. You are a user who normally accesses your remote Windows 2000 network from home. You use a laptop computer with Windows 2000 Professional to connect to a RAS server. You have created a new dial-up connection to connect to the company's remote access server. You want to configure the connection to require secured passwords and to use the Windows logon name and password. What should you do? (Select two answers.)
    a. Configure the security options to enable EAP.
    b. Configure the security options to require secured passwords.
    c. Configure the security options to allow unsecured passwords.
    d. Configure the security options to use the Windows logon name and password.
    e. Configure the dialing options to include the Windows logon domain.
    f. Configure the dialing options to not prompt for name and password.

8. You have a user that uses a laptop from his home to access the network. You are asked to ensure that the computer is properly set up for this access. You install Windows 2000 professional on this computer and create a dial-up connection to use both of the RAS server's modems. When you initiate the dial-up connection and connect to the RAS server, you notice that only one of the modems is actually being used. Which of the following will enable this computer to use both modems when connected to the RAS server?
    a. Configure the dial-up connection to use a SLIP connection.
    b. Configure the company's remote access server to accept multilink connections.
    c. Replace your modems with new modems that support multilink.
    d. Grant your user account multilink permission on the company's remote access.

9. You have a network computer running Windows 2000 Professional and you want to use it to connect to the Internet using a 56k connection. You also want other network users to access the Internet using the Internet Connection Sharing (ICS) feature. Which of the following will enable ICS on this Windows 2000 Professional computer?

  a. Open Routing and Remote Access, click ICS, right-click ICS, and add a New Interface.

  b. In Control Panel, double-click ICS. Configure ICS through the Internet Connection Sharing Setup Wizard.

  c. Open Network and Dial-up Connections, right-click the connection that you want to share, choose Properties, and select the "Enable Internet Connection Sharing for this connection" checkbox from the sharing tab.

  d. Reconfigure the TCP/IP properties for the internal network interface. Set the IP address to an address in the 192.168.x.y range. Configure a DHCP scope on the machine and assign it IP addresses from the same range. Exclude the statically assigned IP address from the previous step.

10. You have five Windows 2000 Professional computers on your network and you want to configure one of them to allow all the computers to connect to the Internet on a 56k dial-up connection. The computers must also be able to connect to the Internet even when the host computer is not connected. Which of the following actions must be performed?

  a. Install the modem and configure the connection to contact ISP.

  b. Check the "Enable on-demand dialing" checkbox.

  c. Enable Internet Connection Sharing on a host computer.

  d. All the above

11. You have a user that uses a laptop to access the network from his home. The computer is running Windows 2000 Professional and has a modem. You configure the modem to connect to the RAS server. The next day, the user claims that he was not able to connect to the network. You believe that the modem is not working properly. Which of the following could you use to test whether the modem is working properly or not?

  a. Use the Diagnostics tab in the modem's Properties dialog box to query the modem.

  b. From a command prompt, run the Net Config Server command.

  c. From a command prompt, run the Net Statistics command.

  d. Use Regedit32 to view the Error Control value in the HKEY_LOCAL_MACHINE\System\CurrentControlSet\Services\RemoteAccess Key.

12. You have a very small Windows 2000 network. One Windows 2000 Professional computer is configured as a dial-up connection to the Internet. This connection will be used by five Windows 2000 Professional computers to access the Internet. You know that there are certain steps to this process. After installing the computer for the shared dial-up connection with Windows 2000 Professional, what are the next steps that you must take to enable all of the computers to share this dial-up connection? (Select two answers.)

a. Through the Network and Dial-up Connections icon, install the modem for the dial-up connection.

b. On the Sharing tab for the connection, select the "Enable Internet Connection Sharing for this connection" checkbox.

c. Install the DNS server service and configure a forwarder to forward all DNS requests to the same DNS server as the machine sharing the Internet connection.

d. Configure the LAN adapter for the machine sharing the Internet connection with an internal IP address (e.g., 192.168.0.1).

Answers and Explanations

1. **c.** PAP will permit you to use plain text passwords. We don't know why you would want to do this because PAP is the least secure.

2. **b.** MS-CHAP v2 provides stronger security for remote access connections by providing mutual authentication between the RAS server and the RAS clients. It also ensures that data passing between the RAS server and RAS clients is encrypted. CHAP does use an encrypted password authentication process, but does not provide for mutual authentication. PAP is not the correct answer because it use plain text passwords.

3. **a.** EAP is the protocol used when you have a smart card installed.

4. **a, b, d.** MS-CHAP uses a nonreversible authentication protocol that uses an encrypted password authentication process. MS-CHAP v2 is an enhanced version of MS-CHAP that uses a higher level of security than MS-CHAP. EAP uses the highest level of authenticated encryption. PAP is a protocol that uses plain text passwords. This is the least secure authentication method.

5. **a.** Configure the client computers to use only TCP/IP for the connection to the RAS server. The question clearly states "The network uses TCP/IP as the only network protocol", which means your network does not support the IPX protocol. When the clients initially connect to the RAS server, they are configured to first connect using IPX, and because your RAS server is not set up to support this protocol, the clients receive an error message.

6. **c.** The dial-up connection of the remote user must be configured to use the default gateway on the remote network. By default, when you dial into the RAS server you have access to the network segment on which the RAS server is located. But if you want access to other network segments, you must enable this feature.

7. **b,d.** You must make sure that the "Validate my identity as follows" is set to require secured passwords. Then, you would click the checkbox below that to enable Automatically use my Windows logon name and password (and domain if any).

8. **b.** The laptop has to be configured to use both modems and the RAS server has to be configured to support multilink connections. This is done in the RAS server Properties dialog box, PPP tab, and the Multilink connection checkbox must be selected.

9. **c.** There is no ICS icon in the Control Panel. You use the Network and Dial-up Connections utility and right-click the connection, choose Properties, and select the "Enable Internet connection sharing for this connection" checkbox.

10. **d.** All the above are correct. First you must install a modem and configure the connection to contact the ISP. Then on the ICS host computer you must enable Internet Connection Sharing. This is done by right-clicking on the dial-up connection, selecting Properties, and selecting the Sharing tab. Then enable ICS. You will also use the same tab to "Enable on-demand dialing", which will allow other network users to connect to the Internet even if the host computer is not currently connected.

11. **a.** Go to the diagnostics tab of the modem's Properties dialog box and select the "Query Modem" to test the modem.

12. **a, b.** First, you create a dial-up connection that the computer will use. The connection must be shared with the other employees to allow them to use the connection. This is done on the Sharing tab for the connection by selecting the "Enable Internet Connection Sharing for this connection" checkbox.

Challenge Solutions

1. The answer is on the Diagnostics tab of the modem Properties dialog box. Use the "Query Modem" button to test the modem.

2. You must make sure that the "Validate my identity as follows" is set to require secured passwords. Then, you would click the checkbox below that to enable Automatically use my Windows logon name and password (and domain if any).

3. To answer this question, refer to Table 11-1, where you can verify that the protocol to use is the PAP protocol, which uses plain text passwords. One important item to note is that this protocol is not normally used because it is the least secure authentication method.

4. Examine Table 11-1 and you will see that the only authentication protocol that can provide mutual authentication between the RAS server and the RAS client is the MS-CHAP (v2) protocol.

5. Examine Table 11-1 and you will see that the only protocol that can be used with smart cards is the EAP protocol.

6. We once again direct your attention to Table 11-1. There are three protocols that can use encrypted authentication: MS-CHAP, MS-CHAP (v2), and EAP. Notice that there are four possible questions that you can receive from Table 11-1.

7. Examine Figure 11-10. Make sure that the "Use default gateway on remote network" checkbox is selected on the General tab of the Advanced TCP/IP Settings dialog box. One important item to note is that this option is configured for this particular dial-up connection and will not affect the other TCP/IP settings for the local computer.

8. Configure the client computers to use only TCP/IP for the connection to the RAS server. The problem clearly states "The network uses TCP/IP as the only network protocol", which means your network does not support the IPX protocol. When the clients initially connect to the RAS server, they are configured to first connect using IPX, and because your RAS server is not set up to support this protocol, the clients receive an error message.

9. Open Network and Dial-up Connections, right-click the connection that you want to share, choose Properties, and select the "Enable Internet Connection Sharing for this connection" checkbox from the Sharing tab, which is seen in Figure 11-11. If you don't enable this option, the other network uses will not be able to use this computer to connect to the Internet.

10. When you configure the computer as an ICS host, it is issued an IP address of 192.168.0.1. If the other computers are not also configured to use ICS, then they will have different IP addresses. When they are configured to use the ICS services they will each receive an IP address from the ICS host in the 192.168.0.0 address range. Disable the shared or the ICS configuration and you should be able to once again access the resources on the local network.

11. The dial-up connection may have been set up to use multilink, but the RAS server itself needs to be configured to use multilink. Now, look at Figure 11-15, on the PPP tab. The Multilink connections checkbox must be checked to enable this feature. If you review the RAS server properties and the checkbox is checked, the modems must be replaced with ones that support multilink.

12. On the Favorites menu in Internet Explorer, click Add to Favorites. Select the Make Available Offline checkbox. Click Customize to specify a schedule for updating that page and how much content to download. Follow the instructions on your screen.

Chapter 12

Optimizing Windows 2000 Professional

These are the areas that are generally testable on the MCSE Server 2000 examination:

1. Deploy service packs.

2. Monitor and optimize usage of system resources.

3. Manage processes.

    *   Set priorities and start and stop processes.

4. Optimize disk performance.

Introduction

Optimizing your Windows 2000 Professional system is very important. You will learn how to use the Windows Update utility. As with other Windows 2000 tools, you must be logged in with Administrator permissions and you must have a Internet connection. This utility will connect you to the Microsoft web site and enable you to download Windows 2000 Professional operating system updates. Next, you will learn how to install service packs with a new process called "slipstreaming". Basically, slipstreaming allows you to install the service pack only once, instead of reinstalling it each time you install a new service on the server.

Next, you will be shown how to use the System Monitor utility. This utility enables you to monitor many different services located on the Windows Professional computer. You will also be presented with some important information about the Performance Logs and Alerts.

Then, we will discuss how to use the Task Manager utility to set process priorities and to start and stop processes. This utility is easy to use and can be accessed by pressing the CTRL+ALT+DELETE key combination and selecting the Task Manager tab.

Finally, you will discover how to optimize application performance on the computer. Also, you will learn how to configure the computer to automatically schedule many different tasks, such as running virus update software. This function can be accomplished with the Task Scheduler utility.

UPDATING WINDOWS 2000 PROFESSIONAL

Your Windows 2000 Professional computer provides a utility to keep your operating system current with the most up-to-date software. The utility is called the Windows Update utility. You should also install the latest service pack to correct software bugs and update new features when they are made available. Both of these actions will ensure that your operating system is current and bug-free.

Windows Update Utility

When you use the Windows Update utility, your computer connects to the Microsoft web site and prompts you to download the latest updates for your computer. *The only requirement to run the Windows Update utility is a connection to the*

Internet. This utility can be accessed by clicking the Start button and selecting the Windows Update option. It is easy to use after you connect to the web site. Simply identify the items to download and install them. *One other item of interest here is that you must be logged on with Administrator permissions in order to perform the download.*

There is another way to ensure that your operating system receives the most current updates. This is to install the *Windows Critical Update Notification utility.* This utility will automatically start when the user logs on as Administrator to the computer and it will notify them if there is a critical update for the computer. The following message is displayed:

> Microsoft Critical Update Notification
> New critical updates are available for your computer. Microsoft strongly recommends that you install these updates now.

Service Packs

Service packs are small programs designed to correct software bugs and to add new features to the operating system. Windows 2000 Professional comes with a new process to install service packs called "slipstreaming". Slipstreaming is a process that allows the user to install the service pack once in a manner that it will not be overwritten if new services are added to the system. *NT Server 4.0 did not have slipstreaming and the service packs had to be reinstalled each time a new service was added.*

If you are not sure which service pack is installed on your computer, simply type *winver* at the command prompt. After you enter this command and press ENTER, a dialog box will appear telling you which service packs are currently installed.

EXAM TIP: It is important that you know that you must be logged in with Administrator permissions and have a valid connection to the Internet in order to properly use the Windows Update utility. There is also another utility called the Windows Critical Update Notification utility that can be installed to automatically notify an administrator of updates. You must also be aware that in Windows 2000, service packs do not need to be reinstalled when a new service is installed. This is because of the slipstreaming process, which Windows NT Server 4.0 did not have. Finally, know that you can check to see which service pack is installed at the command line with the "winver" command.

SYSTEM MONITOR

The System Monitor is a utility used to monitor how your system is performing and identify any system bottlenecks. A bottleneck is any system resource that operates slower than the rest of the system and causes the entire system to run more slowly. To access this utility, you must add it to the MMC as an *ActiveX* control snap-in. The System Monitor utility is used in combination with the Performance Logs and Alerts utility to monitor your computer. Windows NT 4.0 used the Performance Monitor Utility in place of both of these utilities.

Before you can optimize your system, you must first create a baseline. A baseline is a measurement used as a starting point to monitor the performance of your system. You should create a baseline in the following circumstances:

- When the computer is first installed
- At periodic intervals
- When changes are made to the computer's hardware and software

Baselines are used to evaluate your system after you make changes to the hardware and software. Let's say that you have just installed additional memory: A baseline can be used to identify your performance levels before and after the installation. As a general rule, you should create a baseline before and after any change in the computer's configuration. Baselines are created using the Performance Logs and Alerts utility. They can provide valuable information to prevent system problems from affecting overall performance.

The System Monitor utility enables you to view your system's current activity. You can also import a log file to view through this utility. After the System Monitor has been installed, it can be accessed through the Administrative Tools folder by selecting Performance, and then selecting the System Monitor utility. As illustrated in Figure 12-1, the System Monitory utility tracks counters by default. You add the counters manually. There are three different views that you can select in this utility.

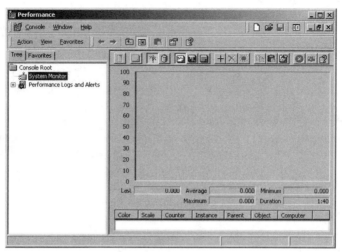

Figure 12-1: System Monitor Utility

Chart – This is the default view and is normally used to monitor a small number of counters in a graphical format. If you have a large number of counters, they could be hard to read in this view. This view is useful when you want to track system performance during a defined time frame.

Histogram – This is a bar graph view that is normally used for viewing large amounts of data. It does not provide a record of performance over time because it only shows current data.

Report – This view provides a logical report view that permits you to track large number of counters in real time. It displays data for the current session only and cannot provide a record of data over time.

Performance Logs and Alerts

The Performance Logs and Alerts utility enables you to create counter logs and trace logs. Counter logs monitor system performance during a given time frame and trace logs monitor performance continuously with periodic samplings. This utility also enables you to configure alerts. An alert notifies you when a counter exceeds or falls below a specified value. After the logs have been created, they can be viewed with the System Monitor. To access the Performance Logs and Alerts utility, open the Administrative Tools folder and select Monitor. Then, expand the node to show the Performance Logs and Alerts utility. Figure 12-2 displays this utility.

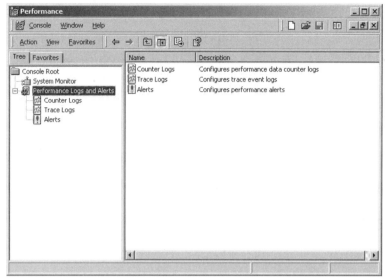

Figure 12-2: Performance Logs and Alerts Utility

John is having a problem with one of his Windows 2000 Professional computers. He decides to use the Performance Logs and Alerts utility to create logs that will identify system bottlenecks. He must use the System Monitor to view the logs. While in the System Monitor utility, he wants to close the utility, but he is not sure that the logs will continue to be written. What will happen if he closes the System Monitor?

Challenge #1

EXAM TIP: Know that the System Monitor utility is installed as an ActiveX control snap-in. Also, know the three different types of views that can be used in System Monitor along with their attributes. Finally, be aware that if you have created some performance logs they will continue to gather information regardless of whether the System Monitor is open or not.

Memory

Lack of memory is the cause of almost all system bottlenecks. A good rule of thumb when your computer is slowing down is to check the memory first. As a program starts, the operating system first checks to see whether the program is in physical memory (RAM). If it is not located in RAM, the operating system then checks the page file (logical memory). If the program is not located in the page file, the system checks the hard disk. Accessing a program from hard disk is much slower than accessing it from RAM. This is where the bottleneck occurs. If your system has sufficient physical memory (RAM) your computer will operate faster because it does not access the hard disk each time a program is started.

A clear sign that you need to add more RAM is when your computer is using excessive paging (swapping between the page file and RAM). Listed in Table 12-1 are the counters that you should monitor to check the performance of your memory.

Table 12-1: Memory Counters

Counter	Description
Paging File>%Usage	You would monitor this counter to determine how much of the page file is being used. If this counter is consistently over 99%, you need to add more RAM.
Memory>Pages/Sec	This counter will show how often the requested information was not located in RAM so that the request was referred to the hard drive. This counter should be under 20 and for the best performance, it should be at 4 to 5.
Memory>Available Mbytes	This counter is used to show the amount of RAM available on the computer. This value should be more than 4 MB.

NOTE: You should use all three counters together to identify whether excessive paging is occurring. If this is happening, adding RAM is usually the solution.

Processor

In a modern computer, the processor is not usually the bottleneck. However, it still should be monitored to be absolutely sure. In Table 12-2, we have identified the most common counters used to determine whether the processor is the source of the bottleneck.

Table 12-2: Processor Counters

Counter	Description
Processor>Interrupts/Sec	If this counter is more than 3,500 on a Pentium computer, it indicates a problem with a program or your hardware. It measures the number of hardware interrupts the processor receives each second.
Processor>%Processor Time	This counter is used to determine the amount of time the processor uses to service system requests. The processor would be identified as a system bottleneck if this value is consistently over 80%.

NOTE: Based on the counters in Table 12-2, if the processor is indeed the bottleneck, you should consider upgrading your processor, or even better, adding another processor (if your system supports multiple processors).

EXAM TIP: Memorize the processor counters in Table 12-2 and what constitutes a bottleneck as far as the processor is concerned.

Multiple Processors

Multiple processors enable your computer to operate faster by sharing the workload among processors. *Windows 2000 Professional can support up to two processors.* After additional processors have been installed, they can be configured to associate a specific process with a particular processor. This can balance the processor load on the computer. This association is called processor affinity, and it is configured through the Task Manager utility. This utility can be accessed by pressing the CTRL+ALT+DELETE and clicking the Task Manager button. This opens the Windows Task Manager dialog box, depicted in Figure 12-3. The figure shows the dialog box with the Processes tab selected. This tab enables you to view all the processes running on the computer.

Setting Processor Affinity – To set the processor affinity, select the process to be associated with a particular processor, right-click that

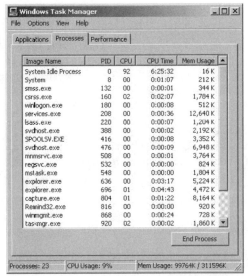

Figure 12-3: Task Manager Dialog Box, Processes Tab

process, and then select Processor Affinity from the pop-up menu. The Processor Affinity dialog box appears, shown in Figure 12-4. Place a checkmark on the processor you wish to handle this process.

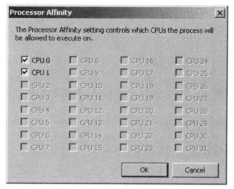

Figure 12-4: Processor Affinity Dialog Box

EXAM TIP: Be aware that Windows 2000 Professional supports two processors. Then know how to set Processor Affinity on your computer.

Disk Performance

You can monitor the amount of time it takes to retrieve data from the hard drive through the Disk Performance utility. This is called disk access time. In Table 12-3, we have listed the most common counters used to determine whether your computer has a bottleneck in its hard drive.

Table 12-3: Hard Drive Counters

Counter	Description
PhysicalDisk>%Disk Time	This counter is used to identify the amount of time the system takes to perform read or write requests. If this counter is more than 90%, you can improve performance by adding another disk controller.
PhysicalDisk>Current Disk Queue	This counter identifies the number of outstanding requests waiting to be processed. If this counter is more than 2, you may have a bottleneck here.

NOTE: *If you believe that you have a disk bottleneck, first check your physical memory.* If you do not have sufficient RAM, excessive paging will occur, which will in turn affect the disk drive performance.

Physical disk counters are automatically enabled in Windows 2000 Professional. In Windows NT 4.0 you had to enable the disk counters through the DISKPERF –Y command. If you wish to enable the logical disk counters in Windows 2000 Professional, you must use the *DISKPERF* command. Physical disk counters are used to monitor the physical disks. Logical disks are referred to as logical disk drives or basic volumes. It is common to configure physical and logical disk counters and then create alerts to notify you when a predetermined level has been reached.

> **EXAM TIP:** Learn what the disk counters in Table 12-3 monitor and know the limits of each. Be aware that the physical disk counters are automatically enabled in Windows 2000 Professional and that to enable the logical disk counters, you must use the DISKPERF command.

Monitoring the Network

In Windows 2000 Professional, by default, you can't monitor the entire network. However, you can monitor the traffic to and from a particular Windows 2000 computer. To monitor the entire network, you must install additional software. The Network Interface Card (NIC) and network protocols can be monitored with the counters listed in Table 12-4.

Table 12-4: Network Monitoring Counters

Counter	Description
TCP>Segments/Sec	Used to monitor the TCP protocol, including the number of bytes sent and received on a NIC.
Network Interface>Bytes Total/Sec	Used to monitor the total number of bytes sent and received on a NIC for all network protocols installed on the computer.

You can optimize your network performance by using only the network protocols that are absolutely necessary. This means that if you are only using TCP/IP on your network, you should not install another protocol such as NWLink. When the additional protocol is installed, each time data is sent from or received by the computer, the packet may be processed against that protocol. This will slow down the network performance. *If your network uses other protocols, make sure the most commonly used protocol is listed highest in the binding order.*

You are the network administrator for a Windows 2000 network. Your network has five Windows 2000 Professional computers. You notice that one computer is reacting slowly to client requests and you must use the System Monitor utility to identify where the system bottlenecks are. In System Monitor you notice the following counters:

% Processor Time (Average): 50%
Processor Queue Length (Average): 1
Pages /sec (Average): 10
Average Disk sec/Transfer: 0.8
Disk Queue Length (Average): 4

Which of the counters is the most likely bottleneck?

Challenge #3

EXAM TIP: There is not much to know in this section, except that adding additional protocols on your computer may affect the network's performance. Also, review all the counter tables so you can solve a combined problem similar to Challenge #3.

TASK MANAGER

As you saw before, the Task Manager utility is used to monitor processes and applications that are running on your computer. Remember that this utility is accessed by pressing CTRL+ALT+DELETE and clicking on the Task Manager button. There are three tabs on the Task Manager dialog box—Applications, Processes, and Performance.

Applications Tab

The Applications tab, shown in Figure 12-5, provides a listing of the status of all the applications the computer at a given time. Notice that each task is listed by name along with the current status of each (i.e., running, not responding, and stopped).

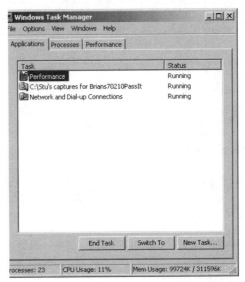

Figure 12-5: Task Manager, Applications Tab

Notice the three buttons at the bottom of Figure 12-5. They each have a specific purpose, as described below.

- *End Task* – This button is used to close an application. First, you must select the application and then click this button to close it. If you have an application that stops responding, you can use this button to close/stop the application, thereby freeing up its memory space.

- *Switch To* – This button is used to make the application window active.

- *New Task* – This button is used to start an application.

Processes Tab

You can use the Processes tab, illustrated in Figure 12-6, to quickly check the performance of the computer, instead of going through the long process of using the System Monitor. On this tab, preconfigured items are collected automatically. You don't have to do anything, just click the tab and monitor the performance. The items listed here deal with the CPU utilization the process is using, CPU processing time, and Memory usage. If you see any indicators here that need attention, then you should use the System Monitor to perform a more detailed check of system resources.

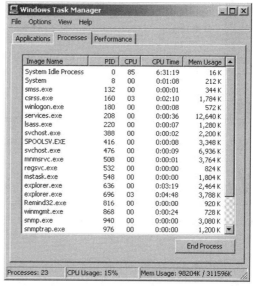

Figure 12-6: Task Manager, Processes Tab

This tab also enables you to set a particular process to be performed by a certain processor. This is accomplished by right-clicking the process and setting the affinity, as discussed earlier. This tab can end a process, end the process tree, or set the priority of the process. It may be necessary to end a process when it starts improperly or freezes. It is necessary to note that, by default, all DOS and Windows 16-bit applications run in the same memory space, called ntvdm.exe. This is important because if one of these applications freezes, then it may affect the other 16-bit applications. Also, note that each 32-bit application runs in its own address space. This ensures that if one 32-bit application freezes, it does not affect the other 32-bit applications.

You have a Windows 2000 Professional computer named PRO1 that is currently running two 16-bit applications. Users access one of the 16-bit applications with app1.exe and the other one with app2.exe. Both of these applications are configured to run in separate memory spaces. You want to create a chart in the System Monitor utility and add the two 16-bit applications, but you are having problems identifying them. Which process will enable you to properly monitor the two 16-bit applications?

Challenge #4

One of your Windows 2000 Professional computers is having problems running a custom application called App1.exe. After you start this application you use Task Manager to review the progress. You notice that when App1.exe is started it starts two child processes: Pro1 and Pro2. You also notice that Pro2 starts one child process: Pro1a. You let the application run a little and you notice that the processor queue is now 4. What steps should you take to eliminate the application as quickly as possible?

As we stated before, The Processes tab can enable you to change the process priority, which will allocate more memory for processes to run in. You may wish to do this if you want a particular process to run quicker than other processes. *To change the priority of a process, right-click the process and select Set Priority from the pop-up menu.* You can select the following priorities—Realtime, High, Abovenormal, Normal, Belownormal, and Low. Be extremely careful when you select a priority, because it can affect the overall performance of your system.

By default, all applications run in Normal mode. Realtime is used for system processes. If you change an application, such as Word, to a Realtime priority, it could affect the system's stability and cause your system to crash. There is also a command-line utility that can be used to change process priority. *The START command is used for this purpose and can be used with the switches listed in Table 12-5.* We have only listed the important switches.

You are the administrator for a Windows 2000 network. You are responsible for monitoring all the Windows 2000 Professional computers in the network. You use the System Monitor to check each computer for bottlenecks. You also download the performance logs into Microsoft Excel. Each time you use Microsoft Excel on a particular computer, it appears to be slow in servicing users' requests. What should you do?

Table 12-5: Start Command-Line Utility Switches

Switch	Description
/low	Used to start an application in low (idle) priority.
/normal	Used to start an application in normal (default) priority.
/high	Used to start an application in high priority.
/Realtime	Used to start an application in real-time priority. You will normally not use this priority because it may adversely affect your system.
/min	Used to start an application in a minimized window.
/max	Used to start an application in a maximized window.
/separate	Used to start a 16-bit application (DOS) in a separate memory space.

EXAM TIP: Read carefully the Challenges in this section and be able to solve them. Remember, Challenges are the same as EXAM TIPS. Also know how and why to change a process priority with Task Manager and the command-line "START" command. Finally, memorize the switches that can be used with the Start command and know what each will accomplish.

Performance Tab

You can use the Performance tab daily to track the computer's CPU and memory usage. This tab provides a graphical display of information, which is preconfigured and is always available for you to quickly check the CPU and memory utilization. The Performance tab is shown in Figure 12-7.

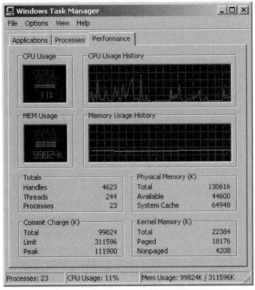

Figure 12-7: Task Manager, Performance Tab

OPTIMIZING APPLICATION PERFORMANCE

If your Windows 2000 Professional computer runs multiple applications at the same time, some of the applications will be given priority. Specifically, foreground applications, by default, are processed (given priority) before background applications. As you have already seen, an application's priority can be changed in the Processes tab of the Task Manager dialog box. You should also recall that you can use the START command to change the priority of applications. There is a third way to change the priority of an application. You can change the priority of foreground and background applications through the Control Panel by double-clicking the System icon, selecting the Advanced tab, and clicking the "Performance Options" button. This will open the *Performance Options dialog box, shown in Figure 12-8.*

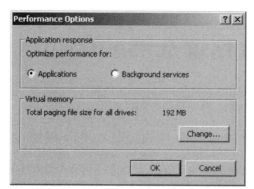

Figure 12-8: Performance Options Dialog Box

In Figure 12-8, the "Applications" radio button is selected. This means that foreground applications are given a higher priority than background applications. One interesting point to note is that if you choose the "Background services" radio button, both foreground and background applications receive the same priority.

You are locally administering a Windows 2000 Professional computer. A very processor-intensive application will run on this computer and must use as much processor time as possible. What can you do to ensure that this application receives as much processor time as possible?

Challenge #7

EXAM TIP: Know that the Performance Options dialog box is used to change the priority of foreground and background applications.

USING THE TASK SCHEDULER UTILITY

The Task Scheduler utility enables you to schedule certain tasks to run automatically at particular times. Most people use this utility to run antivirus software, the defragmentation utility, and the Disk Checker utility. The Task Scheduler utility is accessed through the Control Panel by double-clicking the Scheduled Tasks icon. We won't go through the entire process, but rather we will concentrate on the important points associated with this utility. After you select the "Add Scheduled Task" icon, you will be led through a number of wizard screens. *The most important screen is shown in Figure 12-9. This is where the user name and password that will be used to run the scheduled event are entered. This is important because if you use the wrong user account, the task will not run properly.* Normally, the Administrator account is used when scheduling most recurring tasks.

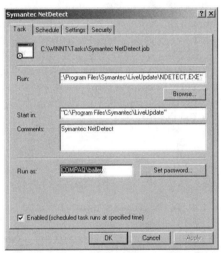

Figure 12-9: Scheduled Task Wizard, User Name and Password to Run Task

EXAM TIP: Know that when you use the Task Scheduler utility to automatically run a particular task, you must use the proper user account to ensure the task is automatically performed.

1. James is a software engineer responsible for three Windows 2000 Professional computers. He wants to load the latest service pack on one of the Windows 2000 Professional computers, but he thinks that it may already be installed. He needs to verify which service pack is currently loaded on the computer. Which of the following command-line utilities can he use?

   a. spverif

   b. winver

   c. verifsp

   d. spconfirm

2. You are responsible for installing software on all the Windows 2000 computers in the network. You update the Service Pack on a Windows 2000 Professional computer and then add Terminal Services. Which of the following must now be performed on the Windows 2000 Professional computer?

   a. Reinstall the last service pack.

   b. No additional action is needed.

   c. Reinstall the operating system.

   d. Reinstall the Terminal Services.

3. You are responsible for ensuring that the 20 Windows 2000 Professional operating systems are current at all times. You plan to use the Windows Update service to make sure the computers receive the most current updates. Which of the following items is the only requirement to use the Windows Update service?

   a. The server needs to be a domain controller.

   b. An Internet connection

   c. The server needs to be a DNS server.

   d. The server needs to be a WINS server.

4. You are the administrator of a large Windows 2000 network. The network has three remote sites, with many Windows 2000 Professional computers at each site. None of the remote sites has an administrator assigned. You must configure each site to automatically notify the other sites that updates are available when an administrator logs on to the computers remotely. Which of the following will provide the automatic notifications?
   a. Installing the Windows 2000 Resource Kit
   b. Installing the Windows Critical Update Notification utility
   c. Configuring system file checker to notify the branch offices
   d. Configuring Windows file protection to notify the branch offices

5. You are the network administrator for a Windows 2000 network. Your network has five Windows 2000 Professional computers. You notice that one computer is reacting slowly to client requests and you decide to use the System Monitor utility to identify where the system bottlenecks are. In System Monitor you notice the following counters:

   % Processor Time (Average): 50%
   Processor Queue Length (Average): 1
   Pages /sec (Average): 10
   Average Disk sec/Transfer: 0.8
   Disk Queue Length (Average): 4

   Which of the following is the most likely bottleneck?
   a. Memory
   b. Processor
   c. Physical disk
   d. Network adapter

6. You have a Windows 2000 Professional computer named PRO1 that is currently running two 16-bit applications. Users access one of the 16-bit applications with app1.exe and the other one with app2.exe. Both of these applications are configured to run in separate memory spaces. You want to create a chart in the System Monitor utility and add the two 16-bit applications. However, you are having problems identifying them. Which of the following processes will enable you to properly monitor the two 16-bit applications?

    a. Add the app1 and app2 instances of the %processor time counter for the process object.

    b. Add the ntvdm, app1, and app2 instances of the %processor time counter for the process object.

    c. Add only the ntvdm instances of the %processor time counter for the process object.

    d. Add the ntvdm and ntvdm2 instances of the %processor time counter for the process object.

7. John is having a problem with one of his Windows 2000 Professional computers. He decides to use the Performance Logs and Alerts utility to create logs to identify system bottlenecks. He knows he will have to use System Monitor to view the logs. While in the System Monitor utility, he wants to close the utility but he is not sure the logs will continue to be written. Which of the following is the correct answer?

    a. You can't close System Monitor when it has logs in it.

    b. Nothing happens: The logs will not be produced.

    c. Closing System Monitor will not stop logs from being produced.

    d. Closing the Performance Logs and Alerts utility will stop logging.

8. Carl is the network manager for a Windows 2000 network that runs some very old DOS programs. One of these DOS programs, called CHART.EXE, will not run properly unless it starts in its own memory space. Which of the following commands will enable you to start the CHART.EXE program in its own memory space?

    a. run /separate chart.exe

    b. run /min chart.exe

    c. start /separate chart.exe

    d. start /min chart.exe

9. One of your Windows 2000 Professional computers is having problems running a custom application called App1.exe. After you start this application, you use Task Manager to review its progress. You notice that when App1.exe is started it also starts two child processes: Pro1 and Pro2. You also notice that Pro2 starts one child process: Pro1a. You let the application run a little and you notice that the processor queue is now 4. Which of the following actions must you perform to completely close the application and the child processes?

a. Use the Applications tab in Task Manager and select the custom application. From the context menu of the application, select Go To Process from the context menu of that process, and set the priority to AboveNormal.

b. Use the Processes tab in Task Manager to select each process of the application that has a child process (App1 and Pro2). From the context menu of App1 and Pro2, select Kill Process.

c. Use the Applications tab in Task Manager to select the custom application. From the context menu of the application, select Go To Process. From the context menu of that process, select Kill Process.

d. On the Applications tab in Task Manager, select the custom application. From the context menu of the application, select Go To Process. From the context menu of that process, select Kill Process Tree.

10. Cindy is the new software engineer for your Windows 2000 network. She just created a new custom application and now wants to monitor the Windows 2000 Professional computer that it is running on to make sure it operates properly. She believes that the processor is overtaxed, but wants to make sure. She accesses the Task Manager, but does not know which counters to monitor to determine whether another processor is needed. Which of the following counters should she monitor? (Select two answers.)

a. Processor > %Processor Time
b. Processor > %Usage counter
c. Processor > Interrupts/Sec
d. Processor > Pages/Sec

11. You are the administrator for a Windows 2000 network. You are responsible for monitoring all the Windows 2000 Professional computers on the network. You use the System Monitor to check each server for bottlenecks. You also download the performance logs into Microsoft Excel. Each time you use Microsoft Excel on a particular server, is appears to be slow in servicing users' requests. Which of the following processes will enable this server to place more priority on servicing requests from users?

    a. Run the start /normal Csrss.exe command before you start Excel.
    b. Run the start /normal Excel.exe command to start Excel.
    c. Use Task Manager to set the priority of the Csrss.exe proccess to above normal.
    d. Use Task Manager to set the priority of the Excel.exe proccess to low.

12. You are the administrator of a small Windows 2000 network. You have a Windows 2000 Professional system with two processors installed. This computer runs two applications that are very processor-intensive. You would like to have each processor handle an application. Which of the following will permit you to assign an application to one processor exclusively?

    a. Right-click on the application executable, select Properties, and select Assign processor.
    b. Right-click on the application process in Task Manager, select Set Affinity, and select the appropriate processor.
    c. Open Task Manager, choose options from the taskbar, select Processor, and assign processes to appropriate processor.
    d. Open Task Manager, chose Performance, choose View all processors, and assign processes to appropriate processor.

13. Donald is the network engineer for your Windows 2000 network. He has a Windows 2000 Professional computer that is running a mission-critical application that is not operating properly. The application is currently running at Normal priority and he wants to configure it to run using the maximum available resources. Using Task Manager, how will Donald accomplish this task?

    a. Right-click the process, select Set priority, and select Low.
    b. Right-click the process, select Set priority, and select High.
    c. Right-click the process, select Set priority, and select Normal.
    d. Right-click the process, select Set priority, and select Realtime.

Optimizing Windows 2000 Professional   **317**

14. You must use Task Manager to stop a rogue application. Which of the following actions will enable you to stop a process?
    a. On the Processes tab in Task Manager, select the process you want to stop and click the End Process button.
    b. Select the process you want to stop in Performance Monitor, right-click, and choose End Process.
    c. Select the process you want to stop in System Monitor, right-click, and choose End Process.
    d. Select the process you want to stop in Explorer, right-click, and choose End Process.

15. You are locally administering a Windows 2000 Professional computer. A very processor-intensive application will run on this computer, but requires as much processor time as possible. Which of the following will ensure this application receives as much processor time as possible?
    a. Put the logged-on user in the Power Users group so that system rights will be increased.
    b. In the system's Environment Variables dialog box, in Control Panel, increase the amount of RAM for user applications.
    c. Under the system's Property sheet found in Control Panel, increase the Paging File initial size to the value currently in the maximum size available in the Performance Options dialog box.
    d. Under the system's Property sheet found in Control Panel, choose the Advanced tab and make sure Applications receive the foreground priority.

Answers and Explanations

1. **b.** The command-line utility winver is used to verify which service pack has been installed.

2. **b.** Because of the slipstreaming process you do not have to reinstall the last service pack in Windows 2000. In Windows NT 4.0 it was a common thing to reinstall a service pack when a new service pack was installed.

3. **b.** The only requirement is to have a connection to the Internet.

4. **b.** Installing the Windows Critical Update Notification utility will ensure that the network sites are notified automatically when the administrator logs on to the server.

5. **c.** In this case the physical disk value is too high and you should consider using faster disks and controllers or use disk striping. If the Current Disk Queue is higher than 2, then you need to take action to lower this. Memory does not seem to be the problem in this case. If the Pages/Sec counter's value is below 20, there is no problem. The optimal performance for this counter should be 4 to 5. The processor does not appear to be the problem in this case. If the %Processor Time averages above 80%, you may have to upgrade the processor.

6. **d.** You can monitor the performance of 16-bit MS-DOS-based applications. However, they are difficult to identify as instances because the program name does not appear. This is because each MS-DOS-based application shows up in its own DOS Machine (NTVDM). You would have to look at the individual threads for the Ntvdm.exe application. An easy way to identify the thread associated with the application you want to monitor is to stop all other 16-bit MS-DOS-based applications and choose the remaining thread. 16-bit Windows-based applications execute in one NTVDM by default, but can be started in separate NTVDMs.

7. **c.** Because the logs were created in the Performance Logs and Alerts utility, the data will continue to log data even if the System Monitor is closed.

8. **c.** The start /separate chart.exe will start the program in its own memory space. Answers a. and b. are incorrect because the command is "start" and not run. Answer d. is incorrect because the start /min will start the program in a minimized window.

9. **b.** This is the best solution. The processes App1 and Pro2 each have child processes, and if you stop these (parent) processes it will automatically stop the child processes.

10. **a, c.** The Processor>%Processor Time counter measures the time that the processor spends responding to system requests. If this counter is consistently above an average of 80%, you may have a processor bottleneck. The Processor>Interrupts/Sec counter shows the average number of hardware interrupts the processor receives each second. If this value is more than 3,500 on a Pentium computer you might have a problem. The Pages/Sec counter is used for memory, and not the processor.

11. **d.** You would use the Task Manager utility to change the priority of the Excel.exe process to low. Changing the priority of a process can make it run faster or slower (depending on whether you raise or lower the priority), but it can also adversely affect the performance of other processes. To change the priority of a process, use the Processes tab and right-click the program you want to change. Point to Set Priority, and then click the option you want.

12. **b.** To assign a process to a processor, use the Processes tab and right-click the process you want to assign. Then click Set Affinity, and click one or more processors. The Set Affinity command is available only on multiprocessor computers. Using the Set Affinity command limits the execution of the program or process to the selected processors and may decrease overall performance.

13. **d.** Setting the priority to Realtime will give the process the highest priority, but this setting may affect the system processes. We would not recommend any setting other than Normal. Setting the priority to Normal is the default and will not change the priority. Even though setting the priority of the process to High will give it a higher priority, it may affect the processes of the system. Setting the priority for the process to Low will make the process run even slower.

14. **a.** While in Task Manager use the Processes tab and click the End Process button. The question calls for the use of Task Manager, not Performance Monitor. You cannot use Performance Monitor to stop processes. It can only be used to monitor the computer's performance. System Monitor and Windows Explorer cannot be used to stop processes.

15. **d.** There are various ways to increase the priority of an application, such as by right-clicking the task in Task Manager and increasing the priority. You can also use the START command to increase the priority. But these are not possible answers. In this case you would use the system's Properties dialog box, Advanced tab, and make sure the "Applications" radio button is selected.

Challenge Solutions

1. Closing System Monitor will not stop logs from being produced by the Performance Logs and Alerts utility.

2. Looking at Table 12-2 you can see that one counter is that the Processor>%Processor Time counter, which measures the time that the processor spends responding to system requests. If this counter is consistently above an average of 80%, you may have a processor bottleneck. The other counter is Processor>Interrupts/Sec, which shows the average number of hardware interrupts the processor receives each second. If this value is more than 3,500 on a Pentium computer, you might have a problem. The Pages/Sec counter is used for memory and not the processor.

3. In this case, the physical disk counter is too high and you should consider using faster hard disks, adding another disk controller, or using disk striping. If the Current Disk Queue is higher than 2, then you need to take action to lower this. Memory does not seem to be the problem in this case. If the Pages/Sec counter's value is below 20, there is no problem. The optimal performance for this counter should be 4 to 5. The processor does not appear to be the problem in this case. If the %Processor Time averages above 80%, you may have to upgrade the processor.

4. You can monitor the performance of 16-bit MS-DOS-based applications. However, they are difficult to identify as instances because the program name does not appear. This is because each MS-DOS-based application shows up in its own DOS Machine (NTVDM). You would have to look at the individual threads (that is, "Thread Processor Time") for the NTVDM.EXE application. An easy way to identify the thread associated with the application you want to monitor is to stop all other 16-bit MS-DOS-based applications and choose the remaining thread. 16-bit Windows-based applications execute in one NTVDM by default, but can be started in separate NTVDMs.

5. On the Processes tab in Task Manager, select each process of the application that has child processes (App1 and Pro2). From the context menu of App1 and Pro2, select Kill Process.

6. You should use the Task Manager utility to change the priority of the Excel.exe process to low. Changing the priority of a process can make it run faster or slower (depending on whether you raise or lower the priority), but it can also adversely affect the performance of other processes. In this case you would set the priority to low so it does not interfere with the users' requests.

7. Under the system's Property sheet found in Control Panel, choose the Advanced tab, and make sure that applications receive the foreground priority. This is done by selecting the "Applications" radio button.

Chapter 13

System Recovery

These are the areas that are generally testable on the MCSE Server 2000 examination:

1. Recover System State and user data.

   - Recover System State data and user data by using Windows Backup.

   - Troubleshoot system restoration by starting in Safe Mode.

   - Recover System State data and user data by using the Recovery Console.

2. Manage and optimize availability of System State data and user data.

System Recovery

Chapter **13**

Introduction

As a good network administrator, you must have a system recovery plan in the event that a computer will not boot. One of your tools is the Event Viewer. This utility has different logs that can be used to troubleshoot the failed system.

To recover from a system failure, you must become familiar with the bootup process. In this chapter, you will learn the most important stages of the bootup process along with the potential errors that can occur during system startup.

You will also be shown how to use the Advanced Startup options to help get the computer up and running. The most important options are—Safe Mode and the Last Known Good Configuration.

You will also be given real-world challenges to help you troubleshoot your network. You will learn how to recover a system using the Windows 2000 Professional Setup Boot disks. These will enable you to utilize the Recovery Console, the Emergency Repair Disk, or to reinstall the operating system.

As a last resort, backups can be used to restore your data. You must know which utility will permit you to perform backups.

SYSTEM RECOVERY

A good network administrator should be able to recover in the event a computer system will not boot. A computer that will not start can be your worst nightmare, especially if you do not have a current backup. To assist you in the system recovery process, you must be proactive and plan for system failure. This plan should include—scheduled system backups, antivirus software, monitoring Event Viewer utility entries, and other troubleshooting techniques. The first item we will discuss is the Event Viewer utility.

Event Viewer

The Event Viewer utility, depicted in Figure 13-1, is used to monitor problems with your computer's hardware and software. This utility also has a log to help you monitor the system's security. It can be accessed through the Administrative Tools folder by selecting the Event Viewer. Table 13-1 illustrates the three log files included with this utility.

System Recovery

325

Table 13-1: Event Viewer Logs

Event Viewer Log	Description
Application Log	This log is used to monitor events pertaining to the applications operating on your computer.
System Log	This log is used to monitor events pertaining to the Windows 2000 operating system.
Security Log	*This log is used to monitor events pertaining to auditing.*

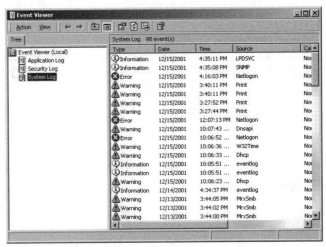

Figure 13-1: The Event Viewer

As you can see, the System Log is shown in Figure 13-1. Notice that this log lists all the events that have been recorded pertaining to the Windows 2000 Professional operating system. The events are listed with the newest entries first. This can be a little deceiving because an older event could have caused a current problem, but it is listed below the most recent events. When we troubleshoot systems using the Event Viewer, we start at the bottom and work our way up the log. Different types of events are listed, such as information, warning, error, success audit, and failure audit events. You can get more information for an event by clicking it. This brings up the Event Properties dialog box, shown in Figure 13-2.

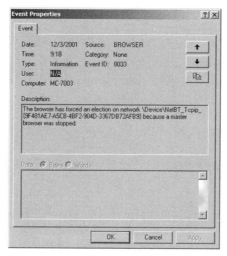

Figure 13-2:
Event Viewer,
Event Properties
Dialog Box

EXAM TIP: Know that the Security Log in the Event Viewer is used to monitor events pertaining to auditing. Don't forget the real-world Challenges. Treat them as **EXAM TIPs.**

The Boot Process

In order to properly troubleshoot a failed system, you must understand the boot process. The boot process starts when you turn on the computer and finishes when the user logs on to the network. We have listed the most important steps in the boot process—the Preboot sequence and the Boot sequence.

Preboot Sequence

Table 13-2 lists the most common problems encountered during the preboot sequence. As its name implies, the preboot sequence starts when the computer is turned on and prepares for the booting of the operating system. It ends when the NTLDR file, which is used to control the boot process, is accessed. Here are the preboot sequence steps:

- After the computer is turned on, a Power On Self Test (POST) routine is performed. This routine actually checks and configures the hardware located on the computer.

- At the end of the POST routine, the Basic Input/Output System (BIOS) locates and loads the Master Boot Record (MBR) into memory. The MBR points to the active partition, which is used to actually boot the system.

Table 13-2: Preboot Sequence Errors

Error	Description
Corrupt or missing NTLDR file	The NTLDR file is corrupt or has been deleted. This file can be restored with the ERD, or the Recovery Console. These utilities are discussed later in this chapter.
Corrupt member	This usually occurs due to a malicious virus. You must restore the MBR with the ERD or the Recovery Console.
No partition is marked as active	If the active partition is not marked as Active, the system will not boot. You would correct this error by running the partitioning program and marking the active partition.

The Boot Sequence

The boot sequence is the actual process that boots up the system. We have listed below the files that are used during the boot sequence. Table 13-3 identifies the most common problems that can occur during this phase.

- *BOOT.INI* – This file is used to point to the boot partition.

- *BOOTSECT.DOS* – This file is used if you have chosen to load an operating system other than Windows 2000.

- *NTDETECT.COM* – This file detects all the hardware installed in the computer and places information about the hardware into the Registry.

- *NTBOOTDD.SYS* – This file is only used when there is a SCSI adapter with the onboard BIOS disabled.

- *NTOSKRNL.EXE* – This file is used to load the Windows 2000 operating system.

Table 13-3: Boot Sequence Errors

Error	Description
Improperly configured BOOT.INI file	This error will occur if you have made disk configurations and the computer will not boot. This file points to the boot partition.
Missing or corrupt boot files	If any of the files loaded during the boot sequence are corrupt, or missing, the boot process will fail. The files can be restored with the ERD or with the Recovery Console (covered later in this chapter).
Unrecognized or improperly configured hardware	If your computer has hardware that is improperly configured, or that is not supported by your operating system, you will receive this error message. You may need to use the Recovery Console to fix the problem.

Configuring the BOOT.INI File

As stated earlier, the BOOT.INI file points to the boot partition of the operating system that will be loaded in the boot sequence. If you make changes to your disk configuration, you must change this file to ensure that it is pointing at the proper partition. When you do make changes to your disk configuration, you will receive a message stating that the BOOT.INI needs to be changed. Table 13-4 describes the BOOT.INI ARC (Advanced RISC Computing) naming convention.

Table 13-4: ARC Naming Convention

Option	Description
multi (w) or scsi (w)	Used to identify the type of disk controller used in the system. The scsi option is used when SCSI adapters do not use the SCSI BIOS. The multi option is used when IDE controllers and SCSI adapters use the SCSI BIOS. The (w) is the number of the hardware adapter you are booting from.
disk (x)	Identifies the SCSI adapter that you are booting from when you use the scsi option. If you use the multi option, this is always 0.
rdisk (y)	Used to identify the number of the physical disks to be used. For IDE controllers, this will be the ordinal of the disk attached to the controller and will be either 0 or 1. For SCSI, this will be the ordinal of the SCSI drive.
partition (z)	Identifies the partition that has the operating system on it. The first partition is always 1.

NOTE: Here is an example of what a BOOT.INI file should look like:

Multi(0)disk(0)rdisk(0)partition(2)\WINNT= "Microsoft Windows 2000 Professional"

This is how it breaks down:

- Multi(0) means an IDE controller or a SCSI controller with the BIOS enabled.

- Disk(0) means it is always 0 when the multi option is used.

- Rdisk(0) means that the first disk on the controller is to be used.

- Partition(2) identifies the system partition as the second partition.

- The rest of the file indicates the folder where the system's files are stored and the operating system that the user sees in the boot menu.

EXAM TIP: Currently, the structure of the BOOT.INI file has not been seen much on the exam. However, this area was hit very hard in Windows NT 4.0 and may return to the Windows 2000 Professional exam.

Advanced Startup Options

The Windows 2000 advanced startup options are provided to help you troubleshoot problems that keep your system from booting properly. You can access these options by pressing the F8 key at system startup. We will list the most important startup options.

- *Safe Mode* – If you are not sure why your computer will not boot, you should use this option to enable you to boot into the Windows 2000 Professional operating system. Running Safe Mode only installs the files and drivers for the mouse, monitor, keyboard, hard drive, standard video, and default system services. This mode will not provide all the normal services, because it is used to help you troubleshoot your most basic system problems and hopefully, identify the problem. After you boot into Safe Mode, it is a good idea to use the Control Panel to check your configuration settings.

- **LastKnownGoodConfiguration* – You normally use this option to restore the system configuration settings from the last time the computer was successfully booted. This option is used when you have improperly configured the computer and it will not boot. One word of caution: When you use this option, you lose any configuration changes that were made after the last time the computer was successfully booted.

Setup Boot Disks

As discussed earlier, the *Setup boot disks* are used to boot to the Windows 2000 Professional operating system when it won't boot on its own. You normally use these when you need to reinstall the Windows 2000 Professional operating system and do not have access to a CD-ROM drive. These disks can also be used to access the Recovery Console and an ERD. The Windows Professional Setup boot disks are not computer-specific, so you can create them on any computer running Windows 2000 Professional. As a side note, these Setup boot disks will not work for Windows 2000 Server. Remember, you need four floppy disks to create the Setup boot disks. Also, as explained earlier, you must use the MAKEBT32.EXE to make boot disks from Windows 2000 or Windows 9x. Likewise, you must use the MAKEBOOT.EXE command to make them from a 16-bit operating system.

Windows 2000 Backup Utility

The *Windows 2000 Backup utility* enables you to create and restore backups of important programs and data. It is also used to create an Emergency Repair Disk (ERD). A backup is a copy of your data stored on another hard drive or a tape. If your original data is lost, or becomes corrupt, you can restore the data from the backup media. The ERD can be used to restore your system configuration information. The Backup utility can be accessed through the Start>Programs>Accessories>System Tools>Backup path. This will bring up the Backup dialog box, illustrated in Figure 13-3.

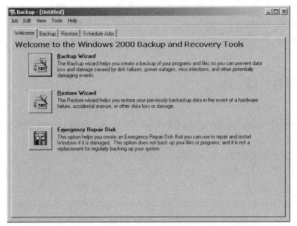

Figure 13-3: Backup Dialog Box

Backup Wizard

One important point about the Backup utility is that in order to properly use it, you must be logged on as an Administrator or as a member of the Backup Operators group. When you click on the Backup Wizard button, shown in Figure 13-3, the first screen produced will be the Windows 2000 Backup and Recovery Tools dialog box. Click the Next button to begin the backup process. Notice that the next screen is the What to Back Up dialog box, shown in Figure 13-4. There are three options to choose from—Back up everything on my computer, Back up selected files, drives, or network data, and Only back up the System State data. We will discuss exactly what the System State data includes in the next section.

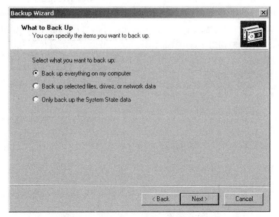

Figure 13-4: What to Back Up Dialog Box

- *System State data* – ***When you back up the System State data, you are backing up the Registry, system boot files, and COM+ Class Registration database.*** There is only one problem in backing up and restoring the System State data—**you can only back up and restore the System State data on a local computer.** You cannot back up and restore the System State data on a remote computer.

- *Backup types* – There are five different types of backup, as described in Table 13-5. The type of backup you should choose depends on how much data is being backed up and how often you wish to perform a backup operation. We have listed only the backup types you need to know.

Table 13-5: Backup Types

Option	Description
Normal	Backs up all files and sets the archive bit as marked for each file.
Differential	Backs up only the files that have not been marked as archived. This type does not set the archive bit for each file that is backed up. To restore with this method you must have the last normal backup and the last differential tape.
Incremental	Backs up only the files that have not been marked as archived and sets the archive bit for each file that is backed up. To restore with this method, you must have the last normal backup and all of the incremental tapes that have been created since the last normal backup.

Emergency Repair Disk

The *Emergency Repair Disk (ERD)* is used when your computer will not boot or
when you need to repair system files. The ERD should be created when the Windows
2000 Professional operating system is first installed. After that, each time the system
configuration changes, you should update the ERD. The ERD can be used to repair the
basic system, system files, the partition boot sector, and the Registry. All of these items
can be repaired, but will only be updated back to the date that the last ERD was updated.

The ERD can be created by clicking the Emergency Repair Disk button in the Backup
dialog box, shown in Figure 13-3. After you press this button, you will be prompted to
insert a blank, formatted floppy disk and choose whether to back up the Registry. The
reason you have an option to select the Registry is because it may not fit on one disk.
*One important item to know is that the ERD is not bootable and, in order to
access it, you must first use the Windows 2000 Professional Setup boot
disks or the Windows 2000 Professional Setup CD to start the system.*
Another important item to consider is that in Windows NT 4.0 the ERD was created with
the RDISK command, which is not available in Windows 2000.

Recovery Console

The Recovery Console is a new feature in Windows 2000 Professional. This utility will
provide you with very limited access to the volumes. When you enter the Recovery
Console, you are not actually booted into the operating system. Instead, you are
provided a command prompt-like interface to enable you to fix your operating system
and provide a normal boot sequence. You normally use the Recovery Console after you
have tried Save Mode and any other troubleshooting methods available. We have
highlighted below the important tasks that can be performed in the Recovery Console.

- *You can format existing partitions or create a new partition.* You would
  perform this function if you were unable to format or create a partition in any
  other manner.

- ***From this console you can fix the MBR.*** This is useful if a malicious virus infects the member on your disks.

- *You can copy, replace, or rename operating system files.* Don't read too much into this type of access. ***Your access is limited, because you cannot copy files from the local drive to a floppy disk.*** This is done for security reasons. You can, however, copy from the floppy disk or CD to the hard drive, or from the hard drive to another hard drive.

- ***The Recovery Console also enables you to enable or disable services and drivers.*** You would disable a service or driver when it prevents you from successfully booting into the operating system.

The Recovery Console can be accessed in two ways. The first way is from the Windows 2000 Professional setup boot disks. To start the process, you would insert the first disk and restart your computer. Then you would ***change the disks when prompted until you arrive at the Welcome to Setup dialog box. At this point, press R to repair the Windows 2000 installation. You will then see a Windows 2000 Repair Options menu. At this time, press C to enter the Recovery Console.***

The second way to enter the Recovery Console is to add the Recovery Console to the Windows 2000 Professional startup options. One word of caution about doing this: In order to use this option you must have installed the Recovery Console before system failure. You can install this option by inserting the Windows 2000 Professional CD and typing ***WINNT32 /CMDCONS*** at the command prompt. This will take you into the installation process. The next time you reboot, the Recovery Console will be added to the Windows 2000 Professional startup options. You cannot add the Recovery Console using the Add/Remove Programs utility. Table 13-6 lists the most important commands that can be used in the Recovery Console.

Table 13-6: Recovery Console Commands

Command	Description
CHKDSK	Used to check your hard drive for errors.
COPY	Used to copy one file to another location, but you cannot copy from the hard drive to a floppy disk.
DISABLE	Used to disable problem services and drivers.
ENABLE	Used to enable required services and drivers.
FIXBOOT	Used to fix the boot sector.
FIXMBR	Used to fix the MBR.
FORMAT	Used to format a partition.

NOTE: We have not listed all the commands that can be performed in the Recovery Console. *You should know that the "EDIT" command cannot be used here for security reasons.*

Challenge #7

Joseph is a professional systems recovery technician for your Windows 2000 network. The network has one Windows 2000 Professional computer that provides mission-critical services to the network users. He installs a tape drive on this computer using the driver that was provided by the manufacturer. After the tape drive has been installed, he reboots the computer and receives this stop error: "irq1_not_less_or_equal". He knows that the device driver for the new tape drive is causing this problem. What process will enable Joseph to fix the problem and return the computer to proper operation?

EXAM TIP: Know how to access the Recovery Console. Also, know how to install the Recovery Console. Then know what access to the system the Recovery Console will provide. Finally, memorize which commands can be performed.

1. Gerry is the system recovery expert currently assigned to your Windows 2000 network. The network has five Windows 2000 Servers and 50 Windows 2000 Professional clients. He has one Windows 2000 Professional computer that is displaying an error message. Because the message is not clear, he does not know where to start the troubleshooting process. Which of the following actions will enable Gerry to obtain additional information about what the problem may be?
    a. Check Event Viewer.
    b. Run the NT Diagnostics utility.
    c. Review the Registry.
    d. Run the diagnostics.exe.

2. You are the administrator for a Windows 2000 network configured for auditing of the success or failure of particular events. The network consists of five Windows 2000 Server computers and 100 Windows 2000 Professional client computers. Which feature will enable you to check the success or failure of events using the Event Viewer?
    a. System log
    b. Security log
    c. Application log
    d. System Security log
    e. Application System log

3. Jeff is the technical expert in charge of system recovery of his Windows 2000 network. He configured each Windows 2000 Professional computer with a separate system partition and boot partition. Both are formatted with NTFS. In the afternoon he reboots one of the computers and receives the error message—"NTLDR is missing, press any key to restart". Jeff must install a new NTLDR and he must ensure that he does not lose any previous system configuration settings. Which of the following processes should he use?
    a. Start the system with the CD-ROM and choose to repair the installation. Then use the Recovery Console and copy the NTLDR from the CD-ROM to the system root.
    b. Start the system with the CD-ROM and choose to reinstall. After installation, copy the NTLDR to the system root.
    c. Start the computer by using the Windows 2000 bootable floppy disk. From the command prompt run the sfc/scanboot command.
    d. Start the computer by using the Windows 2000 bootable floppy disk. Run the file signature verification utility.

4. Tommy, the system recovery guru, installs Windows 2000 Professional on a new computer. He then reboots and the system freezes. He wants to use the Recovery Console, but is not sure of what commands he can use once he's in the utility. Which of the following actions can be accomplished in the Recovery Console? (Select all that apply.)
   a. Copying the boot files from the hard drive to a floppy
   b. Copying the boot files from a floppy to the hard drive
   c. Repairing the MBR for the computer
   d. Formatting partitions

5. Jimmy is the Registry expert on your Windows 2000 network. He has a Windows 2000 Professional computer that he wants to test some system configuration enhancements on. In particular, he wants to improve the TCP transmission speed on this computer. He decides to use the Regedit32 utility to configure an entry for the TCPWindowSize. He makes the change and restarts the computer. The computer boots up to the logon screen, but then it freezes. He believes that his Registry change is the problem and he wants to return the computer to its previous configuration. Which of the following will enable Jimmy to accomplish his goal?
   a. Restart the computer in Safe Mode. Then restart the computer again.
   b. Restart the computer by using the Recovery Console. Run the Fixboot C: command, and then run the Exit command.
   c. Restart the computer by using the Recovery Console. Run the enable winlogon service_auto_start command, and then run the Exit command.
   d. Restart the computer by using the Last Known Good Configuration.

6. Jerry is responsible for performing backups on your Windows 2000 network. All the computers are running Windows 2000 Professional. He needs to perform a weekly backup, making sure that it includes the following items: the Registry, boot files, and COM+. Which of the following is the best choice to ensure the weekly backup includes the required items?
   a. Create a batch file to run RDISK.EXE /s before the backup starts.
   b. Create a batch file to run RDISK.EXE /s after the backup is started.
   c. Configure the Backup utility to back up the System State data.
   d. Configure the Backup utility to back up the system partition.

7. Joseph is a professional systems recovery technician for your Windows 2000 network. The network has one Windows 2000 Professional computer that provides mission-critical services to the network users. He installs a tape drive on this computer using the driver that was provided by the manufacturer. After the tape drive is installed, he reboots the computer and receives the stop error—"irq1_not_less_or_equal". He now knows that the device driver for the new tape drive has been causing this problem. Which of the following processes will enable Joseph to fix the problem and return the computer to operation?

a. Restart the computer by using the LastKnownGoodConfiguration menu option.

b. Perform an emergency repair, select fast repair, and restart the computer.

c. Restart the computer in the Safe Mode, remove the driver, and restart the computer.

d. Restart the computer by using the Recovery Console and disable the driver. Restart the computer, remove the driver.

8. Joni is a member of the Windows 2000 network backup team. She is backing up one of the network's Windows 2000 Professional computers and uses the following backup strategy for all of the data on the computer:

Saturday - Normal Backup
Monday - Differential Backup
Tuesday - Differential Backup
Wednesday - Differential Backup
Thursday - Differential Backup
Friday, the computer's hard drive fails halfway through the backup process.

Which backups would Joni use for the restoration process and in what order?

a. Saturday, Thursday

b. Saturday, Monday

c. Saturday, Monday, Tuesday, Wednesday, Thursday

d. Thursday, Wednesday, Tuesday, Monday, Saturday

9. Kenny is a member of the Backup Operators group on his Windows 2000 network. His network consists of two network segments with one Windows 2000 Server acting as a domain controller on each segment. He has two Windows 2000 Professional computers, one on each segment, called PRO1 and PRO2. Kenny has made some configuration changes to each computer and must back up the System State data on each. PRO1 has an internal tape device to perform the back ups. Which of the following is correct concerning the back up of the System State data of each computer?
    a. Back up both computers .
    b. Back up any computer on the same network segment as PRO1
    c. Back up any computer on a different segment than PRO1
    d. Back only PRO1

10. Jim is the storage manager for your Windows 2000 network. He has an older computer with Windows 2000 Professional installed. It also has a legacy SCSI adapter that is not on the HCL. He installs an updated driver for this device and reboots the computer. He is presented with this stop error—"INACCESSIBLE_BOOT_DEVICE." Which of the following can be used to correct the problem? (Select two answers.)
    a. Start the computer in Safe Mode. Reinstall the old driver for the SCSI adapter.
    b. Start the computer by using a Windows 2000 Server bootable floppy disk. Reinstall the old driver for the SCSI adapter.
    c. Start the computer by using the Windows 2000 Professional CD-ROM. Perform an emergency repair. Reinstall the old driver for the SCSI adapter.
    d. Start the computer by using the Recovery Console. Run System File Checker. Restart the computer. Reinstall the old driver for the SCSI adapter.
    e. Start the computer by using the Recovery Console. Copy the old driver for the SCSI adapter to the system volume and to C:\NTbootdd.sys. Restart the computer.

11. You have a Windows 2000 Professional computer with two IDE 3 GB hard drives installed. Each drive has three partitions with the system partition on the first partition of the first hard drive. The system partition is replicated to the second partition on the second drive. One day the first hard drive fails and you must edit the Boot.ini file so that the system partition uses the replication on the second disk. How should you configure the ARC path?
    a. multi(0)disk(0)rdisk(1)partition(2)\WINNT="Windows 2000 Professional"
    b. multi(0)disk(0)rdisk(2)partition(2)\WINNT="Windows 2000 Professional"
    c. multi(0)disk(0)rdisk(2)partition(3)\WINNT="Windows 2000 Professional"
    d. multi(0)disk(0)rdisk(1)partition(3)\WINNT="Windows 2000 Professional"

12. Jim is the storage manager for your Windows 2000 network. He has an older computer with Windows 2000 Professional installed. He needs to install a new Zip drive in this computer. The Zip drive is not on the HCL. He installs an updated driver for this device and reboots the computer. The system will not bootup. Not even Safe Mode causes the system to boot. Which of the following will enable Jim to unload the driver and return to the normal operating system? (Select three answers.)
    a. Go into Device Manager and remove the Zip drive.
    b. From the command prompt run LISTSVC to disable the Zip driver.
    c. From the Recovery Console, run DISABLE to disable the Zip driver.
    d. Select Recovery Console from the repair disk.
    e. Start the PC from the CD-ROM.

13. You are trying to use the web browser on a Windows 2000 Professional computer to manage a printer. You enter the correct URL address but are unable to see the printer. Which of the following should be performed to correct this problem?
    a. Double-click the connect hotspot in the left pane of the printer's dialog box to view the printer.
    b. Ask the branch office administrator to reinstall the printer by using its URL as the port.
    c. Install Internet Explorer 3.0 or higher on your Windows 2000 Professional.
    d. Ask the administrator at the branch office to install IIS (PWS) on the computer hosting the printer.

Answers and Explanations

1. **a.** Anytime you have a problem with the system, security, or an application, check the Event Viewer for explanations of the problems. The NT Diagnostics utility is not compatible with Windows 2000 Professional. It was used in Windows NT 4.0. If you ever use the Registry, you may find that are not be able to find anything there.

2. **b.** The Security log is used to review auditing of successes and failures. The System log is used to identify problems with the Windows 2000 System. The Application log is used to monitor problems with the applications on your computer. Answers a. and d. were made up.

3. **a.** If the boot sector cannot find Ntldr, Windows 2000 will not boot. This can be caused by moving, renaming, or deleting Ntldr, corruption of Ntldr, or corruption of the boot sector. Under these circumstances, the computer might not respond to input or might display one of the following error messages: "A disk read error occurred", "NTLDR is missing", or "NTLDR is compressed". If Ntldr is damaged or missing", or if the boot sector is corrupted, you can resolve either problem by starting the Emergency Repair Disk (ERD) and following the prompts for repairing the installation. You can also fix this problem with the Recovery Console. You cannot copy a file from the local hard disk to a floppy disk. However, you can copy a file from a floppy disk or a CD-ROM to any hard disk, and from one hard disk to another.

4. **b, c, d.** While in the Recovery Console you can repair the Master Boot Record, copy the boot files from a floppy to the hard drive, and format partitions. However, by default, you cannot copy files from the hard drive to removable media, such as a floppy disk.

5. **d.** This option will enable you to return to the configuration from the last successful reboot. This will return the Registry to its previous (working) condition. The Recovery Console does not permit you to run this command. The commands that can be performed in the Recovery Console are limited for security reasons. Also, using the Recovery Console and fixing the MBR will not accomplish the required result. In this particular situation, the boot record is not damaged. You cannot restart the computer in Safe Mode if it does not boot up to the Logon screen. In this particular case, the Registry was changed and the likelihood of it booting into Safe Mode is low.

6. **c.** Configuring the Backup utility to back up the System State data will include these files. Creating a batch file to run the RDISK.EXE /s command before or after the backup starts will not back up these files.

7. **d.** Answer a. is incorrect because you already logged on. Your current configuration now becomes the LastKnownGoodConfiguration. Answer b. won't work because it is used to repair problems related to system files, the partition boot sector, and your startup environment (if you have a dual-boot or multiple-boot system). The Recovery Console enables you to disable drivers.

8. **a.** You need to restore the last full back up and the last differential backup that occurred just prior to the drive failure.

9. **d.** You can only back up the System State data on a local computer. You cannot back up the System State data on a remote computer without third-party software.

10. **c, e.** If the boot device is inaccessible, then it is unlikely that you will be able to use Safe Mode. Disks created from the Windows 2000 Server CD cannot be used with Windows 2000 Professional. After starting a disabled computer from the setup boot disks, or from the Windows 2000 Professional CD-ROM, you can then use the Recovery Console or the Emergency Repair process.

11. **a.** Multi(0) means that you have an IDE controller that uses the SCSI BIOS. Disk(0) means that since we are using multi, this setting is always 0. Rrdisk(1) means the number of the physical disk to be used, which in an IDE environment is the ordinal of the disk attached to the controller. Partition(2) means the partition number that contains the OS.

12. **c, d, e.** This is a three-part procedure. Start the PC from CD-ROM. Then select Recovery Console from the repair disk. From the Recovery Console, run DISABLE to disable the Zip driver. Running the LISTSVC command from the command prompt will not disable the Zip driver. Going into Device Manager is not possible because you cannot boot up. It is only accessible through Windows.

13. **d.** The computer that will receive the print job over the Internet must have IIS (PWS) installed in order to receive the print job.

Challenge Solutions

1. If you want to learn more information on errors, check the Event Viewer.

2. You need to use the Event Viewer to check the success or failure of events that have auditing enabled. Review Table 13-1 and you will see that the Security log is used for this purpose.

3. Start the computer by using the Windows 2000 Professional computer CD-ROM and choose to repair the installation. Then select Recovery Console and copy the NTLDR file on the CD-ROM to the root of the system volume. Note that you can also correct this problem with the ERD.

4. The answer is multi(0)disk(0)rdisk(1)partition(2)\WINNT="Windows 2000 Professional". To explain further, multi(0) means that you have an IDE controller that uses the SCSI BIOS. Disk(0) means that since we are using multi, this setting is always 0. Rrdisk(1) means the number of the physical disk to be used, which, in an IDE environment, is the ordinal of the disk attached to the controller. Partition(2) means the partition number that contains the operating system.

5. Regardless of what configuration change has been made, you only want to return to the previous configuration. Restart the computer and, from the Advanced Startup Options menu, select the LastKnownGoodConfiguration option. You will be returned to the configuration settings that were used the last time the computer was successfully booted.

6. Simply use Windows Backup utility to back up the System State data.

7. Restart the computer by using the Recovery Console and disable the driver. Restart the computer and then remove the driver. Some of you may have wanted to use the LastKnownGoodConfiguration Advanced Startup option. This will not work because you successfully logged on and then received the error message.

8 The first procedure is to start the computer using the Windows 2000 Professional CD-ROM. Perform an emergency repair. Reinstall the old driver for the SCSI adapter. The second procedure is to start the computer using the Recovery Console. Copy the old driver for the SCSI adapter to the system volume and to C:\NTbootdd.sys, then restart the computer. With the second method, you can access the Recovery Console with the Windows 2000 Professional Setup boot disks, or from the CD-ROM.

9. First, start the PC from the CD-ROM, then select Recovery Console from the repair disk. From the Recovery Console use the DISABLE command to disable the Zip driver. Restart the system, and it should boot normally.

Index

USING THE CD-ROM

This book comes with a CD-ROM packaged inside its back cover. The CD-ROM includes test bank software that features the powerful ExamGear test engine, which provides multiple study modes that simulate the environments you'll encounter with the real MCSA/MCSE exams. This test engine provides both fixed-length and adaptive-mode versions of the exam. Practice again and again until you are really sure that you have mastered the exam material.

THE TEST BANK

This CD contains an excellent test bank of 500 questions that will help you focus on the material from the text and prepare you for the Windows 2000 70-210—Installing, Configuring, and Administering Microsoft Windows 2000 Professional certification exam. The correct answer to each question includes a detailed explanation of why the answer is correct.

The test bank features a free 150-question sample 70-210 Professional exam that will give you a feel for the real exam. You also have the option to unlock the complete 500-question test and get the full range of 70-210 specific questions for the certification. The unlock code is just *$49.95*. Simply purchase online from the eITPrep web site and get your unlock code by return e-mail. Most credit cards are accepted. Place your order at:

http://www.eitprep.com

USING THE TEST BANK

The ExamGear Test Bank is designed to be easy to use. It enables you to select from the following testing modes to efficiently prepare yourself for the exam:

- **Study Mode** - this mode enables you to select the number of questions you want to see and the amount of time you want to be allotted for the test. You can select questions from all the chapters or only from specific chapters. During the exam, you can display the correct answer to each question along with an explanation of why it is correct.

- **Practice Exam** - this mode simulates a real fixed-length MCSA/MCSE exam. Using it, you can take an exam that is designed to simulate the actual certification exam. Questions are selected from all test-objective groups. The number of questions selected and the time allotted are set to match those parameters of the actual certification exam.

- **Adaptive Exam** - this mode simulates a real adaptive-mode MCSA/MCSE exam. You can use it to take a simulation of an adaptive version of the exam. Questions are taken from all test-objective groups. The questions are presented in a way that ensures your mastery of all the test objectives. After you have a passing score, or if you reach a point where it is statistically impossible for you to pass, the exam is ended.

INSTALLING THE EXAMGEAR TEST BANK

The following section provides instructions for installing the ExamGear Test Bank product.

ExamGear requires a computer with the following:

- Microsoft Windows 95, Windows 98, Windows NT 4.0, or Windows 2000.

- A Pentium or later processor is recommended.

- Microsoft's Internet Explorer 4.01 or a later version.

Internet Explorer 4.01 (or a later version) must be installed. (Even if you use a different browser, you still need to have Internet Explorer 4.01 or later installed.)

- A minimum of 16 MB of RAM.

As with any Windows application, the more memory, the better your performance.

- A connection to the Internet.

An Internet connection is not required for the software to work, but it is required for online registration, product updates, downloading bonus question sets, and unlocking other exams.

To install the ExamGear Test Bank software on your computer, run the Setup program found on the CD and follow these instructions:

1. Insert the CD in your CD-ROM drive. The Autorun feature of Windows should automatically launch the software. If the Autorun feature is disabled, click the Start button and choose the Run option from the menu. Go to the root directory of the CD and double-click the START.EXE file. Click the Open and OK buttons.

2. Click the button in the circle and you will see the welcome screen. From here you can install the test bank. Click the ExamGear button to begin the installation process.

3. The Installation Wizard will appear onscreen and prompt you with instructions to complete the installation. Select a directory where you wish to install the ExamGear Test Bank (the Installation Wizard defaults to C:\Program Files\ExamGear).

4. The Installation Wizard will copy the ExamGear files to your hard drive, add the ExamGear Test Bank to your Program menu, add values to your Registry, and install the test engine's DLLs to the appropriate system folders. To ensure that the process has been successful, the Setup program finishes the installation process by running ExamGear.

5. The Installation Wizard logs the installation process and stores this information in a file named INSTALL.LOG. This log file is used by the uninstall process in the event that you choose to remove ExamGear from your computer. Because the ExamGear Test Bank installation adds Registry keys and DLL files to your computer, it is important to uninstall the program appropriately.

RELATED SERVICES

The CD also contains information about other exam preparation tools that can be obtained from eITPrep, including:

- Test scheduling and vouchers
- Additional online and CD-ROM based test banks
- Online, CBT, and audio courses
- MCSA/MCSE Preparation challenge games

Get Certified!

Why Test with VUE?

Using the speed and reliability of the Internet, the most advanced technology and our commitment to unparalleled service, VUE provides a quick, flexible way to meet your testing needs.

You have the experience and the training – now demonstrate your expertise and get the recognition your skills deserve. A Microsoft certification increases your credibility in the marketplace and is tangible evidence that you have the know-how to provide top-notch support to your employer.

Three easy ways to register for your next exam, all in real time:

- Register online at www.vue.com

- Contact your local VUE testing center. There are over 3000 quality VUE testing centers world wide. Visit www.vue.com for the location of a center near you.

- Call a VUE call center. In North America, call toll-free 800-TEST-NOW (800-837-8734). For a complete listing of worldwide call center telephone numbers, visit www.vue.com/ms.

Call your local VUE testing center and ask about TESTNOW! same-day exam registration!

Visit www.vue.com for a complete listing of VUE testing sponsors.

Microsoft
CERTIFIED
Exam Provider

TESTING SERVICES

When IT really matters...Test with VUE!